Praise for
RETAIL GANGSTER

"[An] Editor's Choice!" —*New York Times Book Review*

"[Top] 10 Best Audiobooks of 2022" —*The Washington Post*

"[Top] 16 Mystery, Thriller, True Crime Books to Read (August 2022)" —*Book Riot*

"The Best New Books to Read in September (2022)" —*The Philadelphia Inquirer*

"[Top] 3 Best Audiobooks to Listen to This Month (October 2022)" —*The Washington Post*

"Holiday Gift Guide (2022)" —UrbanDaddy

■ ■ ■

"A compact and appealing account of Crazy Eddie's artificially inflated rise and slow-mo collapse...Subcutaneously, *Retail Gangster* is a tender requiem for a time [past]...But the meat of this limber book is its investigation into the deep family drama and funny money behind Crazy Eddie." —*The New York Times*

"Highbrow brilliant." —*New York Magazine*

"[A] fast-paced, entertaining narrative...Mr. Weiss is an enthusiastic storyteller, and he does a terrific job synthesizing a dizzying amount of information. —*The Wall Street Journal*

"Weiss' irresistible account of the life of Eddie Antar, a small-time huckster and high school dropout who became a wealthy merchant, securities fraudster, fugitive, and convict, is also a tale of the rise of consumer electronics in America and a fond portrait of the sleazy, disintegrating city that was [once] New York in the 1970s."　　　　　—*The Washington Post*

"If you aren't familiar with the saga of Crazy Eddie, fix that immediately [and] read this book!"　　—Helaine Olen, *The Washington Post Opinions*

"A must-read...Weiss deftly weaves the family story, with the New York Zeitgeist of the 1970s and 1980s, along with the rather complicated frauds committed by Sam and Eddie Antar. In other words, he turns the complicated and baffling into [something] simple and understandable. This book is worth your time, and Weiss should be saluted for his work."　　—*Forbes*

"[*Retail Gangster*] is a very good and highly entertaining book, and a very good reminder that the scammers we know now in the start-up world have plenty of history to call their own."　　—NPR's *Pop Culture Happy Hour*

"A rollicking chronicle of malignity, criminality, and family intrigue, [*Retail Gangster*] not only documents Antar's nefarious antics in lucid detail, it also evokes the saga of the Syrian Jews who fled the depredations of their Turkish overlords for the promised land of America in the early twentieth century and prospered, mostly honestly, beyond their dreams."　　—*Commentary*

"Extraordinary."　　　　　　　　　—*The Philadelphia Inquirer*

"[*Retail Gangster*] is a rare business book from which you learn about an important industry and the methods of a criminal enterprise, all while shaking with laughter at the human beings involved as they attempt to rip off everyone in sight from customers to insurance companies to their own family members...Weiss writes up this tale of crime and punishment with great New York verve, delivering a probing examination of a profane way of doing business."　　　　　—*The Washington Free Beacon*

"…Weiss brings his own gifts—a penchant for exhaustive research and a remarkably straightforward style—to bear upon a very complicated and twisty tale."

—*The Federal Lawyer*

"Weiss paints an intricate portrait of greed, aspiration, and complicated family ties…A compellingly readable story about a con artist who 'epitomized the duality of the American Dream.'"

—*Kirkus Reviews*

"Crazy Eddie was one of the most brazen [and] longest-running frauds in history. For twenty years criminal mastermind Eddie Antar fooled everyone he came into contact with—from Wall Street 'masters of the universe' to the government, the media, and the people who came into his stores. Eddie went no higher than junior high school—the first of his many crimes was truancy—but that did not hamper him. He was as brilliant as he was dishonest. As detailed in this enthralling book, Crazy Eddie was a merchandising phenomenon as well as a world-class con game. Eddie might have been a successful businessman had he not sought the American Dream through crime.

Retail Gangster ties together all the strands of the Crazy Eddie story in an immensely readable and enjoyable narrative, filled with fascinating characters, astounding subplots, and more plot twists than a pretzel."

—Frank W. Abagnale Jr., *New York Times* best-selling author of *Catch Me if You Can*

"Eddie Antar, what a shtarker! Whew! It's so strange to me that I am even peripherally a part of the story of Crazy Eddie! How can this be?! I wonder who it was that saw my Zap Comix cover and suggested using it for their logo.

Gary Weiss has done the world a service in having taken pains to lay out in all its sleazy detail the myriad ways these guys conned everyone—[from] customers [to] the government, Wall Street, [and] even each other! Wow! And Weiss did it with humor. I found myself laughing [while] reading 'churning out so much bogus paperwork required dishonesty on an industrial scale.' The shenanigans are often described in this whimsical manner [that]—while revealing bad behavior— is easier on the reader than if Weiss had used an indignant, outraged tone. You know, the absurd tragic comedy of all gross human behavior, layers of chicanery, relentless lying and deceiving, [and] elaborate deceptions [which] Weiss describes. The details are *all* of interest, and the effect is cumulative. Anyway, I want to know it all.

The question arises: How commonplace is such behavior in the business world, in big corporations, in banking and finance, [and] in government agencies? [And] how exceptional, or how typical, is the Antar family? There's no way to know, I guess, unless some[one] does a dedicated, long-term investigation [into] a specific company, organization, or agency. The stuff about investment analysts, 'investment relations,' and all that [is] very informative. I mean, who knew? Being a suspicious character by nature, I [wonder if the Antar family liked] 'the feeling of pulling the wool over the consumers' eyes.' The average working-class person doesn't stand a chance [against] the way things are set up by evil geniuses like Eddie Antar. God help us. We need a frickin' army of investigative journalists like Weiss."

—Robert Crumb, cartoonist and creator of
Fritz the Cat and *Keep on Truckin'*

"I would say that *Retail Gangster* reads like a Grisham thriller, only no one could have invented the absurd characters that populated the carnival of chaos called Crazy Eddie. Alternately hilarious, unbelievable, and jaw-dropping, Gary Weiss's superb book explores the shifting boundaries of truth, lies, love, and betrayal. Between depictions of vicious family drama, pathological greed, and massive fraud, it lays bare the worst of the go-go 1980s, exposing Wall Street analysts and executives as the handmaidens of this deception that wrecked untold numbers of investors. If you want to understand the types of financial dishonesty that will continue to haunt our markets long into the future, read this indispensable history of Eddie Antar and his unbelievable family."

—Kurt Eichenwald, award-winning journalist and *New York Times* best-selling author of *The Informant*, *Conspiracy of Fools* and *A Mind Unraveled*

"An absorbing and revealing treatise on the underbelly of the American Dream, where scam artists and businessmen are one and the same, and the fruits of their labor—in this case, an iconic ad campaign once familiar to all New Yorkers—was the by-product of criminal chutzpah and greed. *Retail Gangster* will turn you inside out and have you reading late into the night."

—T.J. English, author of *Dangerous Rhythms*, *Havana Nocturne*, and *The Savage City*

"A high fidelity dive into the complex and contradictory world of a kid who rode the American dream from immigrant Brooklyn to the coveted throne of New York discount electronics and then to prison. [*Retail Gangster* is] a deeply reported and sensitive snapshot of the retail legend known as 'Crazy Eddie' and of the place that lifted him up and brought him down."

—Matti Friedman, author of *Who by Fire* and *The Aleppo Codex*

"This would be a remarkable work of fiction, except this tale of one man's audacious addiction to fraud is true. *Retail Gangster* is destined to go down as a classic in the annals of public-company fraud. With his history of tracking gangsters, there [is no one] better to tell [this] story than Gary Weiss."

—Herb Greenberg, veteran financial journalist and commentator

"If you [ever] lived in New York City in the late 1970s, [there's a chance] you were driven mad by Crazy Eddie commercials. [City dwellers] shopped [at his store] just to see if he put his money where his big mouth was. [Many] also wondered about the real Brooklyn guy behind the hype. In *Retail Gangster*, Gary Weiss [dives into] the ads and the loud dazzle [of] the truly insane life of Eddie Antar. With brilliant research, confident storytelling skills, colorful anecdotes, and a startling eye for detail, [Weiss gives] a guided tour of audacious treachery and fraud that might have been the template for the Madoffs of the financial netherworld. [Readers won't be able to put down this book] because [they will] keep thinking this [cautionary tale] can't get any more insane. [But] it does. And what's craziest of all is that it's all true."

—Denis Hamill, Former *NY Daily News* columnist and author of *Fork in the Road*

RETAIL GANGSTER

The Insane, Real-Life Story of Crazy Eddie

GARY WEISS

hachette
BOOKS

New York

For the victims

Hachette Books
Hachette Book Group
1290 Avenue of the Americas
New York, NY 10104
HachetteBooks.com
Twitter.com/HachetteBooks
Instagram.com/HachetteBooks

First Trade Paperback Edition: October 2023

Published by Hachette Books, an imprint of Hachette Book Group, Inc. The Hachette Books name and logo are trademarks of the Hachette Book Group.

The Hachette Speakers Bureau provides a wide range of authors for speaking events. To find out more, visit hachettespeakersbureau.com or email HachetteSpeakers@hbgusa.com.

The publisher is not responsible for websites (or their content) that are not owned by the publisher.

Print book interior design by Amy Quinn.

Library of Congress Cataloging-in-Publication Data

Names: Weiss, Gary (Gary R.), author.
Title: Retail gangster : the insane, real-life story of Crazy Eddie / Gary Weiss.
Description: First edition. | New York : Hachette Books, [2022] | Includes bibliographical references and index.
Identifiers: LCCN 2022019041 | ISBN 9780306924552 (hardcover) | ISBN 9780306924569 (ebook)
Subjects: LCSH: Antar, Eddie, 1947-2016. | Crazy Eddie (Firm) | Businesspeople—United States—Biography. | Household electronics industry—Corrupt practices—United States. | Chain stores—Corrupt practices—United States. | Fraud—United States.
Classification: LCC HD9971.5.E542 W45 2022 | DDC 338.092 [B]—dc23/eng/20220427
LC record available at https://lccn.loc.gov/2022019041

ISBNs: 9780306924552 (hardcover); 9780306924576 (trade paperback); 9780306924569 (ebook)

Printed in the United States of America

LSC-C

Printing 1, 2023

CONTENTS

PART FOUR: "There were no files"

The Family

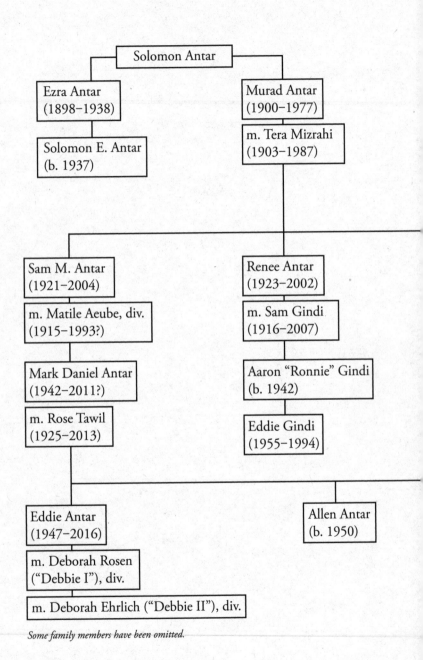

Some family members have been omitted.

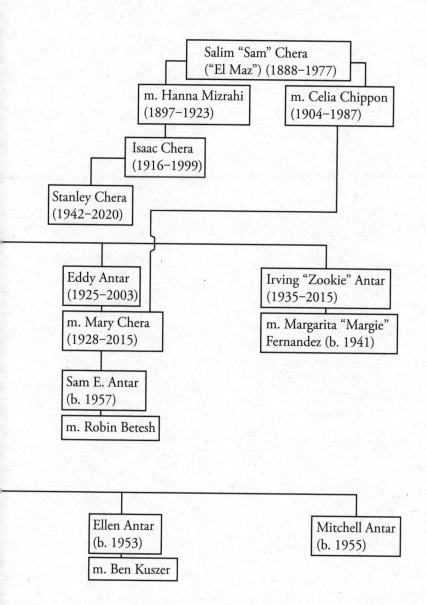

PROLOGUE

EARLY IN JANUARY 1987, THREE MEN OF MODEST STATURE, WEARING TAI-lored suits and long black overcoats, arrived at a five-story town house on East Sixty-Seventh Street in Manhattan. This was the heart of the Gold Coast, which stretched a mile up Fifth Avenue from Fifty-Ninth Street and east for two blocks, a neighborhood (if one could call it that) unique in the city for its ostentatious embrace of unapologetic greed and the good fortune that comes from careful selection of parents. No. 15 was designed in 1904 by Ernest Flagg, a noted architect of the period, as the residence of a well-born man of leisure and occasional biplane pilot named Cortlandt Field Bishop. It was derivative in appearance, with faux Parisian balconies and other frills that were fashionable at the time. Many of the residences in this area had been converted into consulates and private clubs over the years. This one was now the Regency Whist Club. Wealthy men played an obscure card game here, and occasionally they invited for lunch people they wanted to impress.

Sam E. Antar thought that setting aside a town house for playing cards was an absurd waste of prime real estate. But that was none of his business. The people who lived on this street felt that they had to flaunt their wealth. The Antars did not. Sam had an apartment in a middle-class section of Brooklyn. He and his two colleagues were born there, which could be heard when they spoke. They were products of the working class. They didn't call it that. They didn't call it anything. But they wouldn't have minded if other people described them that way, and neither would they have cared if anyone told them that they had achieved the American Dream. It was a cliché, it was trite, it was shunned, it was mocked—but for them, it was true.

They were separated by one generation from the *Bahsita*, the crowded and disease-ridden Jewish quarter of Aleppo, Syria. Their parents and grandparents had run shabby stores in dreary neighborhoods. They overcame obstacles that would have humbled less dogged men. And now they were on the Gold Coast, about to meet one of the most eminent men in their business. *He* wanted to meet *them*.

It was nothing personal; it was a tribute to their company. From the moment its first television commercials aired in 1976, with a revved-up disc jockey named Jerry Carroll screaming, "HIS PRICES ARE INSANE!" Crazy Eddie had been a phenomenal success. It was more than a chain of thirty-two stores, stretching from Philadelphia to New England, that sold stereos, records, VCRs, clock radios, and television sets. It was more than a Wall Street superstar. It embodied the indomitable, sometimes malevolent spirit of New York City.

These men didn't much care. Only the numbers mattered to them. They were hard, cynical men. But it was true—it was provable fact—that Crazy Eddie was as much a symbol of the city as the Brooklyn Bridge and the World Trade Center. Everyone knew Crazy Eddie. Not its reclusive founder, Sam's cousin Eddie Antar, but the Jerry Carroll character and the stores, with their garish yellow signs and "crazy man" trademark, which was plastered on newspaper ads and stock certificates and on T-shirts, mugs, hats, and other memorabilia eagerly snapped up by Crazy Eddie fans. Imagine that—fans of a store!

Eddie and his team had tapped into something. They hadn't planned it, but they had done it. In 1985 a survey found that the Carroll character was better known to New Yorkers than the publicity hound Mayor Ed Koch. A year later, the stores had 99 percent name recognition, higher than Ronald Reagan. Its patrons ranged from ordinary people to celebrities to junkies—a popular brand of smack was called "Crazy Eddie."

And now all they had built might go up in smoke.

The three men were here because Crazy Eddie was "in play." That was a phrase used by the press to denote a company likely to be taken over in the near future. It was an emotion as much as it was a description. If said often enough by the right people or the right media, you *were* in play. Then it had the effect of a For Sale sign planted on a lawn—except that the companies so designated had no voice in the matter. It was happening all over the country. Corporate raiders were buying up companies and squeezing them for every last nickel. They snapped up steel mills, airlines, retail chains, and manufacturers, treating them as if they were derelict houses that needed gut renovation. The people who worked for them were the guts that were renovated.

Crazy Eddie was vulnerable. It was a widely known brand, and it could be bought on the cheap. Its once-soaring stock price had ebbed in recent months, and reports of high-level turmoil encouraged potential acquirers. Sam's widely admired cousin had quit as chief executive officer for unspecified "personal reasons" just a few days before. Reports of Eddie's poor health were circulating in the press. In his absence, the company was run by the newly appointed members of an "Office of the President": Sam, the chief financial officer; Eddie's brother Mitchell, in charge of operations; and Isaac "Ike" Kairey, an old friend of Eddie's, who oversaw the stores. The triumvirate was an unusual arrangement, underlying the executive suite malaise that was said to beset this otherwise pristine and, experts agreed, outstanding company.

Over the years, Crazy Eddie had been blessed with extraordinary profit growth. The result was that its shares soared nearly 1,100 percent in the two years after they began trading in September 1984. Eddie Antar and his team had an almost magical ability to make the cash registers ring even during difficult times. Yet because of the takeover mania that was sweeping the country, its 2,250 employees might be fired in droves unless a corporate savior, a "white knight," bought the company but kept it intact.

Not long after Eddie quit, a very wealthy man named Milton Petrie let it be known that he might fill that role. Oppenheimer & Co., Crazy Eddie's Wall Street bankers, promptly arranged for a luncheon meeting at the Regency Whist Club. This was an ancient and arcane card game, a precursor to contract bridge, a game of skill requiring a prodigious memory. One had to remember the cards that had been dealt. Milton Petrie hadn't forgotten any of the hands he had been dealt in his life. Few had been certain winners.

Petrie had worked his way to the Gold Coast and had far more in common with the Antars than he did with Cortlandt Field Bishop. He was an old-school merchant, and like the Antars he was from an immigrant background. His father was born in Russia, settled in Salt Lake City, and opened a pawnshop in the 1890s. He gave it the grand name Utah Collateral Bank. It failed. No worries. This was America, the land of opportunity, so Jacob Petrovitzky changed course. He moved the family to Indianapolis, left storekeeping behind, and became a cop. His son changed his name but retained the doughtiness. Starting with a hosiery shop in Cleveland, Milton Petrie overcame a rocky start in Horatio Alger fashion, went bankrupt in his early years, but eventually established a highly profitable chain of discount women's clothing stores. He bought more and more chains and became a retailing magnate, but not feared and hated like Sam Walton. His stores were an integral part of their communities, not big-box alien implants.

Petrie was a sharp investor in his later years, buying up Toys "R" Us stock when it sold in the pennies. He was now eighty-four years old, an elder statesman of retailing, a billionaire who lived like one in a grand building around the corner on Fifth Avenue. Laurance Rockefeller was a neighbor.

Sam was impressed by Petrie's background but not intimidated by it. What made him intimidating was that he wasn't intimidating. He was, by all accounts, gentle and generous. He helped ordinary people down on their luck, total strangers he read about in the papers. When a police detective was slain by the mob, he established a trust fund for the cop's four daughters. His will was constantly expanding and, in time, would grow to 120 pages, setting up trust funds and gifts, ranging from $5,000 to $15 million, for 383 people. Petrie did good for the sake of doing good. That gave Sam a weird, unfamiliar feeling.

The three Office of the President members were escorted into an elevator, taken to an upper floor, and ushered into a formal dining room. The old man was taller than expected, towering over the men as he cordially greeted them. His handshake was firm as he peered at each of them with sharp hazel eyes beneath furry brows, but he was stooped and Sam noticed that he looked his age. A butler waited on them.

"So, how is your sick brother?" Petrie asked Mitchell. There was a look in his eye when he said that. Did he doubt that Eddie was really sick? That possibility crossed Sam's mind.

After some small talk about conditions in the industry, Petrie casually asked, "Do you want to do a takeover? How would you feel if I took over your company and kept you guys around?" It was what they wanted to hear, but Sam was uncertain. What was Petrie really thinking? Sam now realized why they were at the Regency Whist Club and not his office. They were in a high-stakes card game, and they couldn't see the hand they were playing. But Sam had the odd sensation that Petrie could see every one of their cards.

As the men and their host ate their specially ordered kosher meals, Sam's anxiety grew. A petrifying thought crossed his mind. That look in his eye. Perhaps he imagined it. Perhaps not. Could Petrie have known that Sam had planted those illness rumors in the press? If he knew that, could he have known all the *other* things they were hiding? That this loud company with the goofy public image was toppling over, bloated, burdened by years of fraud? That Eddie stole from everyone in sight? Even the "crazy man" trademark was swag, an almost exact copy of a Robert Crumb character. The financial statements that Petrie had carefully studied could have been set to music by Dave Frishberg. They were a blizzard of lies.

If Petrie took over Crazy Eddie, there were only two possibilities: he would either uncover the frauds and they would go to prison, or this very decent old man would become their next victim. It was then that Sam identified the unfamiliar emotion that had overcome him—shame.

PART ONE
NEHKDI

CHAPTER ONE

As far back as he can remember, Sam E. Antar recalls watching cash pile up on his uncle's kitchen table. After every trip out of town, his uncle would place the stiff-sided valise onto the table, snap open the brass latches, and out would come the cash.

Uncle Sam—Sam M. Antar—was pretty much head of the family by the mid-1960s, when his nephew started hanging around. Sammy, as he was known in the family, was a slightly built, bookish kid. His father, Sam M.'s younger brother Eddy, wasn't around much. Most days he was two hours away in downtown Bridgeport, the fading Connecticut city where he had a children's clothing store. Sam M. and his sons—Eddie, Allen, and Mitchell—became a kind of surrogate family. They lived not far away, in an attached house on East Third Street in Gravesend, a tranquil Italian-Jewish neighborhood in southern Brooklyn. Sam M. was gone a lot as well, but unlike Eddy he was not tied to a store in a dismal city. Sam M. would be traveling through the country, doing business, cutting deals, and would return not beaten down by demanding customers but "like Marco Polo," with tales of the great and the peculiar that he encountered on the road. Then he would unload the cash.

Sam M. was the eldest son of Murad Antar, the family patriarch. Becoming the head of the family was a birthright, and the cash piling on his kitchen table in Gravesend brought him to that status while he was in his forties. Murad was revered as part of the generation that had come to America from Syria decades earlier. He had done well for decades, but by the mid-1960s his financial fortunes were on the wane. By the late 1970s he owned a sprawling house on Ocean Parkway, not far from Sam M., but not much else. Unlike Murad, a quiet and reserved man, Sam M. was outgoing and bombastic. He was a window trimmer—a designer of store window displays—and that gave him insights into retailing opportunities everywhere he went. He started buying into stores in the 1950s, and by the 1960s Sam M. had a string of part-owned stores from Brooklyn to Jersey City to Nogales, Arizona, selling everything from shoes to toasters to transistor radios.

The window-trimming business and the stores were lucrative, or so he used to say. He claimed to net $10,000 to $20,000 from each of his window displays, good money at the time, though there's no way to know for sure, and Sam M. had a tendency to embellish. Many years later, a federal judge would conclude that he had "obtained a rather clear sense of [Sam M.] as hardworking, ambitious, and highly intelligent. I also found him to be a skillful and inveterate liar." Still, the cash was real enough. He may have lied about how much was in the piles, and if so, what of it? He was accountable to no one, not his family, and certainly not the Internal Revenue Service.

Sam M. would swiftly and expertly sort the bills into denominations, count them, and put them in stacks. Two rubber bands meant fifty to a bundle. Most of the stacks had two rubber bands. A single rubber band meant fewer than fifty bills, and the number would be written in ballpoint pen on the top bill of the stack. He would climb a stepladder in the bedroom closet, lift a loose ceiling panel, and carefully place the cash in the space above it. Or he would put the cash in a file drawer or carefully layer the bills inside a radiator cabinet, snug against the pipes. Some of it went to the bank, and some went to his wife Rose to run the house. But most of the cash went into the ceiling, the bed, or whatever other hiding places were available.

This was the *nehkdi*, as it was known among Syrians, and it offered a number of benefits. The principal one was, of course, that it was not shared with the government. Employees would get paper bags of cash, off the books, sparing everyone involved the nuisance of paying payroll taxes. Since their wages were tax free, without withholdings, employees would take home more money—quite a bit more—than they'd have gotten from employers who paid the same salaries but had a more fastidious approach to the tax laws. Having all that cash around was no big deal. Sammy later recalled: "It wasn't something explained. Our dads didn't sit us down and say, 'This is *nehkdi*.' We just saw and copied, as kids always do. It was part of our early childhood development: reading, writing, and skimming."

A story was told in the family about the time Murad was carrying thousands of dollars in cash on him and believed that somebody was following him. So he left it in a store run by a fellow Syrian. He said, "Do me a favor, can I just leave this bag here?" The man had the bag for more than a month and a half, two months. He finally called up Murad, who said, "Oh, I forgot the money." People leave their checkbooks absentmindedly, and Murad did the same with his cash. That was the message of the story, that and the fact that, at times, the Antar family elder did very well financially.

Nehkdi and aversion to paying taxes were a leftover habit from Ottoman Syria, where few services were provided to the populace by the Turkish rulers except conscription and taxation. Murad and his wife Tera left Syria for America in 1920. It was a good time to get out.

■ ■ ■

The largest Syrian Jewish community was not in the fabled city of Damascus but the less celebrated, but equally ancient, walled city of Aleppo. It was the commercial hub of northern Syria, a way station on the Silk Road to China, and had been home to a sizable Jewish community since biblical times. Most Jewish residents were employed in the *souks* or ran tiny mercantile businesses and lived in the cramped *Bahsita*, the Jewish quarter. But wherever they lived, they were subjected to discrimination. Christians and Jews were *dhimmis*, second-class citizens, "tolerated but not equal." A special tax, the *jizya*, was imposed on the Jewish and Christian minorities. But Muslim Syrians were not exempt from the Ottoman obsession with taking their money.

The pashas—provincial governors—bought their titles and demanded tribute from their subjects like Mafia dons. Pashas "were sent to 'squeeze' the inhabitants of the town, and they were 'squeezed' themselves in return," a nineteenth-century British consul remarked. Jewish communal life under the Ottomans was changing at the dawn of the twentieth century—for the worse. Jewish people had avoided conscription, and the forced assimilation that came with it, by paying a special tax, but that was ended by the Young Turks in the early twentieth century. Then came World War I and still more violence and hardship. A good segment of Jewish Syrians flocked to New York, where they were a tiny minority in a great sea of Jewish refugees fleeing oppression in Eastern Europe.

The center of Syrian Jewish life in early-twentieth-century New York was a dreadful street on the Lower East Side that was "quite unfit for human habitation," according to a *New York Times* editorial published after conditions had improved somewhat. The noise alone made life on this street difficult to bear, but its inhabitants—the poorest of the poor—had little choice. Allen Street was barely thirty feet from curb to curb (twenty-four feet, according to one account), yet the city rammed through the Second Avenue Elevated train line in 1880. That civic improvement gave "the street of perpetual shadow" an ambience "more of a tunnel than a street." Opium dens abounded, and Allen Street had the highest concentration of brothels in the city. One writer observed that "there beneath the roar [of the elevated trains] an open market in human flesh is conducted. In front of every house there stand women of every age and they call to passerby to buy their flesh."

Murad and Tera arrived in New York Harbor on June 20, 1920, on the SS *France*. They traveled second class, as was far more common for immigrants than is now assumed. Doing so meant one disembarked in Manhattan and, unlike third class, avoided the nasty uniformed inspectors at Ellis Island. Murad was listed on the manifest as seventeen and a "teacher." Actually, he was a twenty-year-old merchant, an occupation shared by the bulk of Syrian Jewish immigrants in Syria and in their new home. Syrians avoided the dismal, low-paying garment-assembly plants that abounded in the city and were the principal employers of Jewish "greenhorns." Instead, they usually went into business for themselves. If they had some capital, they opened modest stores. If they didn't, they became peddlers, selling tablecloths, handkerchiefs, and other dry goods from pushcarts and handcarts. A rabbi who worked with Syrian immigrants observed that "though there are many poor in the community, it is on the whole comparatively prosperous."

The two communities, Syrian (they called themselves "S-Y") and Eastern European (known unaffectionately among the Syrians as "J-Dubs"), went on divergent paths in America. "Eastern European Jews showed almost from the beginning of their arrival in this country a passion for education that was unique in American history," observed Nathan Glazer and Daniel Patrick Moynihan in their 1970 book *Beyond the Melting Pot*. "My son the doctor" became a cliché, but not among the Syrians. "The Syrian immigrants, unlike their Eastern European counterparts, did not leap to the educational opportunities which the Ashkenazeem [immigrants from Eastern Europe] sought for their children," observed a Syrian Jewish writer, Joseph A. D. Sutton. Their reluctance stemmed from the assimilation that came with education. Syrian immigrants "wished to avoid as much as possible the acculturation and assimilation of their children, 'Americanization,' that had affected almost all other ethnic and religious immigrant groups." They largely succeeded, and one result was that S-Ys retained a strong Jewish identity and a vibrant religious life into the twenty-first century. That has long been a source of great pride within the community.

Another by-product of the resistance to assimilation was occupational. Though Syrian Jewish youth began pursuing professional careers as the years passed, Sutton noted in 1979 that "as a rule many follow enterprises similar to those of their fathers." That meant joining the family business, which was usually retail, or starting one themselves. "By conforming to their fathers' mores they could look to comfortable and remunerative places in the parents' businesses, and eventually to becoming their successors," he wrote. "Why, then, abandon the traditional mode of life of the Syrian community with its many rewards and satisfactions?"

Why indeed. So it was unremarkable that all of the Antars' six children went to work in stores in their teens, and that only Eddy finished high school. Though assimilation was anathema, American values were embraced. Military service was not feared as it was in Syria, and S-Y lads eagerly joined up after the attack on Pearl Harbor. Sam M. and Eddy both served in the Army in Europe during World War II, with Eddy seeing fierce combat with the engineers during the final bloody months of the conflict. Another son, Norman, served during the Korean War.

After the war, Sam M. married Rose Tawil, the daughter of an S-Y dry-goods salesman. Sam turned twenty-five in May 1946, ready to take his place in the community. The couple settled in Brooklyn near their parents, and began to raise a family. Their first offspring was due at the end of 1947. Many prospective parents agonized about naming the baby, but the process was simplified for Syrian Jewish people. The firstborn son was named after the father's father. The secondborn son was named after the mother's father, and similar rules applied to girls. This resulted in duplicative names, so S-Ys used spelling variations to avoid confusion.*

The community's naming conventions were more than usually impor-tant for Sam M. Antar—because he didn't follow them. A boy was born to Sam M. and Rose on December 18, 1947. He should have been named Mark, which was how Murad was usually Anglicized. Instead, Sam M. and Rose named their newborn baby boy Eddie, which was Ezra Anglicized.

This departure from tradition raised eyebrows, but Sam and Murad had a ready explanation. Murad's long-dead brother Ezra had appeared to Murad in a dream. Ezra had died young in the late 1930s, leaving an infant son, Solomon. The boy had barely known his father. Ezra, deceased but fearful, was concerned that Solomon might not follow custom when he grew up and had kids. What a shame it would be if no child were ever named after him! Ezra pleaded with his brother. If Sam M.'s first child was a boy, could he please name the baby after Ezra? Murad woke up in a cold sweat. Of course he would comply with this small, understandable request from the Great Beyond.

The "dream story" was a beautiful, sentimental tale, and it was also a lie. Sam M. had a secret. Few in the family knew that he couldn't name his baby Mark because he already had a son—his true firstborn son—and had given him that name. Sam M. had already been married and divorced. And his first wife was an affront not just to Murad and Tera, but to the entire Syrian Jewish community—not because of anything she had done, but because of who she was.

■ ■ ■

---

* For that very reason, Sam E. Antar is referred to by his nickname "Sammy" in this book.

Public records sketch out an intriguing if incomplete account of Sam M. Antar's secret family. It's a story that has its roots in the Levant and the quest for a better life in America, very much like Murad and Tera's voyage from Aleppo.

Early in 1942 Sam was employed at a linen shop in Akron, Ohio, probably owned by Murad or a family friend. An hour's drive away in Youngstown, a young woman named Matile Aeube had recently broken with her husband, with whom she'd had three children. She was from Zahlé, a Greek Catholic town in Lebanon's Bekaa Valley, and had immigrated with her new Syrian American husband in February 1930. Matile was young. Very young. The ship's manifest gives her age as seventeen, but public records establish that Matile was fourteen when she arrived in New York Harbor on the SS *Byron*, and apparently was a child of thirteen when she married Joseph Davis back in Lebanon.

The Davises moved to Youngstown and proceeded to have children. The first, a daughter, came when Matile was fifteen. A son and another daughter followed. Joseph struggled to support the family, working first in a candy shop and then as an elevator operator in a downtown office building. The latter job was paying a paltry $1,200 a year in 1940. Marriages survived in less bleak circumstances back then, but this one did not. They divorced sometime after the Census taker came by in April 1940. Then Matile somehow, somewhere, met Sam M., and by the end of 1941 she was pregnant. They were married in Albuquerque on February 25, 1942, and settled in Los Angeles, where Matile had dreams of becoming a dancer. She came without her three children, who remained in Youngstown with her ex-husband.

It's easy to imagine the horror felt by Murad and Tera at their eldest son marrying a Christian Arab woman who was six years older, divorced, already had three kids, and was three months pregnant with his child. The Syrian Jewish community was adamantly opposed to intermarriage even when the non-Jewish spouse converted. In 1935 a Syrian *beth din* rabbinical court in Brooklyn expressed outrage at Jewish-Gentile unions and forbade all marriage-related conversions, which it described as "absolutely invalid and worthless." Any such person, their spouse, and their offspring were not to be accepted in the community. This was not a small matter for a young

Syrian Jewish man, especially if he intended to follow traditional career paths as Sam M. surely did.

Sam M. entered the Army on June 24, 1942. Whether he was drafted—or joined the Army with his wife seven months pregnant—is not clear from the available records. What is clear is that their son, Mark Daniel Antar, was born on August 18, 1942, and that their marriage quickly crumbled after Sam's discharge in July 1945. He and Matia, as she was now known, got a quickie Reno divorce in November, and she married a bit-part actor named Pete Kooy before the ink was dry on their divorce papers.

Thanks to Matia's quick remarriage, the skeletons rattling in Sam M.'s closet gave him no trouble in future years. His firstborn son was never acknowledged or mentioned. It was as if he was a puppy Sam brought to the pound before moving back east. Neither Matia nor Pete succeeded in Hollywood, and both died in obscurity—Pete in 1963, according to public records, and Matia in 1993, according to an online family tree that could not be verified. Defense Department records indicate that Danny Mark Kooy, birth date August 18, 1943—same day and month as Mark Daniel Antar but off by a year—served in the Army during the Vietnam War and died on December 16, 2011. He was buried at Riverside National Cemetery. That is either the child Sam M. abandoned in California or one hell of a coincidence.

Rumors of Sam M. marrying an "Arab dancer" and having a son spread through the Antars decades later, but it's not known if Eddie ever learned the truth, and no word of Eddie's half brother ever became public when Eddie's name was splattered all over the Eastern Seaboard. If S-Y naming conventions had been followed, Eddie would have been named Abraham after Rose's father. The commercials would have screamed, "CRAZY ABIE! HIS PRICES ARE INSANE!" Or perhaps, if Sam M. had treated him like a firstborn, Mark Antar might have become active in the family business. With Eddie no longer the eldest son, there may have been no Crazy Eddie.

It does seem fitting that Eddie Antar's birth was preceded and then surrounded by secrets and lies, because that was the trajectory of his life from the beginning to the bitter end.

Murad used to say, "An Aleppine can sell even a dried camel skin." His grandson would have updated that to "An Antar can sell $30 binoculars for $300." Eddie was schooled in the art of ripping off customers at tourist traps in Midtown Manhattan when he was a teenager—a very young teenager. He wanted to work, not sit in school and learn things that were of no value in the life tradition had set out for him. So he dropped out of Brooklyn's Abraham Lincoln High School, thereby committing one of his first acts of small-scale, winked-at, unpunished lawbreaking.

Many years later, Eddie testified that he dropped out in the ninth grade, and he told a newspaper interviewer that he was fifteen when he was "officially" out of school. If so—Eddie was not exactly known for veracity—that made him a truant. New York State law required that children stay in school until they were sixteen. Like a lot of laws that Eddie would cheerfully disregard in the years to come, the compulsory attendance statutes were enforced, at best, unevenly. Eddie claimed that he fought "battles" with his parents over his school attendance. That's possible—parents were theoretically held responsible when their kids were truants—but it's not likely that Sam M. and Rose would have fought very hard. S-Y kids were expected to work. Eddie was a daddy's boy, a willing adherent to S-Y conventions—when it suited him.

Eddie was a wiry five feet, six inches tall, with an oval face that in later years he obscured with a beard. He had chiseled good looks. He was sure of himself, like the Italian kids who were at the top of the street pecking order. He lifted weights and wore shirts that showed off his muscles. He came of age in the era of fighting gangs, but he never joined one because gangs were for punks who didn't know where they were going. Eddie knew.

Despite his size, Eddie had a definite physical presence. To cousin Sammy he was a protector, the guy who would face down the neighborhood bullies. One day when he was about ten, Sammy was in the PS 215 schoolyard near Sam M.'s house when some Italian kids from the neighborhood started picking on him. Then along came Eddie, who just happened to be walking by. He didn't have to do or say much. He didn't have to hit anybody. Just being there was enough to make them go away.

Eddie had more money than other kids in the neighborhood because he earned it. At about the time he was facing down bullies in that schoolyard, he was being schooled in retailing on the Allen Street of the 1960s. Manhattan had deposited its sleaze at the Crossroads of the World—Forty-Second Street and Times Square—the heart of a wretched stretch of Midtown reaching from Sixth Avenue two interminable blocks west to the Port Authority Bus Terminal. Open-all-night skin-flick movie theaters, porno bookstores, penny arcades, and peep shows were in abundance. Hookers and runaways competed for sidewalk space with muggers and nodding-off drug addicts. Tourist-trap "clip joint" gift shops abounded, many owned by S-Ys, stocking grotesquely overpriced cameras and electronic gizmos alongside 007 knives (an easy-opening mugger favorite) and cheap but overpriced souvenirs.

Later accounts vary concerning the location of the clip joints that gave Eddie his early education. Some say Forty-Second Street, others Times Square, while still others say the vicinity of the Port Authority Bus Terminal. It doesn't much matter, as all were equally grungy back then, and he may have worked in all those areas. He probably worked for several friends and relatives of Sam M. in those sleazy joints, and one was almost certainly Irving "Zookie" Antar, the youngest of Murad's offspring. Zookie was in his late twenties, closer in age to Eddie than he was to his eldest brother. A chubby man who wore horn-rimmed glasses, he wasn't much to look at, but he was fun to be around and he was popular with the younger generation of Antars.

Unlike Sam M., who grew pedantic and stuffy as he aged, Zookie never took himself too seriously. Eddie just acted like a rebel; Zookie was the real thing. At about the time Eddie was learning the art of price-gouging, Zookie's personal life took a difficult turn. In 1962, Zookie married a non-Jewish woman of Puerto Rican extraction. Margie Fernandez converted to Judaism, but it didn't matter. The 1935 edict was still in effect and had been reaffirmed in 1946. So this was a big deal, and marrying Margie affected his ability to earn a living. Yet Zookie was not cast out of the family. It may have helped that Margie was well liked by the family. Change was coming to the S-Y community. Weddings with J-Dubs, once rare, were now becoming more commonplace. So it was not a major issue when Eddie began dating a J-Dub, a classmate from his brief high school career named Debbie Rosen.

Eddie was a talented apprentice during his clip joint years, pulling down what he later claimed was $1,000 a week in commissions. Even if that was exaggerated—other accounts say $600 or $700—that was still handsome money for a teenager living with his parents. "Eddie used to talk about how he'd *saffo* the customers," Sammy recalled. That's S-Y slang for "ripping off." Like tricking them into "paying $250 for a $25 camera." Eddie would say that the camera retailed at $300, and the mark, usually a tourist, would walk away happy. Sure, the sucker would eventually find out he was ripped off, but what could he do about it? He'd be back in Iowa by then. He would never come back to the shop, and if he did, too bad. All sales were final.

After a few years working the clip joints, Eddie entered a graduate school of retailing. His campus was a street in Brooklyn.

Locals called it "the Highway." Kings Highway was an east–west thoroughfare that stretched across the borough, meandering like a long surgical scar. In central Brooklyn it was a shopping street in a neighborhood with an aging, largely Jewish and Italian population. Older adults would sit on webbed lawn chairs in front of their buildings and linger for hours at Dubrow's Cafeteria, chewing carefully their boiled beef and breast of veal and periodically dousing their heartburn with seltzer available without charge at the stainless-steel water dispenser. These people, their cynical and uncooperative adult children, and their truculent grandchildren were Eddie's new customers.

The people who shopped on the Highway were as smart as he was. They knew all his tricks. They wouldn't go into a clip joint on Times Square if it was giving stuff away. The older residents had been poor; some had lived in the Brownsville slums a few miles east. They had emerged from poverty by paying less and watching out for the Eddie Antars of this world. They were, in short, the polar opposites of the camera-toting, shorts-wearing schmucks Eddie had been robbing. They were tough, but Eddie figured he was tougher.

Eddie's commercial debut was a store called ERS Electronics, which was on Kings Highway near Coney Island Avenue. It opened in early 1969, and it was the end product of a series of deals that Sam M. had engineered over a period of years. Sam M. was giving Eddie a lesson in the meaning of family. It began before his son even knew he was in a classroom.

To S-Ys of Sam M.'s generation, relatives weren't people you saw only at weddings, holidays, and bar mitzvahs, people who might show up on your couch when there were domestic troubles, who you sent greeting cards but otherwise were happily forgotten. In the Syrian Jewish culture relatives were friends in the deepest sense, bound by blood or marriage. In days of prosperity, they were business partners. In times of distress, they were lifelines. Relatives and friends did favors for relatives and friends and friends of relatives and relatives of friends. People took care of each other. They helped each other and were compensated in return.

Sam M. impressed these points on Eddie. He wasn't to be just a businessman but a member of a family, an extended family, and he had obligations. Family came before all else. It's not clear if Eddie paid even the slightest attention, even as the family mutual-assistance apparatus worked in his favor, and ultimately resulted in Crazy Eddie. It was set in motion by a routine situation: a storekeeper needed to get out of a lease.

Sometime in the mid-1960s, a relative named Al Cohen needed a favor. Al was a kindly family man who would take his young nephews and nieces on field trips to places like Washington, DC. He was married to Sam M.'s brother Eddy's wife's half sister. By American standards, Sam M. and Al were remotely related. S-Y standards, however, were different. He was a relative, period. Al's problem was that he had a long-term lease that he didn't need anymore. He had set up his son in a store and it went bust. It was on a busy section of Kings Highway. Al was hoping Sam M. could make use of the space. His hopes were fulfilled.

Sam M. was not trying to be nice. By taking over the lease, Sam M. was helping not just his brother's wife's half-sister's husband but his own sister, Renee, her son Ronnie—and himself.

Ronnie had recently gotten married and was ready for a business of his own. But his father, Renee's husband, Sam Gindi, couldn't afford to acquire a lease on a store. Sam M. took over that responsibility and set up Ronnie in Al Cohen's son's old space at 1325 Kings Highway. In return, Sam M. took a one-half interest in the enterprise, giving him another store to add to his list of holdings. Sam M. doubly benefited. He not only gained a source of income, but the deal also solidified his growing stature as head of the family.

Crawford's Decorators was the name of the new Antar-Gindi family enterprise. It was a neighborhood department store. Ronnie would run it. As half owner, Sam M. brought in relatives. His brother Norman was given a concession at Crawford's, a kind of store-within-a-store selling health and beauty aids. Sam M. put Eddie there too, working for Ronnie, selling modestly priced electronics like transistor radios and record players.

Eddie earned a lot less at Crawford's than he did selling overpriced cameras to tourists in clip joints, and he didn't like it. These Kings Highway customers were tough. They were more than tough—they were horrible. They were cheap. They were terrible. Sam M. told him to be patient. His turn to go into business for himself was fast approaching. Eddie was turning twenty-one just before Christmas 1968, and his marriage to Debbie Rosen was set for two weeks later on January 9. Sam M. would put him in business, but, as with Ronnie, it was not a wedding gift.

Sometime in late 1968 or early 1969, Sam M. took over the lease of a defunct TV and appliance store that just vacated 1117 Kings Highway, down the street from Crawford's. Eddie would run the store but not own it. He would not get the customary half interest. His share would be a third. Sam M. would take one-third and Ronnie Gindi another third. There was a logical reason for Ronnie's share. Eddie would be selling consumer electronics, focusing on stereos and components, but he also would be offering the same lower-priced wares that were at Crawford's two blocks away. Family members didn't compete with each other, so that meant Ronnie had to be given a stake in Eddie's business. It would be called ERS Electronics, as in Eddie, Ronnie, and Sam. It opened in early 1969.

It grated on Eddie that he owned only one-third of his own store, but he didn't have much choice. He was starting a family. Debbie was planning to teach in a public school, and teacher salaries were small. But he figured he should do okay, even though it was just a minority stake. The customers on

Kings Highway were stiffs, but he was entering a hot segment of the consumer electronics market. It was a sure moneymaker. Right?

Eddie's nickname was Kelso, after the famed racehorse. It stuck with him from his earliest days to the end of his life. He was the money horse. He would win because he was the fastest, the strongest, and the smartest. That's how Kelso won race after race.

It didn't work like that in consumer electronics. Every race was fixed.

CHAPTER TWO

IN 1969 THE ONLY THING HOTTER THAN SEX AND DRUGS WAS ROCK AND roll. Even the most committed members of the counterculture, rebelling against everything in sight, looked the other way from the capitalist pigs selling the gear that was required to appreciate the music of their generation. Manufacturers were anxious to snare this market of tie-dyed, long-haired, foul-mouthed money spenders. They were willing to look as silly as was necessary to glom baby-boomer bucks. Young people "don't have to go to a favorite hangout like Manhattan's Electric Circus to be in the electronic groove," the *Christian Science Monitor* pointed out in August 1968, in an article titled "Young Buyers 'Dig' Electronics." While young heads were being split at the Democratic National Convention in Chicago, electronics marketers were focusing on entering the skulls of that generation in unsubtle fashion, with products resplendent in "brilliant hues and hep design."

Young people weren't "hep" to anything by then—the word had already gone out of fashion—and were not "into" pandering. What could manufacturers do in such a situation? Well, for one thing they could keep their prices high and fight discounters fiercely. They weren't "hep" to price competition, and they were willing to do everything necessary to attract boomers except cut prices. Manufacturers demanded that retailers sell their products at the prices they determined—the "list price"—and got nasty when their wishes weren't obeyed. A web of state laws, court decisions, and federal statutes, going by the Orwellian name of "fair trade laws," sanctioned manufacturer bludgeoning of retailers in most states, including New York. Discount houses in myriad product lines, from clothing to electronics to appliances, were harassed and sued by manufacturers.

The Eisenhower years set the tone. They have gone down in history as placid, but in that era guerrilla warfare was rampant between manufacturers and discounters. Dispatches from the front lines filled the newspapers. In the late 1950s, the small appliance division of General Electric was spending a half-million dollars a year "tracking down retailers who sell its waffle irons, skillets, coffee makers and other appliances at cut prices." Consumer electronics? That was even more of a no-go zone for discounters. Prices were enforced as rigidly as the party line in Moscow.

"Fair trade" charged ahead in the 1960s with the subtlety of a steamroller. In a display ad for Grand Central Radio, a high-end audio store, shortly before Christmas of 1968, *New York Times* readers learned that they could purchase a Scott 341 70-watt FM stereo receiver with "field effect transistors" and an "integrated circuit IF strip" for $279.95, more than $2,200 in 2022 dollars. Gimbels department store was advertising Magnavox color television sets for $750, about $6,000 in 2022. The market cried out for relief from this craziness, and there were avenues for the truly adventurous.

"Gray market" vendors walked a tightrope between the legal and not-quite-legal, selling brand-name goods at steep discounts to skirt the fair trade laws. In New York, a string of such stores could be found on Canal Street near the Manhattan Bridge. It was a kind of Gray Market Gulch, lined with "import-export" stores that bought goods ostensibly for shipment overseas, which they sold from their dingy, crowded retail outlets at steep discounts. Gray goods did not catch on for various reasons, among them that their wares, manufactured for overseas consumers, didn't carry US warranties and often didn't operate on 110-volt electrical current.

The gray market didn't interest Eddie. He didn't want to operate on small volume in the shadows. So he had no choice. He became an authorized dealer, selling at list price like everyone else. In April 1969, shortly after his store opened, ERS was stocking Panasonic audio equipment and was listed in a *New York Times* display ad as a company-authorized "franchised dealer." He became a vendor of Craig and JVC gear and Marantz stereos and was listed in agate type in the manufacturers' newspaper and magazine ads, alongside dozens of other far-better-known stores. In October 1971, now called Sights and Sounds, Eddie's store was a duly approved dealer for Ampex tapes—as was Crawford's two blocks away, a reminder that he was still competing with his cousin Ronnie.

Being an authorized dealer was like standing in the bread line in Leningrad. You'd get your loaf like everyone else, but you were just going to scrape by. There was no reason to stop at Eddie's store unless you happened to be in the area and needed Ampex tapes. People who lived in Manhattan and the suburbs went to Kings Highway to visit grandma, not to buy stereos. Ronnie sensed failure and pulled out, selling his stake to Eddie for $25,000. Eddie was now the two-thirds owner of a store that was hardly keeping afloat.

Eddie's customers were locals, just as they were at Crawford's, and they were pikers, just as they were at Crawford's. He could see that he needed to break out of the neighborhood-store ghetto. He wanted people willing to spend money, people greedy for bargains, people who weren't smart alecks and deadbeats like the locals. People he could sell. He would need to compete on price, and he would need the major brands—the same ones sold at the big department stores in Manhattan. And that door slammed in his face before he even tried.

Manufacturers weren't selling to discounters, so Eddie and his father worked their contacts. How do you get products that people won't sell you? It wasn't a new problem, and neither was the solution.

You deal with people who don't give a fuck.

■ ■ ■

The van pulled up to a long, squat two-story building on White Plains Road in the northeast Bronx. An elevated train thundered overhead periodically, but this was otherwise a quiet neighborhood with little foot traffic. Eddie and his helpers put the merchandise in the van and did not linger. An impassive, muscular man watched them load and did not offer to help. It had the aura of a heist, or perhaps a transaction in stolen goods. From the standpoint of manufacturers of consumer electronics in 1972, it was a lot worse.

Sam M.'s window-trimming business would have struck out at Corner Distributors. There were no fancy displays in the windows. In fact, there were no windows. They were bricked up. A broad expanse of brown wall faced customers. A long, flat, empty wall. No signs. No advertising. No graffiti. The people who ran Corner Distributors would not have liked that. You did not shoplift there. You did not rob it. You did not deface its walls.

Corner was one of the businesses in New York City of the 1970s with which you did not fuck. It was a category of free enterprise that deserved its own entry in the Yellow Pages. Among them were certain bars in Hell's Kitchen and East New York and social clubs in Little Italy where the windows were tinted and visitors were not welcome. In fiction such as *A Bronx Tale*, strangers intruded upon these places in hostile fashion and were beaten savagely. In real life nothing of the kind ever happened because people did not fuck with them. The rule was to mind your own business. Don't bother them and they won't bother you.

Corner Distributors was in that category not because it sold brand-name electronics, for which it was a duly authorized retailer, but because of its main business. A $15 million-a-year numbers racket operated out of the store, "serving Bronx and Manhattan players for 40 years" at the time of a police raid in 1997. The Corner Distributors ring served 250 numbers spots, located in candy stores and newsstands, where patrons bet on three-digit numbers and winners were paid six hundred to one. "Hundreds of hours of court-ordered wiretaps and intercepted faxes revealed the operation's scope," the *New York Daily News* reported after one such raid. Corner was "pivotal to the success of the gambling operation," police said.

It was a family business very much like Sights and Sounds, old friends and relatives working together. Just as *nehkdi* and avoiding taxation were not viewed as a crime by S-Y merchants, illegal gambling was not considered a wrongful activity by generations of working-class New Yorkers. The Vegliante brothers, who operated Corner, were arrested for running a numbers bank in East Harlem in 1951 and again in 1954. They would have scowled at the depiction of their enterprise as a "racket." It was a business that valued its employees and repaid their loyalty with fair compensation and job security.

One of the operators of the Vegliantes' East Harlem numbers bank, not a family member, a lad of twenty-two when arrested in 1951, was still with the firm and sixty-eight when collared in 1997. His name appears in newspaper accounts of both arrests, but the singularity of that fact was overlooked in coverage of the 1997 bust—that he had grown old in the numbers business. In New York of the 1970s, when murders were so common most did not even get a line in the newspapers, spending one's working life at an illegal enterprise was simply not that big of a deal.

Eddie viewed Corner as a trustworthy and discreet counterparty and recognized that no one would dream of ratting out his new supplier to the manufacturers. The man who managed the numbers bank and Corner, Anthony "Charlie" Vegliante, was described by police as an associate of the Genovese crime family and by his attorney as an "exceptional and exceptionally decent gentleman." There is no reason to doubt either characterization. He was a man of culture and refinement, a devoted art collector who filled his modest Bronx home with treasures that included an autograph collection, thousands of rare books, a Ming vase, and a first edition of writings by the noted Bronxite Edgar Allan Poe.

Eddie knew that the retail outlet was not Corner's only business. It was common knowledge in the North Bronx. It mattered little to the people of the neighborhood and even less to Eddie. Thanks to Corner Distributors and a handful of other suppliers, he was able to stock the sound room of his Kings Highway store with brand-name merchandise that he bought at prices slightly above wholesale. Eddie also bought from overseas vendors and from other retailers at slightly above wholesale, using Sam M.'s contacts.

With Corner and other suppliers lined up, Eddie began his campaign to attract customers down to Kings Highway. He had a plan, which he executed in methodical fashion, step by step. He knew that to succeed in any business where success or failure meant having a slight advantage over the competition, you needed an edge. In the Garment District, the edge came from mob connections that thwarted union contracts. Some of the methods that constituted Eddie's edge were new, some old, some significant earners, and some less lucrative.

Eddie taught one of the oldest, most crucial elements of his edge to a new salesman on Kings Highway named Nick Zippilli. Nick was a neighborhood guy working at the pizza parlor next door, and one day he wandered into

Sights and Sounds. Eddie saw qualities in Nick that Nick didn't know he had. Eddie knew that Nick would be a great salesman, and his judgment turned out to be correct. Part of it was that he could project, put on an act. To sell, at least for Eddie, one had to perform, and Nick could do that. He had worked in nightclubs and as a comedian and singer in the Catskills, a "Martin and Lewis act." He had been a deckhand on a fishing boat in Sheepshead Bay. Those jobs never lasted very long, but in working for Eddie, he found a whole new career path.

Crazy Eddie's method of salesmanship—variations on the tricks and techniques he was taught in the clip joints—changed little over the years. The salesmen (they were pretty much all male) would work as a team. Whenever a customer would walk in the entrance, the salesman who noticed would alert his colleague in a mix of Arab slang and pig latin: *shoof the eye-gay* (keep an eye on the guy). The customer might be a *lot eight* (a crazy person), who'd quickly be ushered out, or a *lot six* (gay person). Or just some *jedge* (jerk) who wanted to use the *tesh* (toilet). Eddie knew how to deal with the common riffraff who came into the store on occasion, the odd *husho* (shoplifter) or *nish* (lowlife). Crime was not to be tolerated. They would *shamble* (mock) such a character and kick him out.

No cash? No problem. The salesman would take a two-buck deposit if a customer was interested in a particular product. If it appeared he was about to leave the store without buying anything and hadn't left a deposit, the word would be passed: *NAD the eye-gay*. Nail the guy at the door. That was a crucial concept. Nick recalled: "His philosophy was that if a customer came in the store, he's supposed to buy. He shouldn't be walking out. He went out of his way to come to that store. There's a reason he's not buying. You nail him at the door." Only if you could keep the customer in the store was it possible to determine if the *eye-gay* was a sales prospect or a *zabba*, a deadbeat who was not going to buy, who was not vulnerable to the *sketch*, the lies the salesmen fabricated about the product. Customers like that weren't worth *hudda* (shit). Waste too much time with the *azab*, the losers, and the salesman could wind up getting *kished* (fired). Eddie demanded, and rewarded, competence.

In Nick's first weekend on the job, Eddie had him stand by the door on Kings Highway, where he had set up a Kenwood receiver with cheap speakers and a low-grade turntable. Eddie told him, "If anybody walks out without buying a stereo system, give them this one for $250." Eddie told him what to say and how to say it. The idea was to be respectful but persistent. The aim was to make the customer feel like he was getting a good deal, a bargain. If a customer was walking out the door empty-handed, you stopped him at the door.

"What were you looking to buy today, sir?"

"A stereo."

"Which one?"

"That one over there."

"Why didn't you buy it?"

"It's just a little more than I'm willing to spend right now."

"I tell you what. See this stereo system right here? It's marked down to $299. You buy it right now, I'll give it to you for $250."

If a customer was responding to an ad offering a Sony stereo, Eddie or his salesman would say, "Done. Come with me." On the way to show him the Sony, he would degrade the product mercilessly. "Don't buy Sony, my friend. Sony is overpriced. You're just shelling out more money for the name. JVC is just as good, but it's cheaper." Eddie wasn't necessarily wrong. Often the other product was just as good. What the customer didn't know was that the lower-priced stereo gave Eddie a higher markup and that the Sony might have already sold out.

This was a kind of "bait and switch," but to Eddie it was just a logical and obvious sales tactic. Besides, customers who insisted upon buying the advertised brand—always a small minority—walked away satisfied. Eddie had a special way of dealing with demanding customers who insisted on brand-name products that were not in stock. Eddie's people called it "lunching."

Merchandise that was put on display could be sold, but the law required that the retailer mark them as "display models" since they had been handled by dozens of customers, sometimes roughly. Most customers avoided such merch and held out for items that were brand-new. Even more stringent rules applied to products that customers returned as defective. If the manufacturer disagreed and returned the unit to the store, it couldn't be put back on sale again. The retailer would have to eat the loss. Law-abiding stores like Macy's offered display models and returned goods at a discount, and they were snapped up by customers who knew the risks that they were taking. Or they were sold at a steep discount to liquidators, which offered them to the public with full disclosure of their origins.

Eddie didn't need liquidators. He had a unique way of getting full price for returns and display models of brand-name electronics. It was called "lunching." The salesman would write up the sale, and then the customer would wait for the product to be delivered at the pickup area. If it seemed to be taking a long time, there was a reason for it. If the customers listened carefully, they could hear a salesman tell somebody to "go have lunch."

While the customer was waiting, the display model or returned unit would be cleaned up with a special cloth so it looked brand-new. Plastic stickers, manuals, and plastic packing filler had been saved when the item was originally received weeks or months before and would be carefully put back in place. The boxes would then be sealed with just the right color and kind of tape, and the staples, which had been carefully extracted when the box was opened, would be replaced to make it seem as if the box hadn't been touched since it came out of the factory. This profit-enhancement technique was called "lunching" because the staple gun and sealing tape were kept in what looked like a lunch bag. The original boxes were kept in mint condition, in a special part of the storerooms set aside for "demo boxes."

Crawford's didn't do lunching as far as Sammy knew. Ronnie was like that. Stodgy. Eddie was the opposite, and more generous as well. Sammy had worked at Crawford's since he turned twelve in 1969, starting at five bucks a day for doing odd jobs. His pay was eventually increased to $10. In January 1971, Sammy started working for Eddie. The pay was $1.75 an hour but Eddie gave Sammy something just as important, a sense that he was part of a dynamic enterprise that had a future, not just another S-Y store. Eddie had a talent for making people feel valued, even when he cursed at them—which he did, frequently. It was part of his persona.

Sammy had the usual adolescent awkwardness. Eddie did his best to draw him out of his shell, treating Sammy to his first sexual experience at age thirteen, a visit to a prostitute that was a memorable bar mitzvah gift. Sammy was never going to be like Eddie, but his cousin didn't mind. Every member of the family could contribute, whether they were bookish like Sammy or Uncle Zookie, who had drawn the wrath of some in the Syrian community because of his marriage to Margie. Unlike Eddie, Sammy took his education seriously. Eddie saw qualities in him that no one else in the family could envision. He viewed Sammy as a long-term investment in human capital.

■ ■ ■

Eddie now had brand-name merchandise, not in very large quantities but enough to get customers in the store. They were starting to come from outside the neighborhood. As his word of mouth improved, there were fewer *zabbas*, fewer jerks who wouldn't buy into the *sketch*. He had salesmen he had trained. What he didn't have was a surefire gimmick. It had to be good. Not original. Good.

Once Eddie told a reporter, "The customers gave me the [Crazy Eddie] name." The reason, he explained, was his NAD tactic—"I wouldn't let a person walk out the door without selling." The story that circulated in the family was that a schoolteacher friend of Debbie's, not knowing they were married, said she went to Sights and Sounds and "bought a stereo from that crazy guy, Eddie." Either version is possible, but it's more likely that Eddie simply stole the "insane" idea. He didn't have to look around for it. By the 1970s, the "crazy merchant" *shtick* was a well-worn cliché in retail advertising.

The most prominent "crazy" merchant in the United States was a California pitchman named Earl "Madman" Muntz, who blanketed the state with irritating radio and television ads claiming that his prices were so low that he was nuts. Muntz began by selling used cars in the 1940s and moved into television sets in the early 1950s. He was still going strong in the 1970s. He "plastered the US with billboards bearing a caricature of himself—a long-nosed figure in Napoleonic hat and boots and red flannel underwear—and such slogans as 'I want to give 'em away, but Mrs. Muntz won't let me—she's crazy!'" Muntz achieved a degree of national repute and was plugged in the 1948 Tracy-Hepburn film *State of the Union*, just as a Crazy Eddie commercial made a cameo appearance in the 1984 movie *Splash*.

Muntz was not a household name in the East, but "insanely low" prices were old hat everywhere by the time Eddie opened his store. In 1962 the sitcom *Car 54, Where Are You?*, set in the Bronx, featured a men's shop with a loudspeaker screaming, "Get a new suit for practically nothing! I'm having a mental lapse! Come in and take advantage of me! Come and take a beautiful suit before they take me away! I've lost my mind!" That was a full decade before Eddie began to go "crazy" so it's not likely he remembered it (even though this was one of his favorite programs), but the *Car 54* episode shows how this approach was already floating through the ether.

Eddie certainly gave the "crazy merchant" a fresh slant. Madman Muntz was garish and hokey. Eddie was cool and hip, as if he was including the audience in his joke. His earliest "insane" ads were childish and stupid, like much great advertising. One of the first appeared in the *Village Voice* on September 28, 1972, a full-page display ad for "Sights & Sounds: Home of Crazy Eddie." At the top of the page was a monkey hanging from a vine clutching a speaker and a banana:

> Has Sights and Sounds Gone Bananas? Sights and Sounds Stereo have really peeled their prices. Crazy Eddie (the top banana) has personally seen to it that Sights and Sound Stereo cannot and absolutely will not be undersold on any sound system.

The ad pitched two brand-name stereo systems, one from Sony and the other from Sherwood, and included a long list of other brands that were supposedly in stock, including Harmon Kardon, Pioneer, Marantz, and Fisher. The Sony package consisted of a STR-6065 receiver, ADC 303 AX speakers, a Garrard SL 72B turntable, and a Shure M91ED cartridge. The list price for all those components, according to the ad, was $827.00. "Crazy Eddie's price: $484.00."

How could he afford to charge so little? It was simple. All he had to do was cheat the government. It was the most powerful component of his edge over the competition. Sammy later recalled that Eddie's approach was simple. Typically, wholesalers charged retailers 60 percent of the list price. So law-abiding retailers would buy a unit for $60 and sell it for the mandated list price of $100, collecting the sales tax. Eddie would sell that same unit for far less than $100, perhaps even less than cost, less than $60. That's because he would collect the sales tax but not turn it in to the government. Thus, as Sammy points out, "even if he sells at cost or below cost, he still makes money."

That's how Eddie could charge so little if customers could not be switched away. While the actual math behind the pricing in the *Voice* ad is lost to history, it probably went something like this: The cost to Eddie, Sammy believes, was probably in the neighborhood of 60 percent of the $827 list price, which came to about $500 ($496.20 to be exact). Customers who could not be bait-and-switched from the Sony package would have paid $484.00 plus $33 (7 percent sales tax), a total of $517.88. Eddie kept that entire sum for himself, including the $33 in sales tax he was supposed to have turned in to the state and city tax authorities. So he'd have still made a small profit of $17.88. It might have been a bit smaller than that, since Eddie paid a little above wholesale to outfits like Corner. But he would still have made a profit. Sammy recalls that "Eddie hated Sony," which refused to sell directly to him in the early days. The *Voice* ad was a way not only to build his business, but also to "stick it to Sony."

Stealing sales tax was a low-risk endeavor in the early 1970s because the forces of law and order had plenty of worse crimes to deal with. At a time when bodies were washing up in New York Harbor and a stretch of Eighth Avenue was known as the "Minnesota Strip" because it was crowded with teenage prostitutes from the Midwest, stealing sales tax simply didn't rank high on the list of law enforcement priorities. Even if the tax authorities suspected it was happening, how would they prove it? Sales tax was rung up with each purchase, so an investigator would not have noticed anything untoward. Some tax was passed on to the state, as *zero* payments would have been a red flag. But it would have been pretty much impossible to prove that large amounts of collected sales tax were being stolen. These were cash transactions, and Eddie's books would have shown nothing of the kind going on. At the time, the government paid attention only when things got out of hand. In the 1980s, Russian mobsters concocted daisy chains of shell companies to siphon off millions of dollars in stolen federal and state gasoline taxes, resulting in a string of criminal prosecutions. The Mafia was involved in that as well. It was far too big to ignore.

Though largely unnoticed, small-scale sales tax thievery was still a crime. Unless a competitor was willing to risk jail, Eddie had the edge. The ad said that he would *always beat a competitor's price*. Had he been honest, he'd have added *because we steal the sales tax*.

Customers had no way of knowing he was doing that. Lunching, if done right, was not obvious to customers either. Neither was upselling—selling stereo systems cheaply and inflating the price of accessories. Eddie taught Nick the art of upselling before he even knew how to write up a ticket for the sale. The aim was to make *"yuck yuck"* on a guy coming into a store. That was Crazy Eddie slang for extra profit, building up the ticket. "I sold the turntable for C-line [a standard price] but I made *yuck yuck* on the cartridge," Nick would happily tell Eddie. High-end cartridges, hi-fi record needles, and cables were marked up by as much as 300 percent, the kind of price-gouging that would have made a Forty-Second Street clip joint owner proud. The store might make a couple of bucks on the turntable, but the cartridge would cost Eddie $7 and he'd sell it for $29.

Eddie's edge worked. He didn't win over the hard-edged locals, who were turned off by high-pressure tactics and savvy to bait and switch, but that was fine. The feeling was mutual. He wanted customers who would buy into his spiel. And there were more of them than there were cranky old farts window-shopping on Kings Highway. The "crazy" device was so effective that Eddie changed the name of the Kings Highway store from Sights and Sounds to Crazy Eddie in 1973. In 1974 he opened a second Crazy Eddie in Syosset, Long Island.

Eddie Antar had turned a corner. With his unconventional sources of supply and unscrupulous (to say the least) methods, he had established himself as a consumer electronics discounter. Kelso was winning a crooked race the only way he could manage, by fighting even dirtier than the manufacturers. Eddie didn't beat fair trade by waging court battles. He did it in

1970s counterculture style—by subverting it. They had the laws. He had a numbers banker in the Bronx and his edge.

Eddie was building a team of people just like himself—hungry young kids wandering through life who had no idea what they were doing, but somehow managed to do it better than anyone else.

CHAPTER THREE

For the baby boomers lined up at Eddie's cash registers, music wasn't a hobby. It was a necessity. It was a way of giving vent to life. Charles Kaiser wrote in *1968 in America* that rock and roll "helped shape a political agenda but its influence was beyond politics. It was by turns steel-edged, sentimental, raucous, melodious, sophisticated, and infantile, sometimes tinged with nihilism but most often blazingly upbeat." Their parents danced to music, listened to it. They lived it. They would lock themselves in their rooms and blast it. Many played instruments, including an ambitious high school student in the suburbs of New York named Larry Weiss.*

Larry was from Massapequa, a bedroom community on the south shore of Long Island. It was as Middle American as one could find in the suburbs of New York City, a place where the houses were freshly painted, the lawns freshly mowed, the parents hardworking, and the kids fashionably ungrateful and rebellious. Larry father's was an engineer at Grumman Aerospace, but Larry was interested in a different kind of technology. Radio was the principal habitat of rock, which transformed that creaky old medium into the "flipside of television in American culture." It helped that Plainedge High School was up to speed in every facet of broadcasting and even had a full-size TV studio. In his spare time Larry played bass guitar in a three-piece band that entertained in cocktail lounges. "We used to say that the people who came to see us were all married but not to each other." Life was good, if busy.

---

* No relation to the author.

While not in school or playing in his band, Larry applied his considerable energy to radio, working at a local station, WGSM, even after he graduated from Plainedge and taking a full eighteen-credit course load at the New York Institute of Technology. He recalls working "pretty much around the clock." During those manic years, Larry learned the peculiar poetry of radio advertising "spots." They had to read right, and they had to sound right, short and punchy—they weren't called "spots" for nothing—getting the message across for listeners driving to jobs they hated and sitting at the kitchen table while the kids squawked. *Giles Chevrolet. Big-G–little I, L-E-S.* Irascible, demanding, unreasonable merchants were his teachers.

Itching to jump-start his career, Larry quit college and moved to radio gigs upstate. He wound up in a Catskills village called Liberty, landing a job at its only radio station, WVOS. After that came a spell in a band with his old high school pal Jeff Gottschalk, and then Larry went into the concert business. In Woodbourne, a short drive from Liberty, an old vaudeville house had come to life on the lingering fumes of Woodstock as the Peace Palace, offering concerts by groups like the Chambers Brothers and organic snacks in lieu of popcorn at the concession stand. Thus began Larry's brief stint as a theater operator, using the old Peace Palace to feature offbeat films like *Pink Flamingos* and live performances.

One of the partners in the venture was an ad salesman at WPIX-FM in Manhattan. His name was Jeff Coleman, and he wanted to be in the concert business, which was a shame because, as Larry later explained, "it was terrible business. We'd make money one night and lose it the next." This was no way to make a living, and Larry began casting about for the next chapter in his life. When the concert season ended, Coleman put Larry in touch with an audio store in Brooklyn that was buying ad spots on WPIX-FM. Crazy Eddie needed someone to handle something called "co-op advertising." Fortunately, that was one of the facets of the ad game that Larry had picked up during his brief but varied career.

By now Larry was getting old—pushing twenty-four—and ready to settle down. He showed up on Kings Highway dressed in "1975 casual," which meant whatever he decided to put on that morning. He correctly guessed that a jacket and tie would have been out of place. He had a dark-brown beard, but it was well groomed and clean—the "dirty hippie" look was no longer in vogue. The store was packed tight with merchandise and customers.

A man about his age with an attitude of studied indifference, who he later learned was Arnie Spindler, was working the cash register.

"I'm looking for Eddie."

"What's your name?"

"Larry."

"Lonnie?"

"Larry."

"Lonnie?"

It was no use. From then on, he was "Lonnie." Anyone who walked into the store would get razzed, whether they were customers, panhandlers, exterminators, or job applicants. It was harmless fun, an S-Y thing. Once Larry went to a Syrian-run store on Times Square. "They had this little trick where they'd walk by fast, and if you weren't looking they'd brush your ankle with something. You'd look around and they'd say, 'Mice.' I knew that trick right away from Crazy Eddie. They would tease everyone."

Arnie directed Larry up the stairs to the second floor. In the rear was a beat-up, musty office with a few old file cabinets and worn steel desks piled high with papers. Two men were in the office, one young, bearded, and unkempt and the other neatly attired, clean-shaven, and middle-aged. Their names sounded identical because they were, except when spelled out. Eddie Antar was the younger man, looking up at Larry impassively. The older man was Eddy Antar, father of Sammy, known around Crazy Eddie as "Uncle Eddy." Sam M. had brought him in as a bookkeeper and to keep an eye on his son.

Their personalities were as different as their names were similar. Eddy was courteous and soft-spoken. Larry recalls: "Eddie was very crude. He was wearing his torn sweater, which he wore for years until it was unwearable. His good-luck sweater. He was very matter-of-fact and very crude and very tough. Uncle Eddy was very gentle and asked the real questions. Eddie was more 'Can you do it?'"

Larry could do it. He was given a desk and went to work. He had no title; his main responsibility would be to obtain for Crazy Eddie the co-op advertising money that Eddie recently learned was owed to the store. While Eddie was engaged in the various sleazy tactics constituting his edge—the bait and switch, the lunching, the sales tax stealing—he was overlooking a perfectly legal revenue-raising mechanism. It was like finding gift certificates beneath a pile of old newspapers. Larry's job was to find still more gift certificates and use them. Whenever a brand was mentioned in retailer advertising, print or broadcast, the store was entitled to a credit against its ad spending if the manufacturer had a co-op ad program. Most manufacturers did, and any retailer was eligible to participate. It seems surreal in retrospect, but manufacturers were about to subsidize Eddie's sabotage of their price-fixing. This fair-trade-fighting gadfly, this nuisance who bought product from a numbers bank in the Bronx, was entitled to compensation from the very companies whose pricing policies he was undermining.

Another irony was that Eddie did not need the inducement of co-op advertising to plug brand names. Ever since he adopted the "crazy" gimmick three years earlier in 1972, he had been pushing brand names in newspaper and radio ads to lure customers. After all, that's what he was selling: top-drawer brands at prices he cut by stealing the sales tax.

In a few weeks Larry garnered about $1 million in co-op advertising dollars. The size of this windfall gives an idea of the magnitude of Eddie's advertising spending. Crazy Eddie was becoming the Antar family cash cow, with Uncle Eddy handling his nephew's two sets of books. One was shown to the government for tax purposes, while the other had the actual numbers, so that the cash could be accurately divided up between Eddie and Sam M. as one-third owner.

Both sets of green ledger books showed that all three Crazy Eddie stores were doing fabulously. The Kings Highway and Syosset stores had done so well that Eddie had just opened in the heart of Greenwich Village, on Sixth Avenue. This was the music capital of the East, and in the mid-1970s it was far grungier than it would be in later years, with a women's prison only recently demolished across from the store location. There were few upscale stores and even fewer audio outlets. Instead, it was the habitat of jazz clubs, revival movie theaters, coffeehouses, head shops, sandal emporiums, book nooks, and record stores. Its streets were swamped with college kids, their pockets stuffed with mom's money, which made it a natural place to sell stereos.

Larry fitted in well with the frenetic atmosphere at this odd little electronics emporium. Eddie remained as curt as he'd been in the job interview. He "showed his appreciation by not firing you," Larry recalls, but Eddie had a fierce determination and charisma that attracted people. He got used to Eddie's peculiarities, like his obsessive working out in the gym he set up in the room adjoining his office and his superstitions. When a lumbering German Shepherd called "Sugar" came into Eddie's life, she was always at his side. He often behaved more like the head of a bizarre family than owner of a retail chain, and in the early days most of his employees were just that—members and friends of the Antar family.

People outside the family were unaware of it, but the boss was a younger, bearded version of Sam M., with some aspects of his grandfather Murad. The difference was that Eddie had a high profile. Sam M. and Murad would never have dreamed of putting their names on their stores. His father still had his own string of stores, including a sizable discount outlet on Kennedy Boulevard in Jersey City, but his holdings were dwarfed by Eddie's growing enterprise. When a Crazy Eddie opened on Fordham Road in the Bronx in 1976, it was Eddie, not Sam M., who put Uncle Zookie in charge. Eddie was clearly eclipsing his father, establishing himself as head of the family through sheer economic power. Sam M. had done that years before, replacing Murad as head of the family, but not at such a young age. Eddie, not yet thirty, had surpassed him, outshined him, and Sam M. didn't like it one bit.

Sam M. was in his midfifties. He might have seemed old to the kids who worked in the stores, but the reflection that stared back at Sam M. in the mirror didn't seem at all elderly to him. He had plenty of productive years ahead. There would have been no Crazy Eddie if it wasn't for him. Eddie wasn't going to replace him as head of the family. He would see to that.

■ ■ ■

Larry, now known around Crazy Eddie as the "advertising guy," noticed right away that Eddie's approach to promoting the stores was slapdash. He would buy radio time and then the stations would produce the commercials, each airing the same refrain that Crazy Eddie would not be undersold. Each station put its own imprint on the commercials, depending on the whims and individual style of the announcers and disc jockeys. Nobody at Crazy Eddie thought to coordinate what the stations were doing. "There was no approach," Larry recalls. "Someone would come up with an idea and do it for their radio station. I saw that as a huge flaw." It made sense to send out a uniform message, a single voice that listeners would instantly associate with Crazy Eddie as they twirled the dial.

Larry had a single, solitary voice in mind. It was a product of Larry's friendship with Jeff Coleman, his former theater partner and radio sales rep. WPIX-FM's Crazy Eddie commercials were being produced at its studios in the Daily News Building on East Forty-Second Street, featuring disc jockeys like Dennis Quinn, Ted David, and occasionally a tall Yonkers native in his early thirties known as "Dr. Jerry" at the station—Jerry Carroll. Soon it became not so occasional. Jerry just clicked. "We found that more and more we were doing stuff with Jerry, because we got a kick out of his delivery." He had a breathless, frantic, rapid-fire way of delivering the ad copy, spitting out a stream of words without garbling any of them. He conveyed urgency, as if heading over to Crazy Eddie was the most important thing a human being could do.

Larry found himself at the WPIX studios regularly to produce commercials featuring Jerry. Before each taping session, Larry would read each commercial to Eddie. He was constantly working out in his office, so Eddie would be peddling a stationary bicycle or hanging upside down, suspended by gravity boots, while he mulled each new ad. "He'd be hanging there upside down, and we'd be talking about commercials," Larry said. "I'd read it to him, and he'd change words around." Eddie always had to change something, always had to put his imprint on the script. It was never good enough. Eddie would change "silly things." A word here and there, or the structure of a sentence. Eddie's tinkering could, and often did, throw off the flow of a commercial.

Larry learned to write a script so that Eddie would "change it the right way." Larry would want the commercial to say, "Now's the time to get the best price ever," so he'd word it, "Now's a time," so that Eddie would have something to fix and make it right. "He had to have the last word."

Television was next. Larry's contacts in radio put him in touch with a small production company called Neshobe Films, headed by an ambitious would-be feature-film director named Mike Fink. If nothing else, Mike had his finger on the pulse of the times. In 1975 he produced *Black Force*, a justifiably obscure example of the 1970s "blaxploitation" film genre. The movie did not garner accolades, but the commercials Neshobe produced for a shock jock named Don Imus were widely acclaimed in the advertising industry. Directed by a talented Brooklyn kid named Jay Dubin, they featured various New York characters, like a guy popping out of a sewer, all saying, "Did you hear what he said this morning?" It was just the kind of approach Larry was looking for.

The decision to run ads on TV was easy. Deciding what to put on the air was a lot harder. Consumer electronics stores rarely advertised on TV, so there was no precedent. The closest anyone had come to Eddie's approach was Jerry Rosenberg, who ran a discount outlet called JGE Appliances. He appeared personally in TV commercials, wearing a hard hat and bellowing, "That's the story!" Definitely not Eddie's style.

Then one day an idea jelled—doo-wop. Fifties and early sixties music was coming back. As the idea began to take shape, Eddie remembered that a customer had written a poem—not much of a poem, but an actual poem—on the Crazy Eddie experience. It included the line "When you think you're ready, come down to Crazy Eddie." There was a nice rhythm to it. Why not turn it into a jingle? Thinking it over in his office, Larry heard the Del Vikings' recording of "A Sunday Kind of Love" come over the radio. He knew immediately—that was it. He ran into Eddie's office and told him. Eddie knew the song and started singing it.

Larry then reunited with his old pal Jeff Gottschalk in the living room of his parents' home in Massapequa. They fooled around with the lyrics and melody at the piano, but there was a problem. The poem's ending, "And so the story's told, Crazy Eddie will not be undersold," did not work. It didn't sound right. Larry's sister chimed in, adding a line to match the tempo. That did it. Soon after, the jingle was taped at a recording studio on Long Island, with the vocals by Jeff, Larry, and their friend and fellow musician John Russo. Larry had the only solo in the song, the line fleshed out by his sister: "And so the story's told, across the whole wide woild."

As time neared to film the commercial, Eddie started having second thoughts. Maybe they should have a spokesman tell people about Crazy Eddie, just as they did in their radio commercials? Larry came up with a sample script for a spokesman commercial and ended it with the line "Crazy Eddie, the man is insane!"

"Eddie freaked out. 'What are you talking about? I am not!' Somehow he took it personally." Larry had never seen Eddie upset like that. He was surprised. After all, Eddie was the one who had come up with the "Crazy Eddie" gimmick in the first place. He was the one who was calling himself nuts. "So we bandied it about, and I said, 'How about "Crazy Eddie, his prices are insane"?'" That became the tagline.

They decided to do both a doo-wop commercial and a spokesman commercial. The next decision was tricky: Who was going to be the TV embodiment of Eddie Antar?

"I said, 'There's only one person we could possibly use. We got to use Jerry Carroll.'" Larry recalled, "And they go, 'Are you kidding?' They absolutely didn't want to use Jerry Carroll." Nobody involved knew Jerry all that well—not the Neshobe people, not Eddie. But Larry had worked with him on the radio commercials and had been in the studio when they were being taped. "Just watching him do radio, the hand gestures and the facial gestures that he used just to get the sound he wanted out of himself, was exactly how I envisioned doing the commercials." Larry talked them into it and offered it to Jerry. He jumped at it.

The doo-wop commercial was filmed by actors who lip-synced along with the song. Jay Dubin had been a film student at Pratt Institute, so he knew the right bathroom, which was near the cafeteria. Both commercials were filmed on the same day, the doo-wop commercial at Pratt, moving to the Village store that night to shoot the Jerry Carroll commercial. The first TV spots hit the air in May 1976.

The doo-wop commercial was nominated for a Clio award, honoring the finest in hucksterism. It became a smash hit or at least as much of a smash hit as a commercial could be. Thousands of Eva-Tone sound sheets—cheap plastic phonograph records—were distributed with the song. There were supposed to be just a few of the Jerry Carroll commercials, but in time there would be hundreds. They became the heart and soul of Crazy Eddie as it soared like Icarus, far too close to the sun.

CHAPTER FOUR

LARRY AND THE CREW FROM NESHOBE WERE FILMING JERRY CARROLL with top-flight 35-mm Panavision motion-picture gear. The purpose was not to preserve him in celluloid for posterity (though they were doing just that) but because putting Crazy Eddie's new spokesman on videotape would have required a far more elaborate and costly setup. A remote unit. Cables across the sidewalk. Film was simpler and produced better quality, but it was sensitive to extraneous sound. Quiet was required on the set.

Sammy wasn't offended when the bearded guy grew tired of his clowning around in the store and ordered him out onto Sixth Avenue. It was after midnight, and the usual street characters were panhandling, peddling the *Daily Worker*, and hanging out at Gray's Papaya across the street. Sammy was used to being extraneous and underfoot. At nineteen he was a late bloomer, socially awkward, and a bit shorter than most of the guys his age. He had done well in school, which didn't count for much among S-Ys but meant a lot to Eddie. Sammy had the ability to intensely focus on a problem, no matter what it was, and spend hours addressing it. When he worked in the stores he was a neat freak, not satisfied until the counters were perfectly clean. Ever since he was twelve, when he started at Crawford's, Sammy had applied that same intensity to pursuing his ambition in life. He would open up his own store, maybe have two or three. Or maybe more. Sammy had an interest in the intricacies of business, the mergers and acquisitions, heroes and villains that he read about in the *Wall Street Journal* and *Barron's*.

Once Eddie gave his brother Mitchell and Sammy some excess merchandise, cassette tapes that they could sell on their own. Sammy proceeded to treat it like a business. They put the tapes in a briefcase, sold them to teachers at Boody Junior High School, carefully toted up the revenues, and split the proceeds, which came to ninety-nine dollars. Eddie saw how his cousin reacted, his enthusiasm, his intensity. One day when Sammy was in high school, Eddie said to him, "We need a brain in the business. This business is gonna grow, and I need a brain to work alongside me."

At the time, few Antars had been to college. The first to do so was Solomon Antar, son of Murad's long-deceased brother Ezra, who had visited him in the make-believe "dream." Solomon had done well for himself despite the early death of his father and had become the family lawyer. He was admired and envied in the family. Now the Antars had a lawyer and they needed a CPA, a certified public accountant, a career Solomon and Eddie both pushed Sammy to pursue. It didn't take much convincing, especially when Eddie told Sammy that he would pay his tuition and expenses and keep Sammy on the payroll while he attended college. In the fall of 1975, Sammy enrolled at Baruch College, the only City University unit that offered a degree in business.

This was an S-Y transaction, not an act of charity or family largesse. There were benefits for everyone involved. Aside from gaining Sammy's loyalty and an implied call on his services, Eddie was showing everyone, including Sam M., that now *he* was the one who wielded clout in the family. He hadn't cared much in the past. But as his economic clout grew, Eddie became aware that he was pushing Sam M. aside—and that was fine with him.

Sammy wasn't clued in to the family dynamics. All he knew was that Eddie was being generous, as he had always been, and he was happy to continue working for him while going to college. He lapped up the coursework with relish while working after school at the Village store, which was a brisk walk from Baruch's urban campus near Gramercy Park. Though Eddie was helping him, Sammy was acutely aware that nothing was handed to you in life and that merely existing could be a gift. He also knew that misery could turn into riches. It had happened in his mother's family, the Cheras.

■ ■ ■

Sammy was named after his mother's father. Salim "Sam" Chera came to America a year after Murad and Tera arrived in New York. He was virtually penniless. Much of his life was a struggle with the poverty that rumbled in the background, but he always managed to survive. He was known in the family as El Maz, "the golden" in Arabic, because he was the sole survivor of seven brothers and sisters. The rest had perished from disease in Aleppo, where medical care was poor and maladies from dysentery to cholera wiped out entire families.

After a sojourn in Colombia with his wife and toddler son, Sam Chera came to New York alone, landing at Ellis Island on February 4, 1921, his uncle's Allen Street address in his pocket. He was scraping by as a peddler when Hanna and Isaac joined him a few months later, arriving on a cargo vessel. Illness continued to haunt him in America, as it had in Aleppo. Early in 1923 Hanna died while giving birth to their daughter Esther. She was only twenty-six. No family members could afford to take them, so Esther and Isaac were placed in an orphanage. Sam remarried a year or so later. His bride was a warmhearted woman named Celia Chippon who didn't mind raising Hanna's two children—even though Sam, who was no fool, told her about his offspring only after they were married. Eight more children followed, and then the Depression hit. The hard times lingered. Sam Chera remained a peddler. In 1940 he was supporting his wife and ten children by selling linen, apparently without any great success as he was seeking work. He was unemployed in 1942, when he was fifty-four.

After the war, the family's fortunes turned. The struggling ended. Isaac became the prosperous owner of a chain of children's clothing stores. Isaac's son Stanley went into business with him. His sister Esther married the genial businessman Al Cohen, who in time would turn to Sam M. to get rid of that lease he couldn't use. Sam Chera was eighty-nine when he died in 1977, the years of disease and suffering far behind him. He was buried in the ancient Jewish cemetery on the Mount of Olives in Jerusalem, alongside eminent Jewish figures from the past.

Sammy knew about this near-endless litany of familial misfortune, but he also knew that all the suffering eventually came to an end and that the Cheras were now anything but impoverished. He knew that part of it was luck and part of it was choices. Stanley's were exceptionally good. He began buying and selling properties at a young age and became a wealthy real-estate developer. But his luck too did not last. Isaac lived into his eighties, but Stanley was not so fortune. A twenty-first-century affliction, no less deadly than the ones that swept Aleppo a hundred years earlier, claimed the grandson of El Maz. Stanley Chera died in April 2020 at age seventy-seven, one of the most prominent early victims of the COVID pandemic.

Had Sammy become close to his cousin Stanley instead of his cousin Eddie, his life would have been entirely different. Relatives were the true teachers in Brooklyn of the 1960s. There were public schools, some quite good, but many were little more than holding pens in which the students were as uninterested in learning as the teachers were in teaching. PS 177 was a middling elementary school, neither elite nor bottom-of-the-barrel. The teachers were largely time-clock-punching mediocrities, though some stood out. Sammy remembered a fourth grade teacher who encouraged him to read the *New York Times* and showered her charges with affection and nurturing. In the following year, he was saddled with a sadistic, abusive teacher who made fun of the children, "making them sit in garbage cans and telling the other kids to laugh at them." Parents had little say over the nightmares their children experienced at the hands of misfits like that. Next came Boody Junior High School, a pressure cooker of racial unrest, where the pupils were older and more violent and the teachers even more prone to lassitude.

Lafayette High School was practically Eton by comparison. Sammy flourished there. He joined the track team. He became an editor of the school newspaper—its largest source of revenue was Crazy Eddie ads—and did well in every subject except music. He didn't hide his business ambitions, which were not fashionable at the time, and in the yearbook photo of his Advanced Placement History class he is called "Sam Capitalist." That was fine with him. He *was* a capitalist. He was going into business. If the other kids wanted to change the world, that was their problem. At Baruch, Sammy would be able to learn the things that mattered to him, things he could use in the Antar family businesses.

Sammy's future role at Crazy Eddie was vague at first. All he knew was that he would be the CPA. At Baruch he learned what that meant. He learned that accountants communicated in their own special language, just like Crazy Eddie salesmen. Accountants had their own standards— "Generally Accepted Accounting Principles"—that they created and administered with minimal meaningful oversight. They could move goalposts or discard them entirely. Their practices were arcane and little understood outside of accounting. Like all professionals, they did not as a rule air their dirty laundry in public. An exception to the rule taught at Baruch, an accounting professor who had already acquired quite a name for himself.

Abraham J. Briloff was dedicated to the accounting profession as a servant of the public, not as a deceiver—a role that, he believed, it too often played. He was born in 1917 on the Lower East Side of Manhattan and was raised in Brooklyn. He had seen poverty in his youth and the abuses of the powerful, and it had left an impression. Deep within him he had taken sides, and he was to be on the side of the small, the powerless, the public, and the small investor. He was the author of well-received books on the foibles of his profession, with titles like *Unaccountable Accounting*. He wrote articles for *Barron's* and scholarly journals, all dedicated to exposing the shortcomings of accounting. He kept a heady pace of writing and lecturing despite a problem that would have defeated a lesser man: he was progressively losing his eyesight.

At Baruch, Briloff brought to life the dry numbers in financial statements. They were not figures in rows and columns but life itself—success and failure, honesty and criminality. Briloff taught that accounting was an exercise not in black and white, true or false, legal or illegal, but shades of gray. In the wrong hands, the numbers could be made to dance. Two and two could equal five—or ten. Or fifty. Or five hundred. Briloff exposed such beauties as "pooling of interest accounting" that "enabled many companies, particularly conglomerates, to report profits that simply did not exist." A dope dealer under the Coney Island boardwalk had the same morals, but would be tossed in the can for offenses far less damaging to society than the legal depredations of CPAs.

Sammy came away from Briloff's lectures with an understanding of the power he would wield as a CPA. Briloff also fed Sammy's growing realization that Crazy Eddie was behind the times. He began to see that while

Eddie was brilliant at marketing, in other ways he was old-fashioned. If you set aside the funky ads and commercials, it was a traditional S-Y enterprise. It was all about cash, bait and switch, evading taxes, and putting relatives on the payroll. There were new ways of doing business that Eddie and Sam M. didn't even know existed.

Numbers were not for nerds. Numbers meant fortunes. The time was approaching when Crazy Eddie would be able to reap all the benefits that America bestowed on its major corporations.

It wasn't inevitable. They had made it happen. They were hitting the big time.

PART TWO
"THEY'VE BECOME FAMOUS"

CHAPTER FIVE

HOWARD SMITH, FILMMAKER AND JOURNALIST, WAS ARBITER OF COOL FOR the coolest newspaper in the coolest city in the world. From 1966 to 1980, he wrote a column in the *Village Voice* called "Scenes" that scoured the garbage-strewn streets of pre-gentrified New York for the cutting-edge and the offbeat, the ridiculous, offensive, and titillating. His approach was straightforward, his prose deadpan, his reporting solid. Young people in Pelham and Great Neck read "Scenes" to learn how to be cool, where to find cool, and what made the cool cool. "'Be-in,' 'love-in,' 'Woodstock,' 'head shop,' 'Yippies' and 'Stonewall' were words and phrases that many *Voice* readers saw for the first time, or nearly so, in Scenes," the *New York Times* recalled when Smith died in 2014. Hucksters were a favorite subject. One column was devoted to hustlers who handed out flyers for massage parlors. (They tended to be ex-cons who worked on commission.) His 1972 documentary on a charlatan evangelist, *Marjoe*, won an Academy Award and cemented Smith's reputation.

The "Scenes" column of March 21, 1977, explored two of the latest exemplars of cool. Half was devoted to Plato's Retreat, "New York's first swinger's club with on-site sex." The second half was a deep dive into his favorite theme, the money-grabbing impulse that propelled the Big Apple.

"Beyond repetition. Way beyond annoyance. Even beyond psychotic outrageousness. . . . In fact, into the shimmering realm of the pop cult has arrived the Crazy Eddie Commercial. Even if you are among the people who hate them, you must admit they've become famous." The title of the column segment was "Crazy Eddie Revealed," but Crazy Eddie (the real one) was not revealed. "Who is Crazy Eddie anyway?" Smith asked, and not rhetori- cally. Larry Weiss, identified as "director of advertising," addressed the issue coyly. "I suppose in the past there was a Crazy Eddie," he said. "There are several Eddies around among the people who work here and own the place." A photo of Jerry Carroll was at the top of the page, and two large photos of commercials were at the bottom, giving Crazy Eddie greater photographic coverage than the infamous sex emporium.

As usual, Smith was not judgmental, snide, or sarcastic. He accepted his subjects on their own terms, and that's how it was with Crazy Eddie. He continued: "Larry had great news for Crazy Eddie fans. For the first time the company would be sponsoring an entire movie on television." That film was *Casablanca*. In a few days, the Bogie classic would be interrupted only by commercials for Crazy Eddie, which had prepared a *Casablanca* spoof for the occasion.

Crazy Eddie had arrived. It was a "pop cult." It had "fans." It was "fa- mous." That wasn't a line of malarkey screamed by Jerry Carroll; it was a verifiable fact reported by a reputable journalist. The Antar family enterprise was getting the kind of buzz usually reserved for the latest girl bands, Andy Warhol, and films by Cassavetes, Godard, and Scorsese. The Highway had been Eddie's launching pad, not his prison, and his edge—especially the sales tax stealing—had worked far more effectively than he or anyone had a right to expect. Stunningly effective advertising had done the rest. A ragtag group of self-taught guys in their twenties, led by a bearded high school dropout, had blown through New York's advertising jungle, disregard- ing conventions, charming their way into the golden reaches of the youth market.

Smith's column wasn't exaggerating. Crazy Eddie really had become a pop cult, really was famous, and the commercials really were hated. The smashing success of Crazy Eddie commercials, which continued to propel the company until its death rattle, was a triumph of youthful energy and inexperience over conventional thinking.

Advertising in the years following World War II was steeped in pop psy- chology and employed manipulation to an almost creepy extent. Vance Packard's 1957 book *The Hidden Persuaders* described how motivational research charted sneaky ways to get products into consumers' hands. Was it mere coincidence that red and yellow packaging had become so commonplace in supermarkets? You better believe it wasn't. The Package Designers Council recommended that merchandise have a "hypnotic" effect, like a "flashlight waved in front of the eyes," and that the colors red and yellow had the desired mesmerizing impact.

Crazy Eddie's youthful advertising director had not been trained in the latest techniques of manipulation. He had spent his career in radio, writing commercials for auto dealers on Long Island, manning the mic for hours on end in the Catskills. Above all, Larry Weiss was a musician and a consumer of audio equipment, and he was the same age as the kids Eddie wanted to bring into his stores.

After he filmed the first two TV commercials in the spring of 1976, Larry made a crucial hire. To buy TV airtime for the commercials, he recruited a studious young workhorse named Larry Miller, who had recently left the struggling E. J. Korvette discount chain. Miller had designed a computer program to aid his media-buying calculations, which was an impressively nerdy feat back then. The two Larrys and Eddie decided to place ads within the commercial breaks of the soap-opera spoof *Mary Hartman, Mary Hartman*, an offbeat comedy that parodied 1970s consumerism. The show premiered in early 1976 and was already a hit. After the first commercials started airing, sales skyrocketed at all three Crazy Eddie stores.

While there wasn't any time to reflect on the subject, and no funds or inclination to conduct market research, Larry Weiss reached some conclusions immediately. One was that "people will do what we tell them to do. And we told them to go to Crazy Eddie. We didn't invite them to Crazy Eddie. We didn't tell them how great it is to go to Crazy Eddie. We *told* them to get a new TV at Crazy Eddie. That's exactly what the commercials said." Apparently consumers, after decades of red packaging and subliminal messaging, had become inured to subtle manipulation. Or perhaps the professional admen, with their three-martini lunches and ulcers, had never been so hot in the first place. The grab-them-by-the-lapels hard sell had worked for carnival barkers in the gaslight era, it had worked for Madman Muntz (whom Larry Weiss had never heard of), and it was working for Crazy Eddie.

Larry and his team had stumbled upon a potent and anything-but-hidden persuader. It turned out that hate was like yellow and red packaging. It brought people into the stores in droves. "I don't think it ever came out at a strategy session, but I realized it back then. What I realized was people love to have something to hate. Especially in a crowd. And it becomes hip to hate. What we did was give people something that was fun and harmless to hate—Crazy Eddie commercials. They loved to hate them!" It's a phenomenon Larry saw replicated time and time again in the years to come. During the Trump years and the 2020 presidential campaign, he observed "a mob mentality to generate hate. Once you generate hate there's a following." The difference was that political hate in the twenty-first century was "real hate. They hated our commercials, but who cares?"

The Hate Factor contributed to the commercials' success. They were dumb, hokey, and, in the case of Jerry Carroll's screamers, downright abrasive. Larry knew how unpopular they were because customers said so, venting on the survey cards they filled out in the stores, saying they hated the commercials and "would never go to your stores." The Larrys and Eddie got a chuckle out of that. Where'd they get the cards? Larry Weiss pointed out to Howard Smith that "people might get irritated by them"—the Jerry Carroll commercials—"but they remember. The screamers always pull the most."

Other retailers occasionally went for the offbeat or the direct, like Jerry Rosenberg's ads for JGE a few years earlier, but audio outlets opted for providing information. They ran newspaper ads that contained long lists of products and their prices. Larry recalls with a bit of lingering disdain that "we called it 'buying the week's business.' We were dead set against it." Eddie had quoted prices in his early ads, but now his pitch was that the customer should consult competitor ads to find the best prices, and Crazy Eddie would beat them. Why advertise prices when other retailers are doing it for you?

So the message was drilled into the public as if all the people out there were recruits at Parris Island. Repetition, repetition, repetition. "Remember our name, remember our name, remember our name. Remember the lowest prices, the lowest prices, the lowest prices. So the minute you want a TV, the minute you want this or that, the first thing that pops into your head is Crazy Eddie. That was the approach. And that didn't require anything other than drumming it in," says Larry. In effect, Crazy Eddie was selling a phone number, 645-1196. That was the number of a pay phone at the Kings Highway store, and later a call center. Customers called there to give the price of a product at a competing store—"and Crazy Eddie will beat 'em! Six-four-five-eleven-ninety-six! Six-four-five-eleven-ninety-six!" Area codes didn't come until the eighties, so Larry could keep it pithy.

Having thrown away the advertising rule book with their "brainwashing lite" customer-conditioning technique, they tried something else that tossed conventions and possibly common sense out the window. They advertised on *Mary Hartman* because of its huge viewership. Their next move was to run commercials when they would be seen by the *fewest* people.

Since the dawn of television, stations had stopped broadcasting early in the morning for a few hours. In the 1960s and 1970s came all-night programming, mainly old movies and reruns of long-canceled TV shows. New technology had made it possible to run all night with limited staffing, sometimes just one employee in the control booth. Ad space was available for the overnight programming, and it was cheap. The new hire Larry Miller pointed out that the cost of advertising to such tiny, drowsy audiences was as little as ten dollars per commercial spot.

Eddie and Larry Weiss jumped on it. They reasoned "that everybody has insomnia. Maybe not every night, but we could just flood the airwaves." They figured that "you're better off hitting a hundred people ten times than a thousand people once." Soon Larry Miller was buying wee-hours time on all six commercial TV stations, and Jerry Carroll was blaring Crazy Eddie's dogma of "incredibly low prices" to audiences of ambulance drivers, swing-shift factory workers, movie buffs, and anyone else unable or unwilling to sleep in the city that never sleeps.

The ad team filmed more screamers, more spoofs. After *Casablanca* came *Saturday Night Fever*. There was no grand marketing strategy and little planning involved. In future years, advertising textbooks would claim that "we had drawn out all these story boards and did all this analysis," says Larry. "What a crock of crap. We would go in there and just start writing. We'd just drum out commercials. I never did a story board, ever."

With revenues climbing because of the drumbeat of TV and radio commercials, Eddie had all the trappings of success except fame, which he did not want. He had a family now. He had three daughters, twins born in July 1973 and a third baby girl in June 1975. They were taking their vacations on the Jersey Shore, just like the other wealthy S-Ys. He was giving money to charity. He was respectable. What more could a young man ask? How could things get better? Perhaps they couldn't. Perhaps they could only get worse. Just as he was getting the *Casablanca* spoof ready for broadcast in February 1977, Larry got the shocking news directly from Sam M. He had just been to the hospital.

Eddie was fighting for his life.

■ ■ ■

Eddie had a family, but a family man he was not. He liked clubs. He liked women. And above all he liked to drink. He was a bad drunk, a nasty drunk. Word spread quickly in the family and in the stores that Eddie had gotten into a fight outside a club and been stabbed in the abdomen. The circumstances were still murky decades later. One assailant or two? Greenwich Village or the Upper West Side? Who did it? Why? Were the assailants gangsters? Whatever the location, whatever the reason, it was not something you want when you're revving up commercials projecting a harmless public image.

Crazy Eddie was supposed to be a fun store, a cool store, a place you could bring the kids, crazy but in a nice way, not in a "founder gets stabbed" way. This absolutely could not get into the papers! Fortunately for Eddie, it did not. His nighttime carousing had never been picked up by the tabloids; he had never sought publicity, and his name simply wasn't that well known. So the stabbing was kept quiet without any difficulty. It was not the only time in Crazy Eddie's early years that the press missed an opportunity to embarrass Eddie. Way up in Vermont, he was involved in a messy dispute that could have tarnished his reputation and raised questions about his integrity.

Four months before the stabbing, in October 1976, Eddie was sued by a former partner in a company called Acousti-Phase, which manufactured a line of speakers at a converted mill in a hamlet called Proctorsville. Acousti-Phase speakers played a role in his bait-and-switch tactics. Customers would come into the stores for a Bose or other name-brand speaker and get talked into an Acousti-Phase product, with its "Mylar dome tweeter" and so on. It wasn't a bad product, but they weren't told that Acousti-Phase was majority owned by Eddie.

Eddie started Acousti-Phase in 1974. Within a couple of years, one of his three partners in the venture, a twenty-five-year-old audio engineer named Richard Rothenberg, smelled a rat. He believed Eddie was mismanaging the assets of the corporation. One of the things that bothered Rothenberg, a Vermont newspaper reported, was that "money was loaned without security to other unnamed individuals." He decided to investigate further. Rothenberg tried to gain entrance to the plant to copy documents proving his case, only to be ambushed by police and thrown in jail for five days. Rothenberg sued the town for false arrest and claimed that the cops were in cahoots with the other partner and Eddie, who told police that Rothenberg had no ownership interest and no right to be on the premises.

Fortunately for Eddie, this unseemly dispute received only local attention. Though covered by the *Rutland Herald*, one of the state's largest papers, this strange legal battle was not picked up by the wire services even though Eddie was identified with Crazy Eddie in the coverage. Without word filtering down I-91 to New York, Eddie's reputation escaped unscathed. In 1982 the Acousti-Phase plant mysteriously burned to the ground, a fire of such ferocity that any clue to the cause went up in flames. Again it received only local attention, and no suspicion wafted down to Brooklyn.

With the stabbing out of the press, Eddie was able to heal in peace. The assault had resulted in a serious, potentially mortal injury that required an extended hospital stay and left him with a ten-inch vertical scar. Larry remembered the aftermath: "Eddie's dad pulled me aside and said to me, 'Don't tell anyone, but you gotta know what's going on.' He came very close to dying right then and there. Doctor said the only thing that saved his life was the fact that he was such a gym nut and a bodybuilder that his abdominal muscles held him together till they could get to the hospital." Apparently, hanging upside down worked wonders on the stomach muscles.

Comic-turned-salesman Nick Zippilli began to see a change in Eddie after the stabbing, a milestone in the transition from "euphoria to paranoia." Eddie had adopted a new circle of friends, seeing less of his pals from Crazy Eddie. He distanced himself from the "old crew," the people he had known since the Kings Highway days and before. It was not the same Eddie. He had become more condescending, more abusive.

Eddie should have been celebrating, not healing. The stores were a money machine, and Eddie was finally unshackled from the state fair trade laws, which were banned by Congress in December 1975. But the end of fair trade was not an unalloyed blessing, as now all electronics retailers were freed from price restraints, and copycats began springing up. There was Meshugenah Ike in Lower Manhattan and Battling Barry on Long Island, who advertised "We drove the other guy crazy." Larry and Eddie sent Barry a case of champagne for the free advertising. Getting ripped off like that was the sincerest form of flattery. But these copycats didn't bother him. He still had his edge and his reputation for low prices. He could, and he did, crush them.

Eddie could take pride in how he was managing the business. He had picked the right people and set them loose, and it was working. He was a salesman, not a manager, but he had a natural talent for manipulating people that a Fortune 500 executive would have paid handsomely to acquire. "We were flying by the seat of our pants, but Eddie was really good at holding all that together," says Larry Weiss. "He was a very charismatic leader. He knew what he wanted, he had a vision, and he was able to get people to accomplish that."

Unlikely people wanted to work for Eddie. In the late 1970s, a man named Brown started calling the Kings Highway offices, pushing for the TV gig, making his case to whoever would listen. Brown was a common name, so Larry had trouble believing that the man with the husky voice on the other end of the line, imploring him for work, was the Godfather of Soul, James Brown. "He just started calling. I couldn't believe it was him," says Larry Weiss with a laugh. "He was relentless. He wanted to be the TV spokesman for Crazy Eddie." These were times of declining record sales and Internal Revenue Service troubles for the performer, and Brown badly needed a job. It was as simple as that. Even legends need to eat.

The idea of bringing Brown on board was tempting. Larry recalls that they "bandied it about" and passed. They were sticking with the screamer, Jerry Carroll, exclusively. James Brown was an unknown quantity as a pitchman. But still. James Brown! "In hindsight, that would have been really cool," Larry concedes. It was a vivid indication of how Crazy Eddie was catching on. And the chain was clicking where it counted most—in the cash registers. Eddie had ambitious expansion plans. In 1977 he opened a new store around the corner from Kings Highway on Coney Island Avenue and another at a prime location in Paramus. In 1978 and 1979 came three more stores in New Jersey and Westchester. Others soon followed on Long Island and on East Fifty-Seventh Street in a well-heeled section of Manhattan.

Every store opening was an event. When the East Brunswick store opened in November 1978, the local paper estimated that twenty thousand people turned out, unfazed by "damp weather and enormous lines." The throngs were lured to store openings by free T-shirts and Frisbees, but the main attraction was the man people loved to hate, Jerry Carroll, in the flesh. "All the advertising really gets to you," one patron remarked as he waited in line. Harry Spero, who joined the advertising team at the end of 1979, recalled: "These store openings were extraordinary. These were holidays unto themselves. We would promote the hell out of them, and there would be lines 'round the block for people to get a free T-shirt. That is the beginning and the end of it. I go back in time and think, 'Who had store openings where people cared enough that they would line up around the block?'" Not to get the hot new iPhone but to get "something that cost us eighty-nine cents to make in China."

For each opening, Harry would print up twenty thousand T-shirts and have to give away another ten thousand vouchers for a hat or some other lesser goodie to the people who weren't first in line. Often thirty thousand people ended up pouring into the stores over the course of three days, sometimes as many as thirty-five thousand. Eddie would join Jerry Carroll at the openings. The star of the TV commercials was actually shy, and one of Harry's jobs was to keep him from being swamped by Crazy Eddie fans. Eddie would be off to the side, watching the crowds. Harry remembered that he "would stand there at the end of a day, or a Sunday, near Eddie, waiting for him to come over and tell me I did a good job. Those were the only times I would do anything like that." And sure enough, his wish would be fulfilled. Every time he did that, Eddie would come over and praise him.

However popular the commercials and the openings were becoming, they were just the public face of Crazy Eddie. Behind the scenes, Eddie was sharpening his edge over the competition. Nothing could stop him, not even rampaging mobs of looters.

CHAPTER SIX

CRIME WAS ONE OF THE PRINCIPAL HAZARDS OF RUNNING A BUSINESS IN New York City in the 1970s, and no Crazy Eddie was more at risk than the store Uncle Zookie ran at 300 East Fordham Road in the Bronx. It was just up the hill from a decaying Sears, a reminder of the days when the area had been a stuffy middle-class shopping district. The surrounding neighborhoods were overwhelmed by drugs and street crime. Fordham Road was the dividing line between a largely black and Latino area to the south and a largely white area to the north, and racial tensions were rising. One hot night, the neighborhood detonated. It was as if a keg of TNT was set off on every block.

On July 13, 1977, rappers DJ Disco Wiz and Casanova Fly were in a park on 183rd Street, a few blocks south of Fordham. They were preparing to battle an upstart rapper, their equipment hooked up to a streetlight, when the power went out. "As gates on the block began slamming down right and left, it dawned on everyone: Blackout! The crowd started yelling, 'Hit the stores! Hit the stores!'" Wiz headed for Crazy Eddie, but not directly. He made a couple of stops along the way. Too late. He arrived to find eight armed guards on the roof. "It was like trying to rob a drug dealer." He hit a sneaker shop instead. Other accounts say that a van was parked in front of the store, with gun-wielding guards on top. Whichever scenario was true, the effect was the same. Looters were not welcome.

Eddie knew that stores selling high-ticket goods were prime targets of looters. When the power failed, he made a flurry of phone calls and rushed shotgun-wielding guards to the Fordham store. They knew how to shoot too. Eddie relied on off-duty cops from the local precincts for security on Fordham Road and some other stores, paying them off the books in cash. So it seems likely that the security force in the Bronx that night consisted of Eddie's private NYPD police force. Other electronics retailers, whose owners were not so quick-witted, were among the sixteen hundred businesses looted that night throughout the city. The street kid in Eddie had kicked in. Punks weren't invading his store. If there was going to be crime at a Crazy Eddie, he was going to be the one committing it.

Eddie was always sure to buy the finest casualty insurance. Store inventory was insured at retail selling price, not wholesale cost. Eddie knew that three things invariably happened to a storekeeper in New York: the roofs will leak, sewage will back up, and pipes will freeze and burst. Water damage was common, as were burglaries. He knew that and so did the insurers. Even when a claim was suspicious, it was usually less expensive to settle than to deny it entirely and risk a court battle. When Eddie put in a claim for all the looting at the Fordham store that didn't happen, it was paid without hesitation. For insurers, fraud was a cost of doing business. The *Chicago Tribune* reported in 1972 that each year, insurance companies "budgeted for a calculated amount of fraud," raising their rates to compensate. Even when entire stretches of the South Bronx were burned to the ground by avaricious and desperate landlords, paying kids twenty bucks a pop to torch their properties, prosecutions were rare.

When Eddie's young cousin Sammy got the call from Eddie late one night about a year after the blackout, he was irritated but not surprised. He was expected to drop what he was doing and rush up to the Bronx. This time it wasn't a riot. There was a flood in the Fordham Road store, and that meant only one thing—it was time to execute one of the elements of Eddie's edge over the competition. It was time to "spike the claim."

When pipes burst or sewage backed up, Eddie would take products that he couldn't sell—discontinued merchandise, returns that the manufacturers refused and that he couldn't unload as lunch—and move them into the store that was flooded. If a broken pipe was discovered in the morning, unsalable merchandise from various other stores would be at the flooded location by the afternoon. Out would come the fire hoses. When the roofs leaked, Eddie was sure to run up a hose to maximize the water flow. He sometimes had the guys dump gear out of boxes and put the contents in sinks filled with dirty water. They would put their shoes in the sinks to make sure the water had a sufficiently putrid quality.

A claim would be filed for all the merchandise, both the products genuinely and legally ruined and all the additional stuff brought in. As was typical for commercial claims, Eddie retained a public adjuster to deal with the insurance company. The aim was to have someone on your side to put your case to the company and get a fair outcome. In return, the adjuster was entitled by law to a piece of the settlement. Eddie would pay extra under the table because he would get extra. The public adjusters that Eddie used were cheerful, cooperative guys like Donald,* who worked for a reputable adjusting firm and received not just a percentage of the claim but a handsome cash kickback from Eddie. He was overweight and out of shape, but that didn't keep him from wielding the fire hose right alongside Eddie's people, wetting down the fresh boxes of discontinued merchandise that Eddie brought in to the flood locations.

Sammy parked on Fordham, which was unpleasantly deserted this late at night, and walked around the corner to the rear entrance on Tiebout Avenue. Vans from the stores were already lined up to offload their merchandise. He pitched in, bringing the heavy boxes into the basement, where he dropped them into the expanding pool of filthy water. Among the people lending a hand was a young guy from the Village store named Vinnie Badalamenti. Donald, the public adjuster, was there too, sizing up the damages, preparing to deal with the insurance company's adjuster. He and the insurance-company man were old pals, and Donald would slip him some cash to keep him friendly.

Though it was a basement in the Bronx in the middle of the night, a festive atmosphere prevailed. One of the guys had a licensed revolver, so the participants in the flooding took turns taking target practice in the basement. If any of the gunshots could be heard outside, it would hardly attract notice, for this was, after all, the Bronx. Donald made sure that everything

---

* Not his real name.

looked right. "This doesn't look wet enough," he said, and proceeded to spit and pee on the boxes.

Fortunately for Donald's bladder, it wasn't necessary to hose down all the merchandise brought to Fordham Road. Some of it had already been waterlogged in previous floods, previously hosed down, and previously submitted for claims. The insurance companies could have taken possession of the ruined, sometimes sewage-contaminated, boxes of forlorn electronics, but they rarely did. So Eddie would put the old, cruddy boxes in storage, hauling them out at times like this, and use them for future claim-spiking. This happened over and over again. The insurance companies would drop Crazy Eddie after the claims were filed—not because they suspected anything, necessarily, but because they didn't like claims. Eddie would just sign up with another insurer. "They didn't talk to each other," Sammy recalled.

Sammy didn't know how many times the moldy old cardboard boxes had been on the spiked-claims carousel, but he knew that Eddie had been recycling waterlogged merchandise since the early days at Sights and Sounds. Once when he was fifteen and working at Kings Highway, Sammy came in on a Sunday morning to find the store drenched in water. Eddie blamed him for letting the water run all night into a stopped-up sink, which overflowed and flooded the place. But Sammy hadn't been in the store Saturday night. "Then I realized what they were doing. They were trying to make me the fall guy for their insurance claim."

Eddie had limits when it came to insurance fraud. He never started a fire in one of his stores, never faked a robbery or sabotaged his own plumbing. Sammy remembered how furious Eddie was when he heard about the Acousti-Phase fire in 1982. He didn't torch the place. What got him mad was not that the plant burned down, but that his Vermont partner hadn't insured it for fire damage. They missed out on a spiking-enhanced windfall.

■ ■ ■

Sammy was glad to see Vinnie Badalamenti in the basement. He was a team player, reliable, always willing to lend a hand. "He was a very good guy, Badalamenti," Sammy said fondly, "a really hardworking kid." Vinnie came dressed for flood work that night, but he was usually nattily attired, wearing a fashionable mustache and neatly styled long hair. Being summoned to help out with the flood showed how much Eddie trusted him. He was always testing the loyalty of the people who worked for him, and Vinnie was passing every test.

It wasn't just Sammy and Eddie. Everybody liked Vinnie. He was an easygoing kid, just a teenager out of high school when he started at the Greenwich Village store, but he had an inner fire, an ambition, that became evident only once you got to know him. Which wasn't hard.

Like most of the people Eddie hired, Vinnie Badalamenti was from a lower-middle-class family, people who had to work hard just to get by. His grandfather Calogero, who came over from Palermo in 1904, ran a fruit store. His father, Vinnie Sr., grew up on Charles Street when Greenwich Village was still an Italian neighborhood. He drove a truck in the Garment District, served in the Army during World War II, and raised his family in a modest two-family house on Twenty-First Avenue in Bath Beach, Brooklyn. He and his wife had six children. Vinnie Jr., born in 1958, was the youngest and the only son. He was not deprived of parental attention, to say the least.

Vinnie Sr. was respectable and conscientious; he expected the same from his son. He enrolled the boy at Xaverian High School, then an all-boys Catholic school where the students wore jackets and ties and discipline was strict. Cut classes and you got expelled. Most graduates went to college, but if young Vinnie had college plans they were not fulfilled. He would go to work, and he would work where his father told him to work.

In the 1970s, the elder Vinnie sold magazine subscriptions, going door to door, and one of his stops was Eddie's Kings Highway store. Sammy remembers him with affection. He was a bombastic little guy a shade over five feet tall and reminded Sammy of Fiorello La Guardia, the pint-size mayor of 1940s New York. When Vinnie Jr. graduated from Xaverian, his father persuaded Eddie to hire him. Vinnie went to work in the stockroom of the newly opened Village store, and in short order worked his way up to the sales floor. It was a good hire, everyone agreed.

Vinnie was sharp and persuasive, charming and knowledgeable, a born salesman. He knew how to relate to whoever came in through the door, whether it was a teenager with an attitude and a wealthy dad, a tourist with a dazed look, or a neighborhood bum wandering in off the street. When the Yippie leader Abbie Hoffman turned up at the store one day, Vinnie showed him a portable radio and cassette recorder and told him it was just right for him if he "needed to flee justice in a hurry." Hoffman laughed, and Vinnie made the sale. Word spread about that. It didn't do his reputation any harm at all.

The Village store was right in the center of the neighborhood and attracted a fair number of shoplifters who had to be ejected. The PATH commuter rail station was across the street, and sometimes punks from the burbs would stop by the store and make trouble. If Vinnie was around, he would help out. Once there was a time when Vinnie got into a fight with some kids outside the store. One of them, a sore loser, summoned his policeman uncle. He took Vinnie into custody and brought him to the Sixth Precinct on West Tenth Street.

A bunch of the guys from Crazy Eddie headed to the station house and kept a vigil for their busted pal. Vinnie's father showed up as well. "My son went to Xaverian High School! How dare you arrest him!" Vinnie Sr. fumed when he got there. "His dad was a pure-hearted guy. Don't make those kind of men anymore," Sammy fondly recalled. It's not clear what happened at the precinct, but apparently Vinnie's father was able to persuade the cops not to book him. An arrest would have given him a police record, an NYPD "B number." Not getting busted for that fracas on Sixth Avenue was a stroke of good luck, the first of several that fortune bestowed on Vinnie Badalamenti in the years to come.

No one at Crazy Eddie cared about that minor scrap. It just showed that he was a tough kid, which was fine. Vinnie had a future with the company. Guys who were smart and dependable were given as much work as they could handle. Vinnie "was very good at what he did. He rose through the ranks." Soon he became "one of Eddie's top guys in inventory controls." It was a natural move for a mature young man with leadership skills.

Sammy was happy to see Vinnie do so well. The family's numbers nerd was growing up. In 1979 Sammy married Robin Betesh, daughter of an S-Y merchant who ran a gift shop on the Atlantic City Boardwalk and then moved into commercial real estate. The newly married couple lived in a rented house a few doors down from Sam M. and Eddie. After he graduated from Baruch in 1980, Sammy began working part-time at Penn & Horowitz, the accounting firm that did Crazy Eddie's books, to get the experience he needed to become a CPA. He was on track to become Eddie's numbers guru, guiding the enterprise's finances, and it was great to have a friend like Vinnie on the team. After all, inventories and inventory controls were crucial to a company's operations, as well as its finances and its relations with bankers and, perhaps someday, investors. Crazy Eddie needed trusted people in that area.

Eddie's faith in Vinnie never wavered. Neither did Sammy's, even after he learned just how ambitious and hardworking Vinnie really was.

In early 1979, not yet twenty-one, Vinnie incorporated what he called Badalamenti Advertising Agency, Ltd. The "Ltd." suffix was only for companies formed in the British Commonwealth, so it wasn't quite accurate, but the sound of it gave his new business a continental flair. It's not clear if Eddie ever found out about Vinnie's ad agency venture. It didn't conflict with Crazy Eddie, so it probably would have been okay. He didn't tell Eddie about a later side business that was definitely not okay.

In 1981 Vinnie decided to go into wholesale consumer electronics with a friend from Crazy Eddie. They called their new company Robad Distributors. It was incorporated in September of that year with Vinnie listed as CEO and operated out of a storefront on New Utrecht Avenue in Bensonhurst. It was the kind of thing a sharp young entrepreneur would do. He had "forged relationships with some of the same vendors and was applying what he learned." The problem was that Vinnie set up Robad while still at Crazy Eddie, which meant he was filling the shelves of his boss's competitors.

Sammy knew that was no good. It was a big conflict of interest no retailer would have tolerated, but he liked Vinnie so he didn't say anything to his cousin. Eddie found out anyway and immediately fired Vinnie, who took his termination in stride. No hard feelings. Everybody, including Eddie, was sad to see him go.

After Crazy Eddie, Vinnie prospered. In the years to come, his little wholesaler gained clients in New Jersey and Connecticut as well as New

York, with eleven employees trucking product to as many as fifteen stores in a single day. In the 1980s Robad went into the retail trade as well, acting as an authorized dealer for RCA and Gold Star televisions, radios, and VCRs. Vinnie's original partner left to become a police officer, but he hired at least one former Crazy Eddie store manager as his business expanded in the 1990s. Vinnie also went into real estate in a small way, buying and managing four commercial properties, and opened a bagel store a few doors down from Robad. Vinnie did so well in his various endeavors that he bought a five-bedroom fifty-five-hundred-square-foot house facing a park in a nice part of Staten Island. He married in the late 1980s and had a son and a daughter.

Vinnie was living well for a small-scale wholesaler, bagel-shop owner, and landlord. Real well. He had some side ventures, just as he had at Crazy Eddie, if one believes indictments naming him as a defendant that were filed with the US District Court for the Eastern District of New York in 2002 and 2012. They contend that Vinnie embarked on a whole new career after leaving Crazy Eddie: the Mafia.

Exactly when Vinnie made the transition from budding entrepreneur to mobster is not addressed in the public record. The indictments suggest that "Vinnie TV," as he was known among the wiseguys, started at the bottom and rose through the ranks of the Bonanno crime family, very much as he had done at Crazy Eddie, which was not mentioned in the court filings he generated and the press coverage he received through the years. He began as an associate, which was the Bonanno family counterpart to the sales floor. He was inducted into the family, and prosecutors contended in 2002 that he had climbed through the ranks to captain, or *caporegime*, running a crew of other mobsters. When he was indicted for a second time in 2012, prosecutors alleged that he had risen to the administrative body of the family and had become "street boss," overseeing the family while more senior Bonannos languished in prison.

What makes Vinnie's career transition remarkable is that there is no evidence that his persona changed very much between his Crazy Eddie days and his future line of work. In the old days he was never a punk, never acted like a hood. In his new line of work, Vinnie was no "Crazy Joe" Gallo or

John Gotti, no preening racket guy in a silk suit. Gotti and a pal were busted in 1984 for beating up some working stiff for honking his horn at them. Vinnie wouldn't have done anything so stupid. He harked back to an earlier generation of mobsters who avoided publicity and tried to remain under the radar. It wasn't a pose. It's how he was. Sammy recalls that there was never a hint of Vinnie doing anything illegal while working for Eddie (other than Eddie-authorized acts such as that episode on Fordham Road). There was no indication that a future mobster was in their midst. Sure, young Vinnie liked gangster TV shows like *Wiseguy* and *Gangster Chronicles*—"he loved mob stuff"—but so did a lot of other people who never got inducted into one of the Five Families.

Despite intensive scrutiny, the feds never nailed Vinnie for narcotics, homicide, or any acts of violence. The charges lodged against him on those two occasions, mainly loan-sharking, racketeering, and extortion, were felonies, but they were not especially heinous by New York mob standards. What are mob standards, you ask? An example can be found in the life and times of a colleague of Vinnie's, a Bonanno mobster named Michael "the Nose" Mancuso. He was twice convicted of homicide, the first time for shooting his wife in the head and leaving her body on a bench in front of Jacobi Hospital in the Bronx. Neither conviction impeded the Nose's criminal career, despite the supposed mobster fealty to "honor" and "family" alleged by Mafia apologists, including the memoir written by the family's founding boss, Joseph Bonanno. The wife-killer Mancuso succeeded Vinnie as head of the family.

Vinnie struck plea deals in both indictments and served two terms in prison, fifteen months the first time and eighteen months the second time. That's the best the feds could do, despite trying their darnedest to decorate their résumés with a "traditional organized crime" conviction. One snippet from a 2012 court hearing gives a flavor of how much effort the forces of law and order deployed to incarcerate the nice kid from the Village store.

As recounted by Vinnie's indignant attorney: In December 2009, the former Crazy Eddie up-and-comer was in a Brooklyn social club, minding his own business, when "between twenty and forty agents descend on the social club wearing DEA [Drug Enforcement Administration] jackets and they come into the social club and they take all the people out of the social club . . . and line them up out in the cold and they conduct a search." They turned up nothing but took Vinnie in a police car to "some kind of warehouse." He was held for hours without being put under arrest. "Now, mind you, this is a man who is supposed to be a high ranking member of the Bonanno family," the lawyer continued, rubbing it in. This account was not contested by prosecutors, who blandly responded that Vinnie's lawyer had never previously raised the issue.

The 2002 and 2012 indictments and subsequent guilty pleas were Vinnie's only brushes with the law after the Village fracas, and the resulting prison terms were his only periods of incarceration. When his sentence was being weighed after he cut a plea deal for the 2002 indictment, Vinnie's lack of a criminal record was a point in his favor. His dad's intervention at the Sixth Precinct had paid off. No question about it, he was a lucky guy. But what made him *really* lucky was not the feds' failure to nail him for anything violent, his modest prison sentences, or even his comfortable lifestyle and loving family.

The luckiest thing that ever happened to Vinnie Badalamenti was that Eddie fired him.

CHAPTER SEVEN

S AM M. WAS PRONE TO MAKING DELPHIC PRONOUNCEMENTS FROM TIME TO time. One of his favorites was "We have the wagon of gold, and people follow us to pick up the specks of gold dust that fall off." Sammy was just another relative following the family gold wagon until a day in 1979 that changed the Antars forever. It was the day of Sammy's Golden Idea. It would send Crazy Eddie onto the road to high finance and all that came with it.

Sammy's Golden Idea involved the *nehkdi*. The volume of cash taken from the cash registers was increasing as Crazy Eddie expanded. Late each night, store managers would stuff greenbacks into satchels and Crazy Eddie yellow shopping bags adorned with the "crazy man" and bring it to Eddy's house in Brooklyn. He would count it up, enter the sums in a ledger, and stuff the bills into mattresses, the couch, and other furniture. All the cash was carefully accounted for. What wasn't used for expenses was profit and went to Eddie and Sam as co-owners. As the chain grew, increasing amounts of the profits, what they called the "net *nehkdi*," were taken to Israel and deposited in bank accounts.

Sammy's schooling in finance at Baruch College persuaded him that the net *nehkdi* could be the Antar family's pathway to wealth. For years, Eddie and Sam M. had talked about getting rich by selling stock through an initial public offering, an IPO. "It was their goal. It was always in their heads. An IPO was the golden goose," Sammy recalled, but it never went past the talking stage. Eddie had no financial training and no knowledge of the stock market. Sam M. and Rose played the market, but for them it was like the trips they took to the casinos in Las Vegas. No one knew much about how the markets worked—except for Sam M.'s nephew.

Sammy's Golden Idea was about Wall Street perceptions. The investment community's view of Crazy Eddie could be manipulated. As described to Sam M. and Eddie by Sammy, it was downright easy. First they had to stop cheating the tax people by skimming off profits. They were saving on taxes but screwing themselves by making it seem as if they were less profitable than they actually were. That's the opposite of what you want to do before an IPO. You want to make it seem as if you are awash in profits.

He pointed out that after the IPO, their wealth would largely consist of Crazy Eddie stock. Skimming $1 million in profits from the company meant saving maybe $500,000 in taxes, but they could make a lot more money by *inflating* their profits. That's because doing so would boost the stock price and the value of their holdings.

It was elementary, literally Finance 101. Sammy was taught at Baruch that investors wanted to see steady year-over-year growth in revenues and profits. The higher the growth in the bottom line, the higher the "price-earnings (P/E) ratio"—the formula that indicates whether a stock is pricey or cheap, like unit pricing in the supermarket. They would want that number as high as possible. After all, they wanted Crazy Eddie to be the filet mignon of stocks, a twenty-dollars-a-pound cut, not cheap like a fifty-cents-a-pound slab of fatty liver. Investors would pay premium prices only if they thought they were getting top cut, without a trace of gristle. They wanted growth, and plenty of it.

That brought him to the crux of his plan. The net *nehkdi* needed to be dialed down slowly, like turning the handle of a faucet. Sammy explained that if "you gradually reduce the skimming, it creates false growth"—the *appearance* of steady growth, an exaggeration of whatever growth had taken place. A mirage. So when they went public, the stock would warrant a higher price-earnings ratio. Not ten times earnings but maybe twenty times earnings. Not ground round but tenderloin.

Apart from reducing the net *nehkdi* to fabricate steady profit growth, there was still "a lot of shit that had to be cleaned up." The company would have to be prepared for public scrutiny. They would need to hire lawyers.

Their financial reports would have to be audited by a well-known, reputable accounting firm. They would need to organize the business better, make it seem more like a modern American corporation and less like a handbag store on Fourteenth Street that kept its cash in a cigar box. They'd have to put employees on the books.

They could still bring out the hoses when a pipe burst, but stealing sales tax would have to end. They would be under more scrutiny as a public company, and the growing size of the chain meant that more employees had to be brought into the scheme, including people outside the family, and it just wasn't worth the risk. They could no longer be as competitive on price, as their built-in, illegal profit margin would be gone. But that was a minor consideration compared to all the other advantages that would accrue for the Antars. "How much money can you stuff in a mattress?" Sammy reasoned. This was America, a nation that encouraged people to buy stock. It meant owning a slice of America. It was celebrated. It was patriotic, like saying the Pledge of Allegiance.

This was Sammy's moment—"my time to shine"—and Sam M. and Eddie bought the idea. "You have to understand, I'm this dorky fucking idiot, but I know what I'm talking about," Sammy recalled. He knew that his role in Crazy Eddie was assured the next time he was at Sam M.'s kitchen table. His uncle and Eddie were looking at him in a new way, with something actually resembling respect.

True, it was securities fraud. It was a federal offense. They could go to jail for something like that. Sammy didn't mention that. He didn't have to—not to guys who stuffed cash in the ceiling, stole sales taxes, and defrauded insurance companies without a second thought. They did not expect to be caught, and if the Antars had any doubt on that score, they had only to look to City Hall for inspiration. The City of New York had done exactly the kind of thing Sammy was proposing, manipulating financial statements to give the public a false picture of the city's health. It was making headlines. The city was still cleaning up the mess.

For years, city officials used accounting sleight of hand whenever expenses outstripped tax revenues. They "would devise a temporary solution by taxing a little here, borrowing a little there, fudging everywhere they could." They gradually moved to ever more brazen fraud. In 1965 Mayor Robert F. Wagner pushed the tax-collection date back one day to shift $45 million into the preceding fiscal year, giving the false appearance New York was living within its means. Another artifice to balance the books was especially cheeky: Over the years, the city shifted $700 million in ordinary spending into the budget for long-term capital spending. Buyers of municipal bonds thought they were financing roads and bridges, when they were actually paying for garbage collection and other things that are supposed to be funded by taxes.

The municipal book-cooking was "tolerated or even suggested by state officials and were certainly not secrets to the banking community." Bond-rating agencies looked the other way. "An investor looking solely at the rating of New York City bonds would have gotten rather misleading information," a 1976 study of New York's fiscal crisis observes. In August 1977, the Securities and Exchange Commission (SEC), the federal agency tasked with protecting investors, issued an eight-hundred-page report accusing past and current officials of employing "budgetary, accounting and financial practices which it knew distorted its true financial condition." New York was "handling its money like a heroin addict, focusing only on its next fix—relying on deceptive accounting, borrowing excessively, and refusing to plan," journalist Ken Auletta recounted.

By 1975 the weight of all that finagling had become too much for the city to bear, and New York City was nearly plunged into bankruptcy. Yet there were never any consequences for the perpetrators. They were not prosecuted, not even sued by the SEC. It was fraud in plain sight, and they got away with it.

■ ■ ■

The plan was put in motion. The *nehkdi* trips to Israel—"pilgrimages to the Holy Land," as the Antars called them—continued, but were fewer in number and stopped completely in 1983. The Reagan administration's tax cuts made the Antars ever more determined to go public, because "Reaganomics" made stock ownership and profiting from stock trades even more enticing than before.

With the help of a consultant named Gerald Newman, Eddie found a Wall Street firm that was interested in bringing the company public. Newman put Eddie in touch with Oppenheimer & Co., a prestigious investment banking house. Preliminary work on the IPO began in 1983. It was tentatively set for 1984, and Sammy worked closely with the two corporate finance executives sent over from Oppenheimer to prepare the preliminary "red herring" prospectus, so known because of a red stripe down the side. That SEC filing would be the bible of the IPO.

For the IPO to succeed, Crazy Eddie needed buzz. Not stories in the *Village Voice* but serious attention from the dailies, business publications, and the trade press. And the company was starting to get just that. One recurrent theme was that Crazy Eddie was driving its competitors nuts. "If there is one name that incites fear and, often, deep-seated rage, within the souls of proprietors of electronics stores in the New York metropolitan area, it is Crazy Eddie, the man whose prices will not be beat," the *New York Times* reported in a March 1982 story that landed on the front page of the business section. Eddie was such a phenomenon that even articles on his rivals—in this case Peter McKean, a Westchester retailer—dwelled on Crazy Eddie and those commercials everyone hated.

"'Every time I turn on the TV or the radio, he's yelling at me. And I'm sick of it,' Mr. McKean said. 'I'm watching TV at night, he's yelling at me. I turn on the radio in the morning, he's yelling at me.'" The reporter followed McKean into a Crazy Eddie store and recorded further evidence that Eddie lived rent free in his head. "He walked outside to his car. He was out of Crazy Eddie, but Eddie was not yet out of his system. 'Do I like the man?' he asked himself. 'No. He's saying, "Don't buy. Get a price and come to me." So he's taken the credibility out of every price that is quoted.'"

McKean would have been happy to know that cracks were forming in his rival's empire. Eddie's bullying, abrasive style was getting old. His advertising guru, Larry Weiss, was increasingly irritated with Eddie. Arguments were constant as Eddie meddled in every aspect of Larry's job. "It was a love-hate relationship," says Larry. He remembers a fight that ensued when he wanted to advertise on WRVR, which was a popular jazz radio station. Eddie "started lacing into me about what an idiot I was and what a horrible radio station it was. Finally, I stood up and said, 'Don't you ever talk that way or I'm outta here!' And everybody in the office started applauding. And Eddie goes, 'He's not gonna quit! He's not gonna quit!'"

He didn't quit. Despite all his yelling and cursing, Crazy Eddie wound up advertising on WRVR. It was how the Antars operated—lots of drama—which was not unusual in family businesses. *Small* family businesses, not retail chains growing as fast as Crazy Eddie. The problem for Larry was that even though he was treated like a member of the family by getting yelled at, he received none of the financial benefits or status of being a member of the founding family. Relatives like Eddie's brother-in-law, Ben Kuszer, and brothers Mitchell and Allen were gaining in responsibility solely because they were family members. Allen was put in charge of the Fifty-Seventh Street store, now the showcase Crazy Eddie, frequently mentioned in coverage of consumer electronics.

Fortunately for Larry, he was able to put space between himself and the bearded, superstitious, angry fitness nut in the torn sweater. At around the time of the stabbing, Eddie relocated Crazy Eddie's offices and warehouse to a former Bohack supermarket at 2845 Coney Island Avenue, way down by Avenue Z. It was almost aggressively hard to reach, a long cab ride from Manhattan and a ten-minute walk from the nearest subway station. By not wasting money on expensive Manhattan office space, Eddie was unintentionally catering to the prejudices of analysts and managers of mutual funds who'd be buying shares in the IPO. Peter Lynch, one of the most successful and influential mutual fund operators of the era, believed that investors should visit corporate offices and "hope that if it's not stuck behind a bowling alley, then it would be located in some seedy neighborhood where financial analysts wouldn't want to be seen." Unless their drivers took a wrong turn on the way to the Hamptons, analysts never came anywhere near Coney Island Avenue.

Larry seized upon the move to create a separate base of operations for his advertising team, hoping that would curb Eddie's constant hectoring. Much of the Kings Highway store moved around the corner about that time, with the old store devoted to record and tape sales, so Larry set up a radio production facility in the former sound room of the old digs. There, a blessed two miles north of Eddie's new headquarters, Larry churned out Jerry Carroll commercials pegged to every holiday, every season, every turn in the weather, one sale after another—"'Crazy Eddie's Greatest Whatever-It-Is Sale Ever!' We'd run that for a month or three weeks and move on to the next sale. There was always a sale." Except "there never was a sale," Larry points out. Prices were the same; only the commercials changed.

In the summer it was "Christmas in August!" Was it snowing outside? A "Blizzard Blitz" radio commercial was recorded in advance, all cued up and ready to go. "Whenever winter weather got extremely severe, I would call directly in to each studio and authorize the on-air staff to run those spots, which claimed, 'If you're crazy enough to come out in this weather, Crazy Eddie is crazy enough to give you the most unheard of crazy deal . . .'"

More stores were planned in Manhattan, more in New Jersey, more on Long Island. The Crazy Eddie flag would soon be planted in Philadelphia and Poughkeepsie, way up in the Hudson Valley. He was running want ads to staff the new stores, but it helped to know somebody at Crazy Eddie. Despite his growing irritation with Eddie, Larry knew that people who worked outside of his boss's orbit had decent jobs and made good money. He felt his brother Ira might want to give Crazy Eddie a try.

■ ■ ■

Ira Weiss was a few years younger than Larry, and like his brother he was always in a band. He started making his living in music after dropping out of Nassau Community College and had a good amount of success, playing keyboard, piano, and organ for a backup band for the Drifters. He was all of twenty when he started touring with the R&B group, which had been around since 1953. Then he moved on to one of the hottest new groups playing the club circuit in the New York metro area, "Razza-Machazz."

Razza-Machazz was a show band, with a four-piece rhythm section that played popular songs, featuring a singer named Jeannie and a talented vocalist named Calogero Palminteri, better known as Chazz. The future movie and Broadway star spent his early years just like Ira, entertaining at smoky, cheesy clubs like the Milky Way Lounge on Central Park Avenue in Scarsdale ("2 Cocktail Lounges, Live Entertainment 6 Nights, Dancing on One of Westchester's Largest Dance Floors"). It was no way to make a living, not for Chazz, not for Ira. After a few years Chazz formed his own comedy group and then found roles off-Broadway before breaking into the big time. Ira continued in music and was playing with a duo when a blizzard threw him out of work. That's what happened in bad weather. Customers couldn't come to the clubs, so the owners fired the bands.

Ira took his brother's suggestion and went to work at Crazy Eddie. He was married by now, and a steady income seemed awfully appealing. By the 1980s, Eddie's best salesmen were making $1,000 a week or more in salary, commissions, and cash bonuses. Commissions came only when they sold service contracts. They kicked in after manufacturer warranties expired and were (and are) a notoriously bad deal for consumers. A good portion of the price went to the salesmen, who could make $500 a week from service contracts alone.

Ira was put in Syosset. At first "nobody wanted me. I was the advertising director's little brother charity case." The audio department manager thought he'd "screw everything up here." But he was wrong. Ira had been working with the best in audio components for years. It's one of the reasons Eddie hired entertainers. They knew the merchandise. Their livelihoods depended on it. "High-end audio equipment is what I *did*," says Ira. Before long he was promoted to video manager.

Despite his success, Ira never really got into it. Part of it was organic to working in sales at Crazy Eddie. "The whole store persona was on making the sale, making the sale, making the sale, switching. It was a big switch thing. He carried all the names. But you sold the big brand names and you made a little bit of money. You sold the alternative and you made a lot of money. Someone came in for a Sony TV; they left with a Hitachi TV. I did what I was told; I was good at it. In reality, does it matter whether someone gets a Sony TV or a Hitachi? Who really gives a shit? But it felt wrong."

Ira had profoundly mixed feelings about the boss as well. "Eddie was a character. There was a strength that came from him, and there was a real tension kind of insanity that came from him. That's the energy I got from him," says Ira. "I was not a huge fan. Most of the people who worked there kind of worshipped him. But, to me, he was not a good human being. That was my impression of him." Eddie had a dark side and a philandering nature that he did not try to conceal. When he met Ira's wife, Debbie, Eddie's "response to my introduction was 'Good name,' and he walked away." Eddie's wife was named Debbie—and so was his girlfriend. Everyone knew it.

At least Ira didn't have to work with Eddie. His brother did. Though their offices were now two miles apart, the arguments with Eddie about stupid things continued and were getting on Larry's nerves. Like the fight they had over the Crazy Eddie that was advertised in the wrong town.

In the spring of 1980, Eddie opened a store at 401 Old Country Road in Carle Place, Long Island, a short distance from Westbury but not in Westbury. "He wanted to call it Westbury. And I'm like, 'It's really Carle Place.'" But Eddie didn't care. Westbury was the site of the Westbury Music Fair, whose events were constantly advertised. To Eddie's mind, that made it better known and much more appealing than Carle Place. So the store had to be there, even though it wasn't. "He says, 'Westbury, Westbury. Nobody ever heard of Carle Place. Everybody knows where Westbury is.' It was back and forth. Eventually, we shot a whole series of commercials calling it Westbury and a whole series of commercials calling it Carle Place, so that we could decide later." Eddie won that argument.

Finally, Larry realized that he couldn't take it anymore.

By 1983 the Jerry Carroll TV and radio ads were getting so much attention, so many inquiries from other companies, that Eddie set up a production outfit called Crazy Ads. One of its clients was 2001 Odyssey, the disco made famous in *Saturday Night Fever*. Commercials were made for Mark Elliot, the brand of shirts you'd wear in that disco. Larry created a jingle for that with John Oates of Hall and Oates. Later in 1983 Larry did some work for a friend of Eddie's. Under his arrangement with Crazy Ads, Larry was due a significant sum of money (he won't say how much) for creating the ad. Then, without saying a word, Eddie stiffed him.

"Eventually, I found out, yeah, we got paid. Eddie just put the money in his pocket. I did all the work. That pissed me off. That was enough." Larry confronted Eddie about it. "He got upset and said, 'Leave me alone.'" That was it, the breaking point. "I just can't trust him. All my trust was gone. I just had to get out of there."

There was no logical reason for Eddie to steal from Larry and drive him away. It was not as if he needed the money. It confounded Larry. "Here's a guy who had enough money to live happily ever after, for his kids to live happily ever after. Their kids and their kids and their kids. And that wasn't enough, and he had to go pull this fraud." What made it stranger was that Eddie didn't want to lose him. He even pleaded with him to stay, but Larry realized it was time to move on.

Larry still marvels at how Eddie ripped him off so casually, so effortlessly. Gerald Newman, the consultant who introduced Eddie to Oppenheimer, no doubt experienced the same kind of emotions.

Newman had a handshake deal with Eddie. That was a mistake. A legal principle ironically called the "Statute of Frauds" requires that certain contracts be put in writing to be enforceable. No matter. Eddie had given his word. Who cares about legal principles when a man gives his word? When the time came to pay, Eddie didn't. Newman sued and lost. Then he appealed to a higher court and lost again. It was a costly education, but Newman learned what everyone close to Eddie would come to realize: Eddie's conscience was on a permanent leave of absence.

"That was just his style," says Larry. "It was the only way he knew how to be." It wasn't personal. Eddie couldn't help himself. You could be close to him, a valued employee or a relative. You could be someone he never met in his entire life. You could even be Robert Crumb, the famed underground cartoonist.

In 1968 the creator of *Fritz the Cat* and *Keep On Truckin'* published a showcase for his work, an "adults-only" comic book called *Zap Comix*. The cover of issue no. 2 was adorned with a goofy, crazy face. Eddie must have liked it because he adopted an almost exact replica of it as Crazy Eddie's trademark, duly registered with the US Patent and Trademark Office. He plastered his slightly altered version of Crumb's creation on everything from souvenir Frisbees and T-shirts to stock certificates and the first page of the IPO prospectus. He used it without a word to Crumb or paying him a penny. Fortunately for Eddie, this act of outright larceny resulted in no blowback. Crumb had a relaxed attitude toward such things at the time, so he didn't make a fuss. "I was sort of flattered by such borrowing of my cartoon images back then," he recalled years later.

For Eddie, stealing was an addiction. Conning tourists in clip joints had been his gateway drug. He moved on to tax collectors and insurance companies, but he didn't stop with rubes and faceless corporations. He stole from Crumb. He stole from Gerald Newman and Larry Weiss. There were never any consequences, which fed his habit.

And he was moving on to the hard stuff.

CHAPTER EIGHT

NEW YEAR'S EVE 1983 WAS CLEAR AND FROSTY. THE TEMPERATURE DIPPED to twenty-five degrees by the time workmen pulled the "brightly lit, 200-pound Big Apple ball" down the pole at One Times Square. The television networks "covered" this annual ritual with soft rock and schmaltz. Dick Clark hosted his twelfth *New Year's Rockin' Eve* on ABC, while Andy Williams anchored on CBS from Times Square. Tradition held firm in the ballroom of the Waldorf Astoria, where Guy Lombardo's son Bill led the Royal Canadians in "Auld Lang Syne" at midnight.

Eddie Antar, who had just turned thirty-six, chose to celebrate the arrival of 1984 with Debbie. He had a choice of two Debbies. One Debbie was his wife, known as Debbie I around Crazy Eddie to distinguish her from Debbie II, his young blonde mistress. Her name was Debbie Ehrlich. Eddie was the father of five young daughters whom he loved deeply—even in her darkest moments of rage and despair, Debbie I was forced to admit that. But he was the same Eddie with whom she had fallen in love so many years before. Still a philanderer.

As usual, Eddie lied to Debbie I about his whereabouts New Year's Eve. He called her in the afternoon to cancel their plans for the evening, telling her that he had to meet some investment types to discuss the upcoming IPO. Debbie knew he was lying. He always lied.

Eddie had been married fifteen years, and he was itchy. Middle age was creeping up on him. His jet-black hair was receding now, and all the working out in the world could not postpone forever the inevitable trip to United Hebrew Cemetery on Staten Island, where the Syrian community's *chevra kadisha* burial society had a section set aside for its dead. Eddie took the traditional route of men with that primal fear. He treated his marriage like a fling, his patient and exasperated wife as if she was a girlfriend he could stand up whenever something better came along.

Eddie would stay out till all hours and then flop on a couch on the first floor of their Brooklyn home, behaving more like an adolescent than the head of a family and proprietor of an expanding chain of highly publicized retail stores. He was not at the hospital when his fourth daughter was born in 1978. It was Valentine's Day. Debbie came home from the hospital to find him asleep downstairs on the floor. "I had to wake him up," she recounted. Eddie was casual about his marriage when he was having fun. Sometimes he would come home. Sometimes he wouldn't. For Debbie Antar, it was a "constantly changing existence."

"He never had a pattern of coming home every single night. He came and went when he pleased. I never kept track of it. This is the way that Eddie was."

Their marriage was now a constant tug between his infidelity and the money that sloshed in her direction. Debbie Antar's mother, Lillian Rosen, was on the Crazy Eddie payroll as a bookkeeper. Debbie herself was drawing $75,000 a year. All of her financial needs were taken care of—their home in Brooklyn, their house in Oakhurst on the Jersey Shore, their vacations, Yeshiva day school for the girls, and many other requirements of an affluent American family. All she lacked was a husband to make the picture complete. "Eddie did what he wanted to do. There was no reason for words. If he wanted to sleep with me, he did. If he wanted to argue with me, he did." Vodka fueled his demons, or perhaps dulled them. All one can say for certain is that he drank, and to excess.

Sam M. sided with Debbie against Eddie. Part of it was irritation with his son's behavior, and part of it, perhaps most, was opportunism. Eddie's growing financial power had steadily eroded Sam M.'s stature. It was deeply humiliating. But he saw a way to regain control of the family. First he would have to break up Eddie's marriage. Sam M. raised the issue with his cousin Solomon, the family lawyer, as early as 1979. "He told me that they should not be living together," Solomon recalled, "and that she should not be subjected to what he called the indignities of life with Eddie Antar."

A promising opportunity to achieve that goal arose a few days before New Year's Eve. Somehow Debbie had found out that Eddie had traipsed off to Florida with Debbie II. She complained to the always sympathetic Sam M., who sided with her and whipped up the rest of the family against his son. Solomon recalled it as "a very, very big uproar at the time as to Eddie's carrying on with this other woman," with Sam M., Rose, Debbie, and Eddie's sister, Ellen, "all demanding that I take action to represent Debbie to obtain a divorce from Eddie Antar, whom they called this animal and other descriptive adjectives."

Then came New Year's Eve. Debbie learned about Eddie's plans for a tryst with Debbie II that evening and was determined to stop it. She brought her daughters to her father-in-law's house in Brooklyn, and "upon arriving at Sam M.'s house that evening, Debbie I advised Sam M. and his wife, Rose, that she intended to drive to Manhattan and confront her husband and his mistress." She went to Manhattan accompanied by Mitchell Antar's wife, Robin, and Ellen Kuszer, Eddie's sister. Ellen was the wife of Ben Kuszer; they jointly owned the Record and Tape Asylums that operated in many of Eddie's stores.

The three women went straight to 401 East Eightieth Street, an ugly highrise building of recent vintage. They arrived to find Eddie's limo parked in the driveway, its engine running. Eddie was sitting inside the vehicle, waiting for his mistress. The irate Mrs. Antar leaped out of her car and screamed at Eddie to get out, kicking the car door, "raging in obscenities." Eddie emerged, and a screaming match began involving all three women, with Eddie bringing the confrontation to a boiling point by slapping his sister across the face. The fight was so loud and disturbing that the doorman called the police. Eddie sped off in the limo before cops arrived to intervene in what came to be known as the "New Year's Eve Massacre."

The family warfare continued the following day. It was a Sunday, but Mitchell and Ben Kuszer were at the Crazy Eddie offices. Eddie confronted them, vowing to throw them out of the business and accusing them of instigating the previous night's confrontation. Then he went to Sam M.'s house and another fight ensued, as Eddie accused his father of fomenting the fracas the night before. Rose and Sam M. were so upset that Rose fainted and Sam M. was hospitalized with a heart attack the following day.

Lying in his hospital bed, Sam M. took Solomon into his confidence, sharing with his cousin the reason he was so anxious for Debbie to leave his son: it would enable Sam M. to take over the company, thereby regaining his position as head of the family.

Sam M., who was no stranger to divorce himself, knew that in New York and most states, the law required an "equitable distribution" of the marital assets, often including business interests. Wealthy fiancés frequently ask their spouses to sign premarital agreements, limiting what they can take in a divorce. Debbie had never signed one. That left Eddie vulnerable.

As later recounted by Solomon, Sam M. believed that Debbie was "in a position to receive 50 percent of Eddie's stock in Crazy Eddie." Since Sam M. owned one-third, "they would both be in a position to fire Eddie from the company and deprive him of his livelihood." One half of Eddie's two-thirds, combined with Sam M.'s share, would give the father and Debbie a two-thirds share of the company. Eddie would be relegated to minority ownership, the same one-third stake Sam M. now held.

Eddie could count too. Even if Solomon didn't spill the beans about Sam M.'s intentions, Eddie was no dummy. If there was going to be a divorce, and that was obvious now, it was going to be done *his* way. Unlike his father, he had the home-field advantage. Eddie proceeded to muscle Debbie with all the subtlety of a jackhammer.

As recounted in a court ruling some years later, in the early months of 1984 there were a series of "arguments, phone calls at all hours containing obscene language, [and] threats to Deborah Antar and her mother." On May 5, 1984, Eddie showed up at Debbie's house with a piece of paper for her to sign. While it's not clear who drafted it, one thing was certain—its contents were perfectly fine with Solomon, who subsequently asserted (Debbie disputed this) that he was Debbie's lawyer, even though he was a full-time employee of Crazy Eddie and Eddie was his boss. He would claim that he went over the terms set forth on that piece of paper and they were okay with Debbie, which she would also dispute.

Now, that piece of paper: it was not a biggie, Eddie assured her. She needn't worry about a thing. There would be a divorce, just as she wanted, but it would be take months to wend its way through the courts, and a fair and wise judge in a black robe would eventually do right by her. "He told her 'it was one year until the time of the divorce, and the judge would take care of everything.'" Eddie stood over Debbie until she signed that nothing piece of paper. He warned her that if the SEC found out about their marital problems it would somehow put the kibosh on the IPO, to the detriment of both of them. So she had to sign. She had to sign! She did.

What Debbie didn't realize was that the document she signed was a separation agreement. Far from being "not significant," it was a crucial document. It set the financial terms of any subsequent divorce, divided up the marital assets, determined visitation, and made perfectly clear that Debbie wasn't getting a single farthing from Crazy Eddie. Some amount of child support was included, but Debbie received what was, considering their marital lifestyle and Eddie's wealth, a measly sum—$35,000 a year in maintenance. That would end when either the youngest child turned twenty-one or Debbie cohabited with another man "for three days, continuous or not." It was "designed to take care of the children and make the wife destitute as the years go by. From day one she has by the Agreement no spendable funds of her own."

Debbie "was frightened and confused when she signed the separation agreement. She tried to read it but really was unable to do so because she was so upset. She was being intimidated by Eddie Antar standing over her in a manner that was threatening and because she had 'always been afraid of him.'" While looming over her, Eddie lied that the "judge will do the Equitable Distribution," when the truth was that the separation agreement determined what she'd get in a divorce. Debbie later asserted that "the agreement was never mentioned again. I was told it didn't get filed and it was not important and I never discussed it with Eddie again, never. I never thought of it again." To help Debbie put the separation agreement out of her mind, Eddie didn't give her a copy of it.

Eddie had worked Debbie like a sucker at a clip joint, promising that she would be showered with riches from the Crazy Eddie bonanza. He'd say things like "Don't worry, you will get your money, and we will have so much money, a butler's lifestyle." Actually, she wasn't going to get a "butler's lifestyle" unless that meant "the lifestyle of a butler." While Debbie was financially penalized if she had a normal social life, Eddie was not to be inconvenienced, his bachelor ways not impeded. He could drop by Debbie's houses in Brooklyn and New Jersey and see the kids whenever he wanted—the separation agreement provided for "unlimited visitation without notice."

From Sam M.'s perspective, the most disastrous aspect of the separation agreement was how it treated Eddie's stake in Crazy Eddie. Debbie was completely cut out of it, ending Sam M.'s fantasy of gaining control of the company and, with it, regaining his position as head of the family. His bitterness would linger for years, but Sam M. could do nothing but accept his defeat. Like it or not, the Antar family's future was bound up with Eddie.

CHAPTER NINE

THE MARCH 1984 EDITION OF THE *JOURNAL OF ACCOUNTANCY* WAS DEDI-
cated to the hardworking people who were lying like hell to get the Crazy
Eddie IPO off the ground. Not literally, of course. But that's how Sammy
Antar read it, with great joy, when his copy arrived in the mail. There it was
in black and white, with the prestige of the American Institute of Certified
Public Accountants behind it: a vindication of Sammy's Golden Idea, the
skim-reduction plan.

The article was called "Going Public—What It Involves," and it described
the "minimum criteria" investors were seeking in IPOs: "Sales of $15 million
to $20 million. Net income of $1 million or more in the current fiscal year."
And then, the passage that justified their years of carefully manipulating the
skim: *an annual growth rate of 30 percent to 50 percent, with the prospect of
continuing growth at that rate for the next few years.*

Crazy Eddie would make the grade—their manipulation of the *nehkdi*
saw to that. Excited as he was, Sammy did not have a cut of the IPO. He
was not directly benefiting by selling shares in the offering. He wasn't even
getting an executive position at first, but that was okay. Eddie wanted him
as his right-hand man, his financial guru. That was enough.

The article talked of 30 percent to 50 percent revenue growth. Crazy Eddie had done even better. Its *profits* had increased in that fantastic range,
thanks to the skim reduction. In 1980 about $3 million in profits was
skimmed off the top. The next year, the net *nehkdi* was reduced to $2.5
million. In 1982 it was cut still further to $1.5 million, and in 1983 the
profits raked in came to just $750,000. In 1984 it would be pretty much

eliminated entirely. With progressively less profits skimmed each year, the actual, for-real 2 percent profit growth between 1980 to 1981 was artificially pumped up to 35 percent. Real profits climbed another 2 percent between 1981 and 1982, and the reduction in the skim ratcheted that number up to an eye-popping 48 percent. Between 1982 and 1983, real-world profits climbed 9 percent. Cutting back on the skim bloated that number way up to a fabulous 35 percent.

The actual profit growth numbers were so-so because even though Crazy Eddie was opening more stores and its revenues were growing, they weren't bringing in bucks fast enough to make up for increased costs. Sales tax was no longer being stolen, depriving Eddie of a competitive advantage. The *nehkdi* manipulation had fabricated great numbers in place of the meh reality. Two and two were made to equal fifty. The numbers in Sammy's worksheets were yelling at the top of their lungs, just as surely as Jerry Carroll was yelling at people on late-night TV. What the numbers screamed was that there was no turning back. From now on, truth was the enemy. Their IPO was built on lies.

Since they were doing everything wrong, Eddie had to be doubly sure that it *appeared* that they were doing everything right. Respectability could be bought, and by now he could afford it. Eddie had a top-drawer underwriter lined up, Oppenheimer, and a top-tier law firm, Paul, Weiss, Rifkind, Wharton & Garrison, at his disposal. It was a politically connected, highly prestigious firm with a stellar reputation. Cahill Gordon and Reindel, Oppenheimer's white-shoe law firm, also decorated the prospectus. KMG Main Hurdman, a large and equally impressive accounting firm, replaced Penn & Horowitz in the midsummer of 1984. Investors would have nothing to worry about with such shiny names hovering around Crazy Eddie.

For months, Paul, Weiss and Oppenheimer guided Eddie through the IPO process. The latter was a paragon of WASP–Our Crowd rectitude, tracing its corporate lineage to predecessor firms that financed railroads and the Union side of the Civil War. The company's current incarnation was founded in 1950 by Max E. Oppenheimer, a German Jewish banker. Its first business was "dealing in blocked German currencies after World War II," but Oppenheimer later gained a reputation for sharp and sometimes adventurous dealmaking, such as raising $40 million for John DeLorean's ill-fated gull-winged sports car in the late 1970s. Oppenheimer had been smudged by DeLorean—everyone involved was suing each other in 1983— but the company was not about to flush its pristine reputation down the toilet dealing with blackguards. Crazy Eddie had to be thoroughly scoped out.

Before selling stock to the public, the investment bank in charge of an IPO engages in a ritual known as "due diligence." The company that is seeking to sell stock must be investigated from top to bottom. To fulfill this requirement, Oppenheimer sent over two corporate finance executives, Todd Berman and Paul Zofnass. Once Crazy Eddie passed muster, Oppenheimer would throw its considerable reputation behind the IPO. Oppenheimer and the other underwriters of the offering, each promised an allotment of shares, would then sell them to favored customers. It was a ritual, but an important one.

Zofnass, thirty-six years old, was the more senior of the two. Berman, just twenty-six, had been with Oppenheimer for only a few months. This would be his due-diligence debut. Both had grown up in the suburbs and were the offspring of prominent families. Zofnass was the son of a bedding manufacturer. He'd received an MBA from Harvard, where he produced Hasty Pudding theatricals and was friends with Al Gore. He joined Oppenheimer in 1978 and had risen to managing director. Berman was the son of a prominent Buffalo surgeon. He had earned degrees from Brown and Columbia and served on the governor of Rhode Island's staff before going into investment banking.

These two men were facing a company very much out of their orbit—a working-class enterprise with arcane family connections and hidden crimes—and to them it was about as familiar as a malarial swamp in the Congo. "The due-diligence guys, Berman and Zofnass, come over, and they're seeing a bunch of Brooklyn thugs running a business," Sammy recalls. They had to play the hand they were dealt. Crazy Eddie was being brought public by Oppenheimer, and that was that. After giving a due-diligence thumbs-up, the next step was another Wall Street ritual—a "road show," in which the CEO and other top executives tour the country, selling its investment virtues to potential buyers of the stock.

Even after fifteen years at the helm of a high-visibility company, Eddie was hardly a standard-issue CEO. He was short and bearded, kept a gym and a dog in his office, and didn't have the foggiest idea how to explain all those numbers he had carefully inflated. This created an opportunity for Sammy. "After meeting with Eddie they said, no, this shit's going to be a disaster, but I was there and I knew how to read a prospectus, because I had been reading the *Wall Street Journal* since I was twelve years old. And I knew that prospectus inside and out. I memorized it. And I knew how to make numbers talk."

The Oppenheimer due-diligence guys were well-acquainted with Eddie's eager if inexperienced cousin. "They said, 'Let's let Sam come along. We'll call him the "staff accountant."'" So Sammy went on the road show. He was still splitting his time between Crazy Eddie and Penn & Horowitz—he would go on Eddie's payroll full-time in June 1984—but he was already Crazy Eddie's top finance person. The "red herring" preliminary prospectus was issued by Oppenheimer in February 1984, and the road show would follow. Sammy's job would be to breathe life into all those numbers, while the Oppenheimer guys, Eddie, and the other Antars expounded on the great things they had done and planned to do. Their audience would be investors, mainly managers of pension funds and mutual funds, as well as analysts working for the funds and for brokerage houses. The latter wrote reports on companies and industries that were distributed to stockbrokers and clients, as well as the business press.

After meeting with analysts and investors in New York, the Antars and the Oppenheimer duo went to Boston, Chicago, Los Angeles, San Diego, and San Francisco, one after another, a succession of hotel rooms, conference rooms, and rubber-chicken lunches. Sam M., swallowing his pride, came on the road with Sammy, Eddie, Mitchell, Zofnass, and Berman. Eddie and Sam M. would make a presentation, working off cue cards prepared by the Oppenheimer team, and then they would answer questions. After the formal Q&A session, there would be informal talks with the people in attendance.

Investors and analysts asked about a lot of things during the road show, but there was a common theme: growth. Was Crazy Eddie a growth company? Did it justify the price-earnings ratio that was contemplated in the prospectus? In other words, was Crazy Eddie caviar or chopped liver? The prospectus said the share price would be in the range of $11.50 to $13.50. That presupposed a generous P/E ratio of about seventy times the previous year's earnings per share (profits divided by total shares outstanding). Definitely a caviar-class P/E. But that price range was only an approximation. The price in the final version of the prospectus could be higher or lower, depending upon the amount of enthusiasm the Antars and the Oppenheimer guys could whip up.

The various elements of Eddie's edge were not public knowledge at this point, with one exception—bait and switch. Questions came up at the road shows about that. These were fielded by Eddie and Mitchell. They adamantly denied that they did any such thing. Of course not! Crazy Eddie tried to give customers what they wanted, and also at times the salespeople tried "to educate the customer as to what's better if we don't feel the customer is buying something appropriate." Not switching customers to higher-margin products but *educating* them. It was a smart line borrowed from Syms, a discount clothier popular with Wall Streeters, whose motto was "An Educated Consumer Is Our Best Customer."

Those questions had been anticipated. According to Sammy, Berman and Zofnass had been in the stores and "were aware that we were in the process of baiting and switching customers." It was a touchy subject and had to be presented in the right way, lest investors get the wrong idea and conclude that Crazy Eddie wasn't as clean as the driven snow. Sammy years later would testify that Zofnass "did not want us to use the words 'bait and switch' to describe our sales practices."

Eddie's presentation skills improved with every meeting, and Sammy kept coaching him on the numbers to downplay the negatives and accentuate the best parts of the prospectus—especially those outstanding, *nehkdi*-fabricated growth numbers. The two men worked well together. Eddie was pleased. Even Sam M., still nursing his wounded ego, was happy with the way things went on the road. The Antars were optimistic until the unexpected appeared to throttle their plans for unlimited wealth.

Someone in the financial press had gotten her hands on the prospectus. That in itself was fine. Crazy Eddie could use the publicity. The problem was that she read it.

CHAPTER TEN

Alan Abelson, the editor of *Barron's*, was a compact man of fifty-eight with a gleaming bald head, a natty dresser who favored pin-striped shirts with French cuffs. Of his many dislikes, the ones that he savored the most were overvalued stocks. When an overhyped, overblown company came on his radar screen, he honed in on it and shot it down. A positive article in *Barron's* was a cause for rejoicing among corporate managements, stockbrokers, and investment bankers, and a negative one was a source of deep despair. Abelson was a one-man court from which there was no appeal. If you wrote a letter to the editor to complain, he would publish a mocking response. If you sued him for libel, he would double down.

On June 4, 1984, the Court of Abelson convened to evaluate the Crazy Eddie IPO. Reading through "Not-So-Crazy Eddie," Sammy realized that they had a problem. After predictably poking fun at the Jerry Carroll commercials, *Barron's* writer Gigi Mahon went to work with a sledgehammer, pounding into rubble every possible aspect of the company, ridiculing its self-dealing and nepotism, and shattering the financial artifice that they were working so hard to promote.

"In the past, Crazy Eddie has been run like, well, a private company," Mahon pointed out with more accuracy than she could have possibly known. She then proceeded to use the prospectus as source material for a dissection of the Antars' intrafamily business relationships. Not the *nehkdi* or the sales tax stealing, not the illegal stuff, but the legal enterprises, which all seemed to be interlinked. All the one-hand-washes-the-other-and-both-hands-wash-the-face mutual assistance that formed the basis of S-Y survival seemed sleazy when viewed from afar. Many Antar family enterprises had dealings with Crazy Eddie, and Mahon made them sound incestuously intertwined with each other, which they were. For instance, Sam M. co-owned a retail shoe chain in Arizona that had gone bust. That had to be disclosed in the prospectus because Crazy Eddie had loaned the shoe outfit money. It wasn't illegal, not even a little bit. It wasn't even unethical. But it didn't look good that Crazy Eddie was used as a piggy bank for relatives.

Months before, when he was assembling the prospectus for Oppenheimer, Sammy had explained to Eddie and Sam M. that they had no choice. They *had* to disclose unflattering details. Leaving them out was not worth the risk of discovery. If an omission was uncovered, it would give regulators a slam-dunk securities fraud case. "We didn't want to give the feds low-hanging fruit," Sammy points out. Besides, who actually read the fine print in prospectuses? Mahon did. She even denigrated the crown jewel of the IPO prospectus: the increase in profits, carefully crafted and nurtured through paring down of the net *nehkdi*. Mahon quibbled with the growth figures and then prophetically observed that "if there's anything to worry about with Crazy Eddie, it's whether it can sustain that kind of growth."

On the piece went, detail after unflattering detail. There was Eddie's salary, which at the time was awfully rich for a company of its size—a five-year contract paying $300,000 a year. Then there was the matter of a chief financial officer. The prospectus disclosed that Crazy Eddie didn't have one, which was not true. Sammy was already CFO—the de facto CFO—and had been since he graduated from Baruch in 1980, even while working part-time for Penn & Horowitz, Crazy Eddie's pre-IPO auditors, gaining the experience required to become a CPA. He had done well at Baruch, and scored in the ninety-eighth percentile in the CPA exam, but it wouldn't have looked very good if the prospectus said, "We've got Eddie's kid cousin lined up for CFO, but he's just out of college and training to be a CPA." So instead the document pretended that a hunt was on for a CFO. That may have looked even worse.

In the last few brutal paragraphs, Mahon examined the all-important pricing of the IPO. As far as the Antars were concerned, this was more important than everything that preceded it. Self-dealing, rich salaries, no

CFO, none of that mattered if *Barron's* felt that the IPO was fairly priced. The verdict of the Court of Abelson was no. Despite the *nehkdi*-inflated earnings growth, *Barron's* asserted that investors would be overcharged if they paid the stock price contemplated in the prospectus. Mahon concluded: "You might get rock-bottom prices in the store, but you don't necessarily get them in the stock."

The *Barron's* piece was personally painful for Eddie and Sam M. Not only was Crazy Eddie raising money for itself in the IPO, but Eddie was selling 466,667 shares and Sam M. was selling 233,333, reflecting their two-thirds/one-third split of the company. As spelled out in the prospectus, Eddie would get about $6 million from the IPO. Even after selling so much stock, Eddie would still own 53 percent of the company. That was not unheard-of for a company going public, but it was yet another thing that didn't look so good.

Eddie reacted calmly. He didn't write an angry letter to the editor, which would have been pointless. When a product wasn't moving off the shelves, or got a bad write-up in *Stereo Review*, he cut the price. After talking with Zofnass and Berman, he agreed to lower the IPO price from $11.50–$13.50 to $8 a share. The company went public on September 13, stock symbol "CRZY." Slashing the price attracted buyers, as it did on the sales floor. The offering sold out at its $8 price, and the stock rose quickly to $9.125. The IPO did so well that Oppenheimer exercised an "overallotment option" and sold another 300,000 shares to lucky customers. The odor of creepiness wafting from the *Barron's* piece quickly dissipated.

The thumping delivered by *Barron's* demonstrated the crucial role the press would play in Eddie's personal financial health. Clearly, he needed help interacting with the media, preferably someone who could deal with investors and analysts as well. He needed a public relations/investor relations professional, commonly and unkindly known as a "flack."

The Oppenheimer connection brought Eddie a man of fifty-three by the name of John Edmund Colloton. They met at the Fifty-Seventh Street store and then proceeded to Dewey Wong, Eddie's favorite Chinese restaurant. Ed Colloton knew what animated CEOs. He went to work on this bearded little man with bad table manners. He told Eddie that elevating the stock price would be his one and only objective. As he later put it: "There is no benchmark for corporate excellence. There are no awards accompanying a stock rating. The P/E ratio is considered the judgment of the investing community on the performance of the company. There is no other yardstick." After hearing that, Eddie was ready to hire Colloton on the spot.

He couldn't. First Colloton had to deal with a conflict of interest that made him even more irresistible to Eddie: hiring him would screw the competition. Colloton's employer, Investor Access Corporation, represented one of Eddie's direct competitors, the Circuit City electronics chain, and Colloton just happened to work on that account. To represent Eddie he needed to get permission from Circuit City's chairman of the board, Alan Wurtzel, who had been struggling to compete with Crazy Eddie in the New York market. Wurtzel quickly and predictably said no.

Colloton was as sold on Eddie as Eddie was sold on him. After Wurtzel turned down his request, Colloton quit his job and started his own company, setting up shop in an Art Deco office building at Fifth Avenue and Forty-Second Street. It was an old-money, old-fashioned venue that exuded respectability. Crazy Eddie would be the first client of the Colloton Group, established in October 1984, purveyor of glad tidings (and spin when things did not go well) to the media and the Street. There would be other clients, but Eddie would consume the bulk of his time. Henceforth, Colloton would generate press releases, court the media, schmooze with analysts, and create the kind of image enhancement that Crazy Eddie urgently needed. Not everyone at Crazy Eddie was as enamored of Colloton as Eddie was, however. Sammy found him to be slovenly and annoying. Colloton would pepper him with questions on every possible subject, some of which he felt were stupid.

Like the Oppenheimer due-diligence guys, Colloton came from a white-bread background that was worlds apart from the Antars. The son of an industrial products salesman, Colloton dwelled amid the manicured lawns and country clubs of Larchmont in Westchester County. He had spent his entire adult life in public relations, joining the St. Regis Paper Company after graduating from Fordham University in 1954. He worked there for more than two decades and then for a succession of independent PR firms.

He was an avid amateur yachtsman. He had the right connections, the right broad and insincere smile, the right firm handshake. He drank to excess and once got his name in the paper for boozily driving into a succession of parked cars. Except for the alcohol, Eddie had nothing in common with Colloton. But that was fine. He was brought on as an emissary to the alien worlds of media and finance, not as a drinking buddy.

Once again Eddie was displaying a talent for hiring the right people. Reflecting on Colloton years later, the veteran corporate hype observer Kathryn F. Staley wrote: "He was the best: smooth, enthusiastic, helpful. He knew all the analysts on the Street and was always available with the latest word from Eddie Antar. He made it easy to be an analyst. Wall Street analysts just wrote down what Ed Colloton told them and did not bother with all that messy financial stuff. Then they could revel in the sales charm of Eddie Antar himself and feel comfortable that everything was okay."

It was a marriage made in stock fraud heaven, or so it seemed to Eddie at the time. But as Eddie knew, or should have known, making a marriage work was not one of his talents.

■ ■ ■

The *Barron's* piece was mercifully brief in dealing with one of Eddie's side ventures, a Caribbean medical school that was in the process of defaulting on every debt it owed. A company that sold TVs and clock radios, whose commercials were parodied on *Saturday Night Live*—Joe Piscopo's "Crazy Edelman" spoof aired in October 1983—was in the doctor-training business? It was bizarre. Eddie had become involved in the school through its "director of admissions," a psychologist friend of Eddie's named Isaac "Ike" Kairey. It had to be mentioned in the prospectus because Crazy Eddie had made interest-free loans to the school and to a related entity that provided it with "recruiting and other services." The latter was run by brother-in-law Ben Kuszer, who operated the Record and Tape Asylums—the only thing even remotely medical-sounding on his résumé.

As with Crazy Eddie, Eddie had an edge over the competition when he created the University of St. Lucia School of Medicine. His target customer base consisted of American college graduates who yearned to be doctors but couldn't meet the strict admission standards of US medical schools. Mexican schools were a popular alternative but required fluency in Spanish for at least part of their programs. A medical school that taught in English had already opened on Grenada, but political instability there, culminating in a US invasion in October 1983, opened the door to competition. Like Crazy Eddie, the St. Lucia school offered an irresistible bargain. Instead of "crazy prices," it built up its customer base by offering crazy admission standards.

Eddie launched the school in April 1983 with a reception at Manhattan's Water Club overlooking the East River. In attendance was the prime minister of St. Lucia, John G. M. Compton, along with other officials from the island nation. Ads were placed in newspapers throughout the United States, and enrollment ramped up quickly. By September 1983 the school enrolled 127 students, and a second class of 41 students arrived in March. Newspaper ads touted the school as "A Great Adventure in Medical Education." It was not intended to be ironic. The would-be doctors arrived on the island to find that they were the victims of a clip joint hustle. Students were promised that a new lecture hall was coming, that a new library was coming. "They really sold the place," one student later recounted. But when they actually got there, "there was nothing."

Despite charging steep tuition and cheating its students, the school failed to make money. Eddie abruptly pulled the plug in March 1984, leaving "a number of unpaid bills and students who are worried about getting back the thousands of dollars that they paid." The students were promised slots at the Grenada medical school when the one on St. Lucia closed, but only 37 of the 168 St. Lucia students were academically qualified. Eddie's admission standards had been a bit too insane. The fiasco infuriated government officials in St. Lucia, who had backed the school from its inception. Prime Minister Compton was particularly incensed; he had not only attended that Water Club reception, but posed with Eddie in the college catalog and was given an honorary degree when the school first opened.

Sammy discovered just how angry St. Lucians had become when Eddie summoned him into his office on Coney Island Avenue not long after the school closed. Eddie had Sammy shut the door behind him. He opened a desk drawer and proceeded to pile a stack of greenbacks—$20,000—on his desk. "Mitch Pinto is in jail down there," Eddie said calmly, as if he was ordering a box of Milk Bones for Sugar. He gestured toward the stack. "Get him out."

Mitch was a trusted Crazy Eddie old-timer, a former manager in the high-volume Syosset store. In Eddie's eyes that qualified him to work as a medical school administrator. Mitch was taking the fall for the fiasco on the island—it wasn't clear why—and had been tossed behind bars because of all the unpaid debts. Sammy booked the next flight to St. Lucia with the bribe money carefully tucked into his carry-on luggage. When he arrived he was relieved to find that Mitch had already been released from the St. Lucia lockup. However, he was not yet out of legal jeopardy and expected that he'd be arrested again.

Sammy took a chance. He gave Mitch the $20,000 to pay off the local police and fly himself off the island on a single-engine plane. Sammy believed Mitch could be trusted with the money, and he felt vindicated when Mitch handed him back a thousand of it before he left the island. After all, Mitch could have just pocketed the leftover cash.

Mitch's jailing, payoffs, and absconding looked more like the actions of a drug dealer than a medical school administrator and would have drawn damaging publicity if it had leaked to the press. Fortunately for Eddie, the people in St. Lucia just wanted to put the whole nightmare behind them and weren't going to make a fuss about an absconded medical school administrator. Mitch went back to work for Crazy Eddie, and the medical school controversy died down.

The ebbing of the Caribbean crisis might have given Eddie a sense of security, a feeling that he had finally gained control over the disparate threads of his life. If it seemed that way, it was a fantasy. Eddie remained in a life-or-death struggle with his worst enemy—the man who faced him every time he looked in the mirror.

CHAPTER ELEVEN

EVEN THOUGH THEY WERE NOW SEPARATED AND LIVING APART, EDDIE's relationship with Debbie had changed very little. It was a terrible relationship before they separated, and it was a terrible relationship now that their marriage had crumbled.

There were still bitter quarrels. He still barged into Debbie's houses in Brooklyn and Oakhurst at any hour of the day or night. However, despite all the bitterness, their physical intimacy didn't change from what it had been before the separation and continued even when they were fighting. As Debbie later said, "There were many times when we were arguing and we didn't go through reconciliation and we had relations."

At first, Eddie was happy with the one-sided status quo. Then his facade started to crack. He started talking about all the stress he was under because of the IPO. He gave Debbie the impression that there had been a grueling procession of road show meetings, which he described in heartrending terms—sometimes ten meetings in two days, meetings in airports, one in the morning, one in the afternoon in a different city, and yet another in the evening in still another city. All the meetings were exhausting, dizzying. The whirlwind of activity made Eddie reconsider their breakup. He had an idea.

Eddie came to Debbie's house in Oakhurst late one weekend night in July 1984 with a proposition. He wanted to settle down with both the Debbies in his life. He asked her "if he could have children with someone else, and if I would allow him to live with someone else part of the week?"

Debbie Antar had heard many words coming out of Eddie's mouth, wheedling and excuses, lies and abuse. But never anything like this. She

Gary Weiss

reacted with horror and disgust. Eddie reacted to her reaction by falling into bed like a child. He remained there, weeping, for three days in a full-blown attack of self-pity, a performance worthy of Brando. To no great surprise, it didn't work. Debbie wasn't going for it. The status quo of quarrels, empty promises, and lies resumed and continued through the end of 1984. Then came the New Year and another "massacre."

Early in the morning of January 8, 1985, one day before their sixteenth wedding anniversary, Eddie and Debbie had a face-off that was far worse than any they'd had before. As usual, Eddie dropped by her Brooklyn home at one or two o'clock, banging on the door and demanding to be let in. That led to the usual argument about Eddie's annoying habit of dropping by unannounced. Then they squabbled about money, as usual, but Eddie wasn't in the mood to make any more empty promises.

"You will get nothing, and I will break your arms and legs!" he screamed. The first part was rare honesty. The second part was hyperbole, or so she thought. Eddie had never been violent with her.

Debbie went upstairs, climbed into bed, and pulled the covers over her head. That did not end the fight. Their fights did not end until *Eddie* wanted them to end. He followed her upstairs and screamed again.

"You will get nothing!"

That didn't work, so he started whining.

"You can't go to a lawyer!"

"I am going to a lawyer."

"You will not get anything," he said. "You will get nothing. I will get Sammy [Solomon Antar] to do it"—the divorce—"whether you like it or not."

Eddie yanked off the covers. Debbie pulled them back and cried out, "Leave me alone!" Eddie pulled off the covers again. Debbie pushed him away, and Eddie hit her hard on the left side of her face. The force of the blow sent Debbie reeling back onto the bed. Her head "was spinning." As Debbie lay there, crying, Eddie went on a rampage through the bedroom, ripping the venetian blinds from the windows, and tearing out two of the closet doors before storming out of the house. Debbie later recounted that she sobbed for the rest of the night.

The next afternoon, Eddie showed up at the house. In just a few hours he'd had Solomon Antar draw up divorce papers. Then came a replay of the separation agreement browbeating. "You wanted a divorce, here it is," he told Debbie, ordering her to sign the legal papers he brought with him. "You wanted a divorce and here is your divorce." Debbie asked Eddie about her money. For the umpteenth time, he lied that the financial details of their divorce would be determined by a judge and that it was nothing for her to worry about. "The judge takes care of the equitable division," he replied. "The court will take care of it when it gets filed." In the eight months since she signed an unimportant piece of paper the previous May, she hadn't learned that it had parceled out their assets, with Debbie getting a big hot slice of bupkis.

Debbie signed the papers. As with the separation agreement, she did not get a copy. Seventeen days later, on January 25, 1985, the divorce decree was signed by Richard O. Huttner, a justice of the Supreme Court of the State of New York. Debbie was unaware of this. She did not know that she was now legally single again. She did not know that all the financial arrangements involved in ending their marriage had long since been tied up with a bow, concluded, finished. So the arguments continued, as did the lies. "Trust me," Eddie would tell her. "Don't worry and you will get your money." Yet again, she believed him. She swallowed whole his lie that "the judge would look at the finances and give me what I deserved."

Eddie's assault left Debbie with a black eye and discoloration of the left side of her face, which she tried to cover with makeup. Yet she was not ready to completely cut the cord. Later that month, Debbie traveled to Acapulco with the kids on a school-sponsored trip during the winter recess, and she let Eddie drive her and the girls to the airport. While they were in Acapulco, Eddie called. He just wanted to see if everything was okay. "I will come down with Richie to check," said Eddie. She did not object.

Eddie came to Acapulco, accompanied by his pal Richie Dayon. The Dayons were old friends of the Antars. Richie's dad—a jovial, heavy man named Al—was a flamboyant swindler who graduated from selling fake watches from his Forty-Second Street clip joint (for which he was indicted in 1957) to running an elaborate stock fraud ten years later (for which he was indicted in 1971). Richie, a few years younger than Eddie, was something of a sidekick. Eddie would often stay at Richie's house, and whenever Debbie wanted to reach her ex-husband in future years, she would contact Richie to get ahold of him.

They had a pleasant time together. It was as if they were a normal couple and not in the death throes of a marriage. Eddie rented a boat, and they spent a day on the tranquil Pacific—he and Debbie, Richie, their friends, and the kids, water-skiing and sunning themselves. At night they enjoyed a "luau-style" dinner. As usual with Eddie, there was no discussion of plans for the night. He would decide. "Let's go," he said.

They went—the kids to bed and Eddie and Debbie to a disco, and then they spent the night together in Debbie's suite. In the morning at breakfast, Eddie sat at the other end of the table from Debbie and regaled their friends with the magical qualities of levitation performed by Crazy Eddie stock since the IPO. If their friends weren't impressed, they should have been. In barely four months, share prices had doubled. Then, he and Richie flew back to New York, and Debbie and the girls continued their vacation.

It would be the last time they slept together. That part of their relationship was over. But Eddie was not completely out of Debbie's life. He continued to visit the kids as often as he wanted without notice. And they never stopped fighting about money, with Eddie now feeding her the line of hogwash that she'd get her equitable share of the marital assets "when the case goes to court."

After she learned that the case *had* gone to court and that she was divorced,* Debbie still entertained the fantasy that a treasure chest of Antar gold was waiting for her somewhere, and Eddie maintained that illusion through a new series of lies. First the divorce papers weren't complete even though they were divorced. Then the papers were complete, but the case hadn't yet come up on the court calendar. Having abandoned his brief flirtation with the truth ("You'll get nothing"), Eddie resumed promising

---

* Exactly when Debbie learned that she was divorced is unclear. Debbie would later insist she didn't know until she read about it in a Crazy Eddie SEC filing toward the end of June 1985. Ruling on one of the many lawsuits that spilled out of the company in future years, a judge found her story to be "highly implausible."

that Debbie would get "half of our marital property." He would say, "Don't worry, you will have plenty. We [will] make multiple offerings and we sell the stock and you get half. Multi-millions of dollars."

Despite all that had happened, Debbie still relied on Eddie to tell her when her "equitable" share would supposedly "come up" in court, since she was planning to appear before the judge without a lawyer. Why she trusted Eddie to explain court procedures to her, and did not consult a divorce lawyer, was still a mystery decades later. By the 1980s, lawyers were advertising on TV and in subway cars. There were page after page of divorce lawyers in the Yellow Pages. She could afford a lawyer—and Eddie might have been compelled to pay her legal fees if she was properly represented. But instead she decided that she would go it alone, with the "expectation . . . that after the divorce became finalized I would get half of what we owned at the time of the divorce."

When Debbie started questioning Eddie's "court calendar" hokum, Eddie invented a new series of excuses. According to Debbie, "He began to say there is a problem with taxes and how he paid taxes once and he doesn't want to pay it twice. 'Why should the government get all the money?'" The solution to this problem—really *their* problem, as he described it—involved Benel Distributors, owned by his sister, Ellen, and brother-in-law, Ben Kuszer, which operated the Record and Tape Asylums. Eddie told Debbie that she was due at least $8 million in Benel stock. Maybe even $9 million. It's not clear what "tax strategy" Eddie was conjuring up out of thin air, but Debbie believed him. "I felt guilty about having to give it to the government. He said we can keep it for ourselves and the kids."

She clung tenaciously to his lies. It was as if Debbie had fallen in love with the imaginary world that Eddie had created for her—a prosperous, secure life that was coming her way not as a gift but as an act of justice. Throughout 1985 she was no more able to see through his falsehoods than any of the suckers who bought returned merchandise repackaged as "lunch." But unlike the unwary customers in the stores, she knew that he was a compulsive liar.

Debbie's self-delusions were in full flower not long after the Acapulco trip, when she learned that Eddie had recently sold a chunk of stock in a public offering that Oppenheimer engineered in March 1985. Investor enthusiasm, whipped up with Ed Colloton's expert help, was so rabid that the share price had almost tripled since the IPO and was now $21 per share. Eddie sold 600,000 shares for himself and another 240,000 as custodian for family members. Some of the shares sold by Eddie were held in trust for his mother and other Antars, including the children of cousins. Other relatives were selling their own shares as well. Sam M. sold 150,000. Eddie's brothers, Allen and Mitchell, and brother-in-law, Ben Kuszer, were selling stock held jointly with their wives.

The rest of the shares were in Eddie's name alone, as you might expect of a man who had just gotten divorced. He was netting $14.5 million, and it was all his. As for Debbie, she got nothing. But she believed she had a stake in Eddie's shares. It was *their* stock dump. Some years later, she recounted, "The stock sold, and he made a lot of money, and he came home"—they were divorced, but still he "came home"—"and we were very happy, and he said, 'It is ours. We all did great. Isn't it great? The stock is doing great.' He made me feel like it was us who were doing great. It was our stock." Incredibly, "I believed him."

Debbie trusted Eddie, but he certainly didn't trust her.

In June 1985, Eddie sold 300,000 Crazy Eddie shares, worth $8 million, that were held in custody for their children in an account controlled by Eddie and Debbie. Eddie wanted to transfer the proceeds into an account he had set up in the Cayman Islands, and he didn't want Debbie to know about it. But how could he do that? She would have to sign account documents.

Eddie found an easy solution to his problem. Debbie's mother, Lillian, worked for him, and he had her sign her daughter's name on the Bank Leumi account papers. He could have forged her signature himself, but Eddie was no dope. Why should he take such a risk? The money was now safely, quietly salted away under Eddie's control, and Lillian never told Debbie about it. Eddie got away with it, succeeding in what was later described as "a preparatory effort by Eddie to steal the $8 million from his own children."

CHAPTER TWELVE

LIKE EDDIE'S FORMER AD GUY LARRY WEISS, DEBBIE HAD BEEN EXPOSED to the reality of Eddie that he concealed from the public and most of the people who worked for him. The salesmen, managers, stockroom clerks, cashiers—most were in the dark. For all they knew, their boss was an odd-ball, a strange but charming and magnetic dude who ran next to his limousine for the exercise and let Sugar lick visitors whether they liked it or not. Just as Sugar was a nice dog, just untrained, they believed that Eddie was a good person, just rough around the edges. Not a bad person. Certainly not a criminal.

Among the fortuitously not-clued-in employees was Larry Weiss's successor as head of Eddie's successful advertising campaign. Harry Spero arrived at the end of 1979 to take charge of co-op advertising for the Record and Tape Asylums. Ben Kuszer operated them, but it was Eddie who interviewed him for the job. He asked just one question: "Do you know what co-op advertising is?" He did. End of interview. He was hired, starting the following day. That was New Year's Eve, Harry pointed out. Eddie didn't care, so he went to work.

Like a host of Crazy Eddie employees, Harry had a background in entertainment, in his case going back a generation. His father, Herman, was a TV producer in Cleveland, where his roster of shows included some of the first televised prizefights and a syndicated rock-and-roll show called *Upbeat*. When he was a kid, Harry would come home from school to find his dad mixing cocktails for the likes of Chubby Checker and Gene Pitney. Harry went to college in Toledo but didn't find the experience quite as satisfying as playing drums in a nightclub trio. He moved to New York with the hope of breaking into the entertainment industry, which he proceeded to do. He was hired by Don Kirshner as a songwriter, going on to run an RCA record label before moving into artist management with Cyndi Lauper and John Robie as clients. Eventually he left entertainment for one of the least stable corporate environments on earth. He was not yet thirty when he passed Eddie's one-question job interview.

Expansion—and Larry's departure—did not result in substantial change to Crazy Eddie's Jerry Carroll–oriented ad strategy, though there were subtle differences in approach. Prices started to creep into the ads, even coupons. Harry borrowed from the old *Rocky and Bullwinkle* cartoons, introducing puns and satire into the Carroll TV spots. As demands on his time grew, Eddie largely abandoned micromanaging the TV and radio commercials, which had created so much friction with Larry Weiss. But he was still Eddie, still unpredictable.

Harry learned that the hard way when he devised a surefire way of saving money for the company. They were advertising seven days a week on radio and TV. Why not go off the air on Mondays? He went to the office on Coney Island Avenue, expecting to be showered with praise. "We could save ourselves almost $3 million in advertising," he said.

Eddie looked at him. "Why would you even bring this up to me?"

"Because wouldn't you like to save $3 million?" asked Harry, genuinely puzzled.

"I would never, ever consider that," Eddie said flatly.

Harry was stunned. "One day you don't advertise. I'm betting you're not going to cause us to lose 1 percent worth of business."

"Get out of my office."

"I don't understand."

"You don't understand 'Get out of my office'? How about 'You're fired'?"

Harry went home. No sooner had he told his wife that he had lost his job when the phone rang. It was Ben Kuszer.

"Harry, what are you doing to me?"

"What are you talking about?"

"Why would you get into a discussion like that with Eddie?"

"I'm trying to save the company money."

"We don't want you to save the company money."

Ben instructed Harry to come into the office at nine the next morning to meet with Eddie. Harry pointed out that Eddie never got into the office before ten and usually much later. "Harry. Come into the office at nine o'clock," Ben replied, and hung up. Harry did as instructed, expecting to wait an hour.

Eddie was there at exactly 9:01. Ben was in the office with him, shaking his head at the errant employee being called on the carpet. "Well, what do you have to say to me?" Eddie asked.

"I apologize. I won't bring this up again. It was a silly idea. I was just trying to save the company money."

"What are you talking about, saving the company money!" Eddie exploded.

Harry apologized again, which made Eddie calm down. He went back to work, having been forced to eat crow for a perfectly good idea that would have been welcomed (or at worst ignored) at any other company in America. For Eddie, Harry's effrontery in actually suggesting something was an opportunity to cut his underling down to size. It was his way of exerting control over people. For Eddie, it wasn't enough to reject an idea he didn't like. He had to throw in a dash of humiliation.

Over time, Harry learned how to cope with Eddie. It was worth the effort. The company was being heralded as a rising star after the IPO, and Crazy Eddie was clearly destined for great things. A favorable piece in *Forbes* was cherished on Coney Island Avenue when it appeared in October 1984, as the magazine was investor-focused like *Barron's* and happy to take down overhyped companies. A *New York Daily News* article in December was even more welcome because it quoted an analyst by the name of Richard M. Lilly. He just loved Crazy Eddie. Citing an expected "45% return on net worth in its current fiscal year," Lilly said he was "very impressed" with Crazy Eddie.

Lilly's name didn't mean anything to most *Daily News* readers, but his views counted a great deal to the people who mattered to Eddie, the ones who were buying Crazy Eddie stock. Though he worked for a small brokerage firm, Raymond James, Lilly had a reputation for carefully researched reports that made him highly regarded as an analyst. His stamp of approval gave a significant boost to Eddie's quest to elevate the stock price. Lilly, of course, had no idea that he was extolling a company that had been juiced up by fraud for years—lies no less brazen than the ones being showered on Debbie every time she asked about her "equitable."

With the benefit of hindsight, it's tempting to blame analysts like Lilly for not deducing that something wasn't quite right at Crazy Eddie. But not even the most clairvoyant analyst could have detected—without an inside informant—what was happening in the inner sanctums of upper management. Even Ed Colloton, experienced as he was, never learned what was going on behind the scenes, though he picked up clues on occasion. For instance, Eddie was not just curious about the stock price; he was obsessed. He would call Colloton daily, sometimes twice a day, sometimes three times a day. What was the stock price? What was the trading volume? How was it doing? Eddie's calls were incessant and repetitive. But Colloton was paid to swallow that kind of thing.

Colloton was working hard to make his stock-focused client happy. He had prepared a dynamic and enticing marketing program that he used to peddle the virtues of the company to the Street and the business press. It was based on a simple (and, as far as he knew, accurate) premise: that Crazy Eddie had generated profits with the reliability of a twenty-one-inch Sony Trinitron. It had never disappointed. Not only had every year been a lot better than the previous year, but its sales and profits had increased every fiscal quarter throughout the history of the company.

That was the Crazy Eddie Story. A classic story. An American story. The story of a scrappy retailer that had beaten the odds. Its "underlying assumption was that Crazy Eddie was one of the real success stories of special retailing. Eddie Antar put together a unique business that was growing fast, expanding geographically, at the time when the consumer electronics business was perhaps at its zenith."

Eddie pushed that "never-fail, always-growing" line himself when he met with analysts, usually at the store on East Fifty-Seventh Street where he had first met Colloton. He would guide each of the analysts on a tour throughout the store, department by department, explaining how the business operated and how inventories were maintained by a state-of-the-art computer system. And it was never a group of analysts; it would be one at a time, during which each had Eddie's undivided attention. Eddie would spend up to two hours doing these "one-on-ones," making every analyst feel like the only person in the world.

In coaching Eddie for his new life as a public company CEO, Colloton underlined the importance of the principle of "no surprises." If in the future profits weren't performing as brilliantly as always, the Street would react by taking a scythe to the share price. That of course would directly slice into the Antar family's wealth. So it was imperative that any negative tidings were handled tastefully, so as not to unduly upset the Street.

If bad news were to arise, it would have to be "signaled" to Wall Street by Colloton. He would prep analysts for any earnings shortfall and then spin it as best he could afterward. That, he assured Eddie, would lessen the severity of a stock-price decline. Far from being objective or dispassionate, the stock market reacted emotionally to bad news, very much as children do when denied ice cream before dinner.

Eddie readily accepted Colloton's advice. He had five daughters. He knew there was only one way to handle bad news when an innocent child looks up to you with hopeful eyes.

You lie.

PART THREE
"RIP THEIR EYES OUT"

CHAPTER THIRTEEN

As 1985 began, customers crowded into the Crazy Eddie Record and Tape Asylums, clamoring for the hottest new records—Bruce Springsteen's *Born in the U.S.A.* and Madonna's *Like a Virgin*. Eddie's own theme song was from an iconic single that hit the charts in December: "Money Changes Everything." Cyndi Lauper sang it. Eddie Antar lived it. He was rich now, stinking rich for the first time in his life, and he was determined to stay that way.

"Maximizing shareholder value" had become a catchphrase in the corporate world, and Eddie was on board. He was anxious to maximize shareholder value for one shareholder. The reports cranked out by brokerage house analysts would do the maximizing for him. The rubbish they wrote was based on numbers. *His* numbers. Those numbers were vitally important in early 1985, since Crazy Eddie was nearing the end of its first fiscal year as a public company on March 3. Annual reports of newly public companies are always closely scrutinized, and in this case there was an additional reason the numbers would be examined thoroughly—the company was selling stock. There was to be yet another public offering, scheduled for mid-March. This was the stock offering that got Debbie so excited.

Companies offer stock to the public after IPOs to raise money or give insiders a chance to dump their shares. Eddie was planning to do both. He put 1.2 million shares on sale, one million belonging to family members—mostly himself. Two hundred thousand more shares would be sold to raise money for the company. So the numbers in the March 3 report would have to be darn good.

By now, analysts thought they had Crazy Eddie all figured out. They realized that the "insanely low prices" advertising spiel did not reflect reality. Most customers didn't like to negotiate for the lowest price. But they came into the stores anyway because of the Jerry Carroll commercials. Thus Crazy Eddie had a reputation for low prices "without the financial burden of consistent price competitiveness." As fraud expert Kathryn Staley observed some years later, "Analysts liked the feel of pulling the wool over the consumers' eyes." They realized that Crazy Eddie was a hype machine that bamboozled customers. But what they didn't know was that *they* were the real chumps. They had swallowed the profit growth numbers in the IPO prospectus, which were fabricated by Sammy's Golden Idea. And they were about to become suckers again.

As the fiscal year drew to a close in late February of 1985, Eddie realized he needed to act right away if the value of his shares was to be properly maximized. He needed to buff up the numbers, really make them shine. To accomplish that objective, he met separately with two of his key aides, both trusted employees who had been with him since the early days on Kings Highway. Both were named Dave. One of the Daves was honest. The other was not. That character trait was immaterial, for what Eddie needed now was loyalty and obedience.

Eddie knew that Dave Panoff was loyal, obedient, and dishonest. His official title was "director of service," but arguably his most important function was "director of warranty fraud." When customers brought in items for repairs that had an expired warranty, he'd give the units back to them, tell them that they were out of luck, and file claims with the manufacturers anyway. He would alter the dates of purchase so the manufacturers would be forced to pay for the repairs. He also billed manufacturers for parts that were not replaced and put in claims for merchandise that was not repaired when the customer thought the product was defective but it wasn't.

Panoff once estimated that around 40 to 50 percent of Crazy Eddie's warranty claims to manufacturers were phony after he took over the returns department in 1976. Churning out so much bogus paperwork required dishonesty on an industrial scale, a man capable of cheating manufacturers and customers with equal élan. It also required loyalty and obedience, for he

personally didn't see anything wrong with it at the time. But I didn't really question any more than that. He just said it was something that was important to do."

It was indeed vitally important. Despite his lack of a financial background, Eddie had picked up a basic principle of Accounting 101: the relationship between inventories and profits. Before preparing financial statements, retailers add up the contents of their warehouses and stores. That number is used to determine a line item in financial statements known as the "cost of goods sold." It is calculated by taking the starting inventory, adding purchases, and deducting the ending inventory. The result of that calculation is subtracted from sales to compute profits.

If the ending inventory is a big number, it means that the "cost of goods sold" number is small. The smaller a company's costs, the bigger its profits.

What this simple arithmetic meant was that $2 million in bogus inventory translated to $2 million in fabricated profits in the financial statements of Crazy Eddie as of March 3, 1985. Pretax profits were coming in at $10.3 million, so if Neiderbach was able to comply with Eddie's request, he'd be inflating the bottom line by nearly 20 percent. Bigger profits meant higher share prices, which meant a lot if you were the biggest shareholder, Eddie Antar.

None of this dawned on Dave Neiderbach. He had never taken a financial course in his life. The only crime he knew that was committed in warehouses was pilferage and burglary, which Eddie did not tolerate. Eddie would force veteran, trusted salesmen to take polygraph tests to prove that they weren't walking away with merchandise. Dave didn't know that the warehouse on McDonald Avenue, a dreary Brooklyn street with an elevated train roaring overhead, was as valuable to Crazy Eddie's financial posture as Fort Knox was to the US government.

This Dave had a particularly tough task ahead of him, as he would not be filing false pieces of papers like Panoff, but would have to actively deceive auditors from KMG Main Hurdman. They would be right there in the warehouse, checking to be sure everything was done correctly. While Dave may not have grasped the inventory-profits equation, they certainly did.

The tedious work of counting up the boxes in the main warehouse began on a Saturday morning. Dave and about a dozen of his employees did the work, watched by three accountants from KMG Main Hurdman. The boxes were counted by hand, with the quantity, brand, and model of each product compiled for entry into the clunky computer system. The accountants used standard procedures to determine that everything was being accurately toted up, performing what were known as "test counts." They would take a complete count of a particular make and model and then check their numbers against Dave's when he was done. About twenty such test counts were performed. The products were chosen at random.

The auditors did not, of course, tell the warehouse guys which products they were test counting. Dave came up with a solution to this problem. He had a few of his people "give the auditors a hand because it was very difficult to count anything in that building because the merchandise was so piled up and jammed up all over the place." Then they would report back to Dave and tell him which items the auditors were test counting. It was a simple matter to avoid those items when he was inflating the inventory numbers. He performed that task with the flick of a No. 2 pencil, changing the quantities of products in the warehouse and adding items that weren't actually there. He focused on high-ticket merchandise to make the number of required changes fewer.

All these falsifications created a problem for the guys who ran Eddie's growing roster of stores, because they relied on the computerized record of the stock in filling their shelves. Dave was a studious and responsible manager and realized the inventory would eventually have to be made right. After complaints started coming in from the store managers, who saw stuff in the terminals that wasn't in the warehouse, Dave asked Eddie when the inventory tabulations would be corrected. Eddie told him "we would change them back, but we couldn't do it yet." Dave asked him four or five times that year and always got the same answer.

Eddie did have a problem, and it was much bigger than the one Dave was complaining about. Since he had bloated the inventory numbers by $3 million through his warehouse machinations, Crazy Eddie began the new fiscal year in the hole by that amount. To avoid taking a $3 million earnings penalty during the upcoming fiscal year, Eddie would have to inflate inventories again by $3 million just to break even. He had to feed the beast. If profits were genuinely terrific, it wouldn't have mattered. But the problem with reality was that it couldn't be controlled. It just happened.

■ ■ ■

Ed Colloton had no idea the inventory numbers were being falsified. All he knew was that he had landed in PR pig heaven. He had a client who was a little wacky, more than a little temperamental, and obsessed with the stock price, but well worth the hand-holding. True, fires occasionally had to be put out. There were bothersome rumors.

Colloton heard from his former client Alan Wurtzel, the Circuit City chairman, that Crazy Eddie was engaged in a shady business practice called "transshipping." If true, it meant Eddie was selling product at slightly above wholesale prices to other retailers or to wholesalers. Why would Crazy Eddie do such a thing? Why would he sell at cut rate to his competitors? Colloton didn't understand the logic of it and consequently didn't pursue the point with Wurtzel. If he had, he would have learned that transshipping was used to inflate sales. Which would have made it even more nonsensical. Eddie had no reason to do anything like that—after all, his sales were fantastic! His spectacular fiscal 1985 earnings release, which he distributed to analysts and the press in early March 1985, said precisely that.

Still, Colloton felt that he had to get at the truth, so he asked Eddie, who reacted with righteous shock. Of course not! When analysts (who had heard the same rumor) asked him about it, Colloton relayed Eddie's firm denial. It was preposterous! Nonsense! They believed him. The vicious rumors were quashed then and there. Such tittle-tattle was beneath Ed Colloton. His ethics met the highest standards of the investor relations and public relations professions. In furtherance of that imperative, he never bought or accepted from the company a single share of Crazy Eddie stock.

Though the foul transshipping rumors were quashed—and they weren't true, not then—after a while Colloton began to wonder about the charismatic CEO who performed so well when meeting analysts. There was something in particular that really bothered him. Even though Colloton was careful not to trade his client's shares, Eddie had no such scruples. He was repeatedly dumping large blocks of stock on the market.

Stock sales by corporate insiders, especially CEOs, created a problem for people in the investor relations field. Colloton would have to explain those transactions. They looked bad. As he later put it, "The sale of stock by the chief executive of a successful, fast growing retailer with a steadily appreciating price of his stock is highly unusual, and generally suggests a lack of faith in the future earnings of the company and a corresponding drop in the stock price." When CEOs do things like that, "it is generally presumed that he knows something that the investing public does not."

Insider sales had to be disclosed, but not with any great speed. At the time, such trading was reported on a monthly basis, within ten days after the close of each calendar month in which the sale or purchase occurred. But Colloton picked up on Eddie's share dumps right after they happened from his contacts on Wall Street. Word would leak from the fraternity of traders and stock salesmen that Bear Stearns, which handled Eddie's stock transactions, was offering blocks of CRZY stock for sale. Colloton would then call Eddie, and he would confirm that he was selling stock. His explanation every time was that he "had a right to diversify his portfolio." That was the story Colloton would give investors and analysts who heard the same thing. The onus was on both Eddie and Colloton to make that bland explanation credible.

They had their chance sometime after Eddie's post-IPO stock sales began in the spring of 1985. Eddie's sale of 600,000 shares in the March 1985 stock offering had netted him $12.5 million. A large owner of Crazy Eddie stock was so disturbed that he arranged to meet with Eddie and Colloton at a restaurant in Lower Manhattan to talk about it. As usual, "Eddie was very persuasive." The meeting with the investor, who represented a respectable institution, was such a success that he bought even more Crazy Eddie stock.

Eddie's stock sales came up yet again in May 1985, and something happened that left Colloton with a bad taste in his mouth that no amount of scotch could wash away.

The occasion was a luncheon meeting with a group of investors at the Intercontinental Hotel in Manhattan. This was an important gathering of important people, made up of sixty to seventy investors and analysts. Eddie, accompanied by his brother Mitchell, would be addressing the crowd and taking questions. On his way to the hotel, Colloton borrowed a small tape recorder from the Fifty-Seventh Street store. When the meeting began, he turned it on. His motive, he would insist, was utterly benign. "I normally taped CEO addresses, particularly questions and answers, which can become very difficult to follow in a crowded room."

As anticipated, someone asked about the stock sales. Eddie's response could not have been more reassuring. It was exactly what the people attending the conference had wanted to hear. "The stock was sold to diversify his own portfolio." That would be the end of it, Eddie pledged. No more stock sales. *Finito.* "He gave his word to the investment community that such sales were over," Colloton later recalled.

After lunch, Eddie walked up to Colloton and snatched the tape recorder out of his shirt pocket. He took the tape out and handed it back to him. "Don't ever do that again," he warned Colloton.

No CEO had ever done anything like that before. Though his doubts about Eddie were fueled by this incident, Colloton did not act on them. "A doubt is a process. A seed process," he later reflected. Colloton was too happy with the money coming in to allow that seed process to germinate. If he had any doubts, he drank them away. He shared them with no one, not even when Eddie proceeded to break the solemn promise he had made at the Intercontinental.

In September 1985, Eddie sold 428,550 shares. Then he sold another 600,000 at the end of October. Colloton dutifully announced the news in a press release on October 30, 1985, under the header "Crazy Eddie Chairman Diversifies Holdings." The release ended with this carefully worded reassurance: "The company also was informed by Mr. Antar that he had no current intention to make any further sales of the company's common stock." No *current* intention.

Colloton was doing his job, which was to spread the Crazy Eddie Story, not the doubts that were gnawing at his insides. Eddie did not expect that reneging would gain traction in the press, and he was right. Two months later, it was mentioned in a lengthy and generally favorable article on Crazy Eddie in the *New York Times* the day before Christmas 1985. The *Times* reported that Eddie "ruffled feathers" by breaking his promise, but that was it. Eddie was waving a red flag, but no one was paying attention.

By the end of 1985, Eddie's marital problems had leaked to analysts. It was not a big deal—many CEOs had broken marriages—but they wanted to know if these reports were true. So they'd take Colloton aside and ask him, always privately. "Most analysts are honorable gentleman," Colloton explained. When such queries came his way, he knew just what to say: "I told them it was none of my business."

Eddie's problems with his divorced spouse actually were Ed Colloton's business, because Debbie was in a position to undercut the Crazy Eddie Story. It was a story of success. It was an American story, a rising-to-greatness story, a tale of the American Dream. An abused and ripped-off ex-wife was not consistent with the narrative that Colloton was promoting.

All the major analysts were enamored of Crazy Eddie. Every one of the top names was on board: Drexel Burnham Lambert, Mabon Nugent, Goldman Sachs, Morgan Stanley, and Salomon Brothers. When Drexel Burnham's retailing analyst Barry Bryant commenced coverage in December 1985, he rated Crazy Eddie superior to all the other consumer electronics chains. Better than Circuit City. Better than Federated Group. Better than Newmark & Lewis. Only Crazy Eddie was rated a "buy." Bryant cited the company's "above-average growth prospects."

Bryant's research was widely circulated among investors and the media, and his enthusiasm was infectious. A few months later, Wersheim & Co. analyst Robert J. Schweich outgushed the gusher from Drexel. He noted that Eddie "relishes beating earnings estimates, and we see no reason to deny him this pleasure if the company continues to perform exceptionally well." All a large investor had to do was to examine the columns of numbers that festooned these analyst reports. They told an uplifting story of phenomenal growth.

And what sound figures they were! Schweich, a highly regarded retailing expert, was not one to fall for accounting gimmicks. Behind the screaming, hokey commercials was a responsible company that kept its ledger books neat and tidy. "We judge the results no less than outstanding," he wrote, "given the company's known conservative accounting practices."

CHAPTER FOURTEEN

SAMMY'S JOB WAS TO EXPLAIN TO ANALYSTS WHY THE COMPANY WAS DOING so well, why its accounting methods were as solid as a crystal vase, and why the numbers in the financial statements pointed toward a glorious future (though he was cautious with forward-looking statements, being careful not to overhype). He took the top people from the top firms to the top restaurants in the city. He walked them through the numbers if they needed help, giving them as much time as they desired, and he did it cheerfully. He was happy in his work.

Eddie had kept his promises and given him a position and a title that reflected his vital role at Crazy Eddie. The "hunt for a CFO" mentioned in the IPO prospectus was forgotten, and neither the media nor analysts noticed that Eddie had settled on a candidate close to home. What difference did it make? The numbers were terrific! So the "CFO hunt" vanished, and after getting his CPA certification, in July 1985 Sammy became an officer of the company—controller. He started wearing suits, which he bought for $600 at Jimmy's on Kings Highway. He was a Brooklyn kid at heart, a hard-nosed bargain hunter, and he knew it was silly to buy suits at Brooks Brothers. Jimmy's was cheaper but just as good. He had a big, clunky, but indispensible mobile phone. And cars. Everyone got luxury cars because of their Crazy Eddie wealth, and top executives like Sammy got theirs from the company. Sammy's company-supplied car was a BMW. Eddie, of course, had a limo and driver.

Sammy's family shared in his good fortune. Robin and his sons now spent the summer at a house in Deal on the Jersey Shore. Since the public school system was even worse than it was in Sammy's youth, the Antar boys went to a highly regarded Yeshiva day school. Robin gave birth to their second son, Leon, in May 1985, and their oldest boy, Eddy, was turning three in July. Their youngest, David, would come in January 1987. Robin was making a name for herself as a sculptor.

The whole Antar family—the uncles and aunts and cousins and nieces and nephews, their friends and spouses of friends, and relatives of their friends and spouses—was reaping the rewards of the Crazy Eddie bonanza. Rori Sassoon, daughter of Eddie's brother Allen, remembers a happy and even idyllic childhood, with all the cousins playing together and vacationing together at the Jersey Shore. The affairs of the adults, their dramas and troubles, were kept far from the kids.

It was good that the younger generation wasn't in the loop. The Antar family's money machine was fueled by fraud. Fortunately for Eddie, Sammy, and the small nucleus of people carrying out the frauds, the front line of defense against what they were doing was as formidable as the French Army General Staff in 1940, but not half as well dressed.

The Securities and Exchange Commission of the 1980s had many dedicated lawyers and accountants, but it was outnumbered, outgunned, and poorly led. Turnover among enforcement lawyers was high, for the pay was mediocre and the workload was heavy. The SEC was tasked with overseeing a vast swath of Corporate America. It was on the lookout for bad actors of all kinds: sneaky floor brokers at the stock exchanges, nefarious trading by greedy amateurs and cynical pros, and, last and least, fibbing on financial statements.

Accounting fraud simply did not get SEC juices flowing. This was the epoch of Michael Milken and Ivan Boesky and traders being led away in handcuffs as the cameras whirled. John S. R. Shad, SEC chairman since 1981, focused on insider trading, saying he would come down on it with "hobnail boots." Stamping out corporate fraud would have required not footwear but reading glasses. The amount of paper falling on the SEC every year was overwhelming. Between 1981 and 1986, the number of corporate filings reviewed by the agency climbed 71 percent to 10,526, with most of that growth after 1984 as the bull market exploded. In 1981 the SEC reviewed 325 10-K annual reports. In 1985 the number was 2,135. In that year, SEC enforcement actions actually declined over the year before. Of the 269 cases filed, just 20 percent involved inadequate financial disclosure.

That said, SEC lawyers did go after corporate fraud from time to time. Nothing motivated government lawyers as much as career-enhancing publicity, but they needed a visible, juicy target. They needed to be taken by the hand by informants and shown what was happening. They needed a lot. But it did happen.

Sammy didn't give the SEC much thought, and he didn't worry about KMG Main Hurdman either. Ever since its fresh-faced young auditors started dropping by Crazy Eddie's offices, Sammy did his best to ensure that they did as little damage as possible. Year-end audits took about eight weeks to complete, and Sammy had a strategy to ensure that the auditors were unproductive and distracted during that time. Having once been an auditor himself, he knew that this kind of work was shunted to the most junior employees. They were usually in their twenties and tended to be single and, at the time, almost exclusively male. Sammy encouraged his female underlings to get acquainted with these overworked and underpaid people, to flirt with them, and to let themselves be taken out to lunch and dinner to discuss accounting issues, with Crazy Eddie picking up the tab. The charm offensive made the Antar family enterprise "more likeable to our auditors and corroded their professional skepticism. They did not want to believe we were crooks. They believed whatever we told them without verifying the truth," Sammy recalled.

The auditors seemed almost as feckless as the brokerage house analysts, whom Colloton could always count on to tell the Crazy Eddie Story just the way he liked. Analysts paid close attention to rising "comparable store sales" as the chain expanded. Was each cash register in the chain raking in more bucks, or were the numbers so good because there were more cash registers? Analysts were looking for increased customer enthusiasm, not sales gains that were a by-product of expansion. To make that distinction, they kept an eye on sales figures of stores that had been open at least twelve months. Colloton had Eddie publish comparable store sales numbers in every quarterly news release. It became an essential part of the Crazy Eddie Story.

In his first report recounting the virtues of Crazy Eddie, the one in which he'd rated it his only "buy," Drexel Burnham analyst Bryant pointed out that "Crazy Eddie achieved the highest comparable store sales record in this fiscal year" due to its "unique merchandising ability." Drexel stock research was considered among the best in the business. So when Bryant six months later predicted 35 percent profit growth based on "comparable store sales growth in the low double digits," it raised expectations for other analysts and professional investors.

Such high hopes presented a challenge for Eddie. Not only would he have to keep the inventory inflated by at least $3 million, to account for the fiscal-year-end inflation by the Daves in late February and early March 1985, but he would also have to gin up comparable store sales. Those numbers would have to be sparkling to keep analysts bubbling over with good feeling.

First things first: the inventory situation needed work. Early in 1986, just before the end of the fiscal year, Eddie assembled Sammy, Eddie's brothers Mitchell and Allen, Sam M., and Ben Kuszer. A new plan was hatched to keep the inventory numbers artificially high. Everyone agreed that it was a big improvement over the year before.

■ ■ ■

Fraud is not always a great, cynical master plan, with sinister characters gathering in smoky bars to hatch their schemes. The people involved can be ordinary, not criminals, willing to do a favor for a friend, a colleague, or an employer. Willing to look the other way. Willing to not think too closely about what they're doing.

Such a person was Leonard Rubin. He led an unremarkable, stable life. His only employer had been a large and reputable company called Wren Distributors, which was the exclusive wholesaler of Sharp Electronics products in the New York area. He started out driving a truck for the company when he was in high school. Now he had an impressive title (senior vice president), but it was humdrum work, requiring a person not easily bored, not minding tedium and routine for the sake of a paycheck. He worked the books. He worked collections. He interacted with all the major electronics retailers—Macy's, Abraham & Strauss, Newmark & Lewis, the Wiz, PC

Richard—but most of his time by the mid-1980s was devoted to the biggest buyer of Sharp products, Crazy Eddie. Wren sold Eddie clock radios, home audio systems, TVs, "anything with a battery or a plug." It had been a profitable relationship going back to the early 1970s, and a very routine one except for its size.

The mechanics of this relationship were straightforward. Orders would be placed by phone or in person. Delivery was prompt. Paper was generated—a packing slip for each shipment, produced right away, and an invoice a day or so later. Everything was then entered into the computer. It was a continuing relationship, so flexibility would be shown. On rare occasions a large customer would want more time to pay an invoice. But the invoice would always go out promptly. It was never delayed—except when an order came in from Crazy Eddie in February 1986 for $2 million in merchandise. The product was to go out immediately, but not the invoice. Instead, the invoice would go to Crazy Eddie in March. It was an unusual request, but Rubin did it as a favor.

Rubin did not know that he was playing an unwitting part in a book-cooking scheme for which he would have to testify under a grant of immunity. For now, Wren's late billing of its biggest client was a piddling detail. To Eddie it was not picayune at all. It meant that $2 million in merchandise would be boosting Crazy Eddie's inventory just before the end of the fiscal year on March 2, 1986. Since it wasn't immediately being billed or paid for, Eddie would be able to inflate profits by $2 million. There would be other inventory-inflation efforts in early 1986, and the Wren scheme was simplest to execute.

Dave Neiderbach, the scrupulous warehouse manager, also had a role to play in the 1986 inventory inflation. He was another ordinary man caught up in a fraud without knowing he was caught up in a fraud. As the months went on, he was getting fed up with Eddie's stalling when asked about changing back the inflated 1985 inventory numbers. Dave didn't like that he had been forced to screw up the figures for which he was responsible and that were so vital to his friends in the stores. And now Eddie was telling him that he would have to do the same thing all over again—and a lot more of it.

One day in February 1986, Eddie summoned Dave to the Coney Island Avenue offices. They walked around, just the two of them, and Eddie asked

Dave if he "could do basically the same thing I had did the year before." Only this time it wasn't $2 million in nonexistent inventory; it was $6 million. It was hard to say no to Eddie. Dave's answer was the same as the last time. He would try, but he needed help.

After the meeting he was given the assistance of another longtime Crazy Eddie employee. Arnie Spindler had worked several jobs over the years and was manning the cash register when Larry Weiss arrived for his job interview on Kings Highway years before. His relationship with Eddie was frosty, and he had quit and returned a couple of times, but he had moved up in the company nonetheless. Arnie had worked with Dave Neiderbach on the inventory a year earlier, but not to inflate it. He was getting a promotion.

Like the two Daves, Arnie was summoned to a private meeting with Eddie on Coney Island Avenue. The boss, talking in a low voice to not be overheard, told Arnie to "go to the warehouse to watch the auditing team work the inventory and then to inflate the figures" with Dave Neiderbach. Eddie "kept stressing how important it was."

"I want you to know I will remember this in the future," Eddie assured him.

This time the vital work would be performed at a spanking new facility in South Plainfield, New Jersey. There was more merchandise and paperwork than the year before, but the mechanics were the same—changing numbers, watching the auditors, checking to be sure that figures weren't altered for the test counts that the young accountants would be conducting. It was a long, laborious process consuming an entire day, beginning at seven in the morning and stretching until eight in the evening. Dave and Arnie changed the numbers to inflate the inventory, picking costlier items as Dave had done a year earlier, and seasonal goods less likely to screw up the stores.

As before, a record was made of the phony counts so that everything could be made right as Eddie again promised. Dave gave that list to Mitchell so he could work with the stores if they had a problem ordering goods from the warehouse. The auditors compiled a list of their own, showing the merchandise they had test-counted. Arnie generously volunteered to make a photocopy for them (and made a couple of copies for himself). By the end of that long day, $6 million in nonexistent goods were officially part of the Crazy Eddie inventory.

Once again, the phony inventory caused problems in the stores. Once again, Dave asked Eddie if he could fix numbers. Once again, Eddie told him he could make the numbers correct, but not right away. Frustrated, Dave asked Mitchell to ask Eddie to make the numbers right, and Mitchell got the same answer. Didn't Eddie want accurate counts? Why was he lousing things up for his store managers? Dave told the managers that the reason for the bad counts was that the computer was overworked and "not in great shape at that point."

At about the time Dave Neiderbach was getting his inventory-bloating instructions from Eddie, so was the other Dave. "Service manager" and reeps warehouse boss Panoff was called to Coney Island Avenue for another closed-door meeting. "You'll have to do it again this year, but you'll have to do it more this time," said Eddie.

"How much more? How much is involved?"

"I need $3 million this year," Eddie replied.

Dave Panoff complied. Then something unexpected happened—the auditors actually did their job. They caught a discrepancy in the count at one of the reeps warehouses. Panoff learned about it in a call from one of Sammy's people. This concerned him, but not for long. He called Eddie and then Sammy. Both told him not to worry about it. After a few days of agita, it appeared that they were right. Sure the numbers didn't add up, but what's a little bad arithmetic between friends? Panoff was reassured that the accountants were on the team, doing their part to make the financial statements look good.

Panoff later recalled: "It was explained to me what the auditor decided to do, since clearly the inventory was invalid, they just diminished the value of that warehouse by $2 million. Basically, they took whatever the figure finally was, the total, and they cut it down by two million, thinking that would compensate for any mistakes that had been made. That was it. That closed the matter."

The auditors from KMG Main Hurdman were giving Crazy Eddie the benefit of the doubt, assuming that the warehouse people were not crooked, just sloppy. It would not be the last time this large and prestigious accounting firm cut Eddie more slack than he deserved.

■ ■ ■

Sam M., now sixty-four, was acutely aware of his son's struggle to pad the financial statements and keep them padded. He realized that the frauds were like hungry rattlesnakes that needed to be fed, lest they strike and kill. While Eddie was vulnerable, this was not a time for settling scores. Though Sam M. had largely cashed out his stock holdings, he still owned 403,000 shares, making him the fourth-largest shareholder, so his own wealth depended upon the stock price staying as high as possible. He would need to work with Eddie to keep their fortunes safe.

So Sam M. joined his son when he convened another meeting of family members to discuss the coming crisis. Yet another stock offering was planned for sometime in March 1986, right after the end of the fiscal year. There was no margin for error. Failure meant disaster. The company was selling stock, and Eddie and Sam M. would be dumping a good chunk of their shares as well. It was a formal stock offering with three underwriters, not Oppenheimer this time, but better. Their old firm was fine, but Crazy Eddie was in the big leagues now, and Eddie and Sammy opted for larger and more prestigious banks: Wertheim & Co., Bear Stearns, and Salomon Brothers.

If the stock offering was to be a success, Eddie and his team needed to make comparable store sales look a lot better than they really were—which meant inflating them by $2.2 million. Each store had its own separate corporation and bank account, and the right store accounts would need to get an infusion of funds so that it looked as if customers were marching in and buying stuff. But where would the money come from?

After batting around a bunch of ideas, it was eventually decided that $200,000 in merchandise would be sold to a wholesaler called Gateway Marketing, with the proceeds funneled into the Fordham Road store, which was tracked for comp-store sales purposes. That left $2 million. Quite a large chunk. Sammy came up with the idea that carried the day: "Why don't we recover the money that we skimmed previously? You're going to get it back when the stock price goes much higher than the amount you're putting back in the company." *Nehkdi* had been accumulating in Israel, though it had tapered off before the IPO. Why not reverse the flow of money, bring it back and inject it into the company to prop up comparable store sales?

Putting their rivalries, jealousies, and irritation with Eddie aside, the Antars worked together to pull off this plan. On February 27, 1986, three days before the end of the fiscal year, Eddie transferred $1.5 million from one of his accounts at Bank Leumi in Israel to an account at the bank's branch in Panama City, Panama. The transfer was executed in the name of a Panamanian company called Aeronautics Traders Corporation. The following day, the Panama City branch issued ten drafts to Crazy Eddie totaling $1.5 million. By shuttling the money through a country with tight bank secrecy laws, Eddie figured he had made the transaction untraceable back to him. Sam M. pledged another half million from his private stash.

The task of fetching that money from Panama fell to the family lawyer, sometime domestic counselor, and corporate general counsel Solomon Antar. The funds came in the form of bank drafts, which were delivered to Eddie and then to Sammy, who had them deposited in store bank accounts. Eddie paid sales tax on the Panama cash infusion to give it the appearance of actual sales.

All the frauds in early 1986 were standouts. The warehouse inventory was inflated by $6 million, the reeps inventory by $3 million–$4 million, and last-minute store-inventory bloating added about the same amount. Altogether, the financial statement fictionalizing totaled $12 million–$14 million in fabricated profits. These were all great numbers. In fact, the numbers were *too* great. Eddie had been far too enthusiastic. They needed to boost profits by only $3 million or so to account for inflated inventory the previous year. The rest was gravy, a waterfall of it. They were coming in with numbers that were much too high by somewhere between $10 million and $11 million, all of it crammed into the fiscal quarter ending March 2, 1986.

If allowed to stand, that would have conveyed a ridiculously high profit margin of 40 percent in the final quarter, and Crazy Eddie had never experienced such profitability before. It would look suspicious.

It turned out that fine-tuning that number was easy. Eddie and Sammy met with two of their outside auditors, who recommended simply not reporting all the profits. Sammy and his cousin readily agreed. They created a "cushion" or "rainy day fund," known more formally as an "allowance," that could be used to offset losses in the future. "It was like 'money in the bank,'" Sammy recalled. As one of the accounting firm's execs said to Sammy at the time, "No public company got sued for underreporting earnings." By deducting about $7 million–$8 million from their profits, Eddie and Sammy were able to prevent their numbers from seeming just a bit too insane, and they also created wiggle room for the future.

After all the bloating and auditor-sanctioned de-bloating, Crazy Eddie reported pretax profits of $26.5 million, when the real number was $20.5 million. Even before those numbers were released, a comp-store sales gain of 10 percent was announced for the months of January and February 1986, far better than the actual number (4 percent). Analysts loved good post-Christmas numbers. On the strength of the comp-store bonanza alone, elevated by the "Panama Pump," the March 1986 stock sale was a blowout blitz. Eddie cashed out 720,000 shares, earning him a bit over $18.1 million, while Sam M. netted $5.3 million from his 200,000 share sale. "Not bad for a $2 million 'reinvestment,'" Sammy later pointed out.

By setting aside their differences and working together, the Antar family had been able to rescue Crazy Eddie from itself in its time of need. Everyone played a role, including Eddie's brother Allen, who had been on the outs with the family for marrying a non-Jewish woman whom he later divorced. He deposited funds in store accounts using deposit slips supplied by Sammy. Sam M. ultimately came up short on his $500,000 pledge, but he coughed up half that sum with the rest from Ben Kuszer.

The frauds of early 1986 were a triumph. But the Antars could not rest. Even after a feeding, the fraud rattlesnake did not feel sated. It only grew hungrier.

CHAPTER FIFTEEN

SASSON COHEN WAS EVERYONE'S IDEA OF AN IMMIGRANT SUCCESS STORY. He was born in Jerusalem and immigrated to the United States in early 1976 at the age of twenty-nine. His education consisted of three years of high school in Israel, and his grasp of English was tenuous even decades later. That might seem like a recipe for failure. But anyone betting against him would have failed.

Thanks to a dogged work ethic and a talent for seizing opportunities, by the mid-1980s he was president of a wholesale electronics distributor called Zazy International. It was based in Manhattan and sold products to retailers as far away as the Caribbean, Taiwan, and Bermuda. Success did not come easily. Sam, as he was now known, had to scramble to stock the hottest products, the ones consumers were clamoring to buy. Zazy was just another small wholesaler as far as the giants of consumer electronics were concerned.

Fortunately, Sam had a friend who could help.

Wholesaling was all about relationships. Knowing people who knew people. One of the people Sam knew, a friend who'd been in the business for many years, worked for an electronics retailer called Tops Appliance City. His name was Abe Grinberg. In May 1986, Abe introduced Sam Cohen to a friend of his, Allen Antar, who worked for the retailer everyone knew by then. Sam had never done business with Crazy Eddie. He was happy to meet. So was Allen Antar. So was Abe Grinberg. The three men got together in Brooklyn for a chat, and the gods of retailing now smiled upon Sam Cohen.

At the meeting, Sam Cohen later recounted, it was agreed "that we'll start working together. That I'll start taking goods . . . goods on a wholesale basis. And as long as things go well, that work goes well, I'll feel very good about it. They'll feel very good about it and that will be excellent." The good feeling was infectious. Allen told him "that I have every possibility of developing and becoming bigger, that their company has every existing type of merchandise and that I would be able to get anything that I wanted." Zazy became a wholesale customer of Crazy Eddie in June 1986.

Thanks to the kindly people at Crazy Eddie, Zazy no longer had to wait in line with the other wholesalers. Sam was getting the hottest merchandise, the biggest brand names. As a large retailer, Crazy Eddie's days of scrounging for top-drawer product were far behind it, and now it was "the first to receive all new merchandise that comes on the market." Zazy now had first dibs on the best VCRs, TVs, and stereos, which it would buy from Crazy Eddie and resell quickly to other stores at a profit. If it struck Sam as odd that a retailer would sell first-rate goods to a wholesaler who would then sell them to his competitors, it didn't bother him very much. Nor was Sam concerned by the odd little requests that came with this business.

Zazy was making big purchases, $250,000 at a time, yet Allen asked that payments be divided into checks for $20,000 to $50,000. Not a problem. Allen also didn't want the checks to be dated. "He explained to me they're a company that only sells to consumers and they can't show, from a public perspective they can't show they're selling wholesale. And if the checks are small, they could put it through the stores of Crazy Eddie afterwards. No one would know that they're selling wholesale. I agreed because we were doing excellent business together."

That was putting it mildly. Zazy was buying 80 percent of its merchandise from the very nice and accommodating people at Crazy Eddie. During 1986 and 1987, Sam Cohen delivered $20 million in hundreds of undated checks, in payment for the splendid merchandise that Sam chose personally at the retail chain's warehouse. Why was Crazy Eddie being so nice to Zazy? Sam didn't know, and he didn't stick his nose where it didn't belong.

Sam Cohen was playing a more or less (probably less) unwitting role in Eddie Antar's struggle with crummy comp-store sales numbers. Under

Eddie's direction, the small, undated checks from the sales to Zazy were deposited into the separate bank accounts of the older Crazy Eddie stores whose sales were tracked for comp-store-sales purposes. It was a larger and more elaborate version of the Gateway Marketing scheme early in 1986. Since the checks were undated, the Antars could insert whatever date most benefited the cause of doctoring its financial statements.

Zazy helped tremendously in that vital task during the new fiscal year. Unlike the Panama Pump a few months earlier, dealing with Zazy did not require travel. It was conveniently located in an office building on Twenty-Fourth Street, just off Sixth Avenue. And Sam Cohen's help came in the nick of time. Eddie was again dipping into the well of goodwill on Wall Street. There would be yet another securities offering, in June 1986. Not a stock offering but something more complicated and fancier sounding: convertible debentures.

Again Eddie employed the three prestigious investment banks that so ably managed the March 1986 stock offering—Wertheim & Co., Bear Stearns, and Salomon Brothers. All the proceeds from the sale would be going to the company. Though Eddie and Sam M. weren't selling stock this time, their wealth was largely tied up in CRZY shares, and they had no intention of holding on to them for all eternity. If comp-store sales faltered, that would hurt the offering, tarnish Crazy Eddie's reputation on Wall Street, and put a dent in the stock price.

The convertible debentures going on sale in June would be marketed to the brokers' wealthiest clients. Debentures were a bit like bonds, with Crazy Eddie borrowing from the public, but had a feature designed to add to their sales appeal. Investors would loan Crazy Eddie money, and the company would pay an interest rate. If the buyers wanted, they could convert that loan into fabulous Crazy Eddie stock. The higher the price of the stock, the lower the interest rate the company would pay debenture buyers—another reason to keep share prices healthy.

Swindling those investors required more phony figures. That's where Zazy came in, providing $650,000 in small, undated checks that were deposited in store accounts to inflate comp-store sales figures for the fiscal quarter ending June 1, 1986. After that mission was accomplished, Colloton issued a press release on June 3 announcing a splendid 10 percent increase in comp-store sales, which was sufficient to bamboozle the market. The debenture offering a few weeks later was a hit, raising $81 million for the company, $9 million more than initially anticipated, thanks to the company's inflated share price. Zazy had been a friend, and that was appreciated, as was Grinberg for the introduction. He was brought on as director of marketing. He had a bright future at Crazy Eddie as long as he did as he was told and kept his mouth shut.

The Zazy scam went flawlessly, but sometime later it almost blew up in their faces. An anonymous caller tipped off Salomon Brothers, one of the debenture underwriters, that "merchandise was being skimmed" via fraudulent transactions with Zazy. In reality, merchandise wasn't being skimmed; Zazy was actually doing something worse. Salomon then contacted Jim Purcell, the Paul, Weiss partner assigned to Crazy Eddie. He insisted that Sammy "call in" KMG Main Hurdman audit partner Al Ferrara and outside director Jim Scott and "investigate it by proper means." A probe of the Zazy dealings was the last thing that Eddie wanted. Sammy gave KMG a phony excuse, and the threat evaporated. Ferrara would later testify that he was never asked to do an investigation.

Eddie's sweetheart deal with Sam Cohen was stirring up internal dissension. By catering to Zazy in return for those vital small checks, Eddie was depriving his own stores of prime merchandise. Store managers complained. The warehouse inventories were already unreliable, and now they couldn't get the gear customers wanted because Zazy walked off with the hottest products. Mitchell sided with the store managers. Eddie told everyone to shut up. The fraud came first. Every dollar Crazy Eddie got from Zazy went straight into comparable store sales, and high comparable store sales meant happy analysts, and happy analysts meant higher stock prices, and higher stock prices meant more money for Eddie Antar.

■ ■ ■

Crazy Eddie was now a Wall Street star. Thanks to the phony numbers, CRZY stock doubled in the first half of 1986. The company was regularly plugged in financial columns as a hot investment and was mentioned twice by a *New York Times* investing column in the space of two weeks. That was nice, but this was golden: on May 19, 1986, just as Eddie was gearing up to hoodwink the debenture buyers, a widely followed Wall Street newsletter slobbered all over him. At fifty dollars an issue, the *Wall Street Transcript* was for people who wielded big bucks and wanted to know what the other big-bucks wielders were buying. Those people loved Crazy Eddie. The "only issue," noted a Montgomery Securities analyst, "is can they really meet the estimates that everyone is using."

At the end of the issue, the *Transcript* announced "awards" for top CEOs in the retail industry. These reflected not the personal opinion of the *Transcript*, but rather the collective wisdom of Wall Street. Sam M. Walton of Wal-Mart got the gold, Sol E. Price of the Price Club got the silver, and Eddie Antar got the bronze. Ed Colloton made sure that this was not kept secret. "The comparison to Wal-Mart and its chief executive Sam Walton, a retailing legend, is made by many observers," gushed a long and flattering article in a New Jersey newspaper in July 1986.

Crazy Eddie now had all the trappings of the corporate colossus that it was fast becoming. Its headquarters moved in the fall of 1986 to an industrial park in Edison, New Jersey, a sterile location not popular with the staff (the closest restaurant, Harry Spero sourly recalled, was a Ponderosa steak house). Eddie had financed the new building with $7.8 million borrowed on favorable terms from the New Jersey Economic Development Authority, so it made financial sense to get out of Brooklyn. But he never liked it and was rarely in Edison.

The company now had a personnel department, and it already had a chatty internal newsletter. The *Crazy Times* celebrated birthdays and anniversaries, group photos and softball games, and it contained useful articles such as "How to Handle a Maff at the Store Pick-Up Window" ("maff" was Crazy Eddie slang for an item that was out of stock). It singled out worthy employees and recorded morale-building events like the annual "Awards Night." Sammy was a winner in June 1986 along with his dad and the loyal and cooperative Dave Neiderbach, who like Sammy won laurels for managerial talent.

In the stores, far from the pressure cooker of Eddie's inner circle, Crazy Eddie was a collegial environment that demanded street smarts over formal education. Former store manager, later newspaper reporter and author William Westhoven reminisced that "even a high school dropout could rise to upper management if they emulated their retail rabbi and worked as hard as he did." Some of the new people coming in were fresh out of high school and, as Harry Spero observed, "didn't have the benefit of a proper education. They attended Crazy Eddie University." By mid-1986 there were two dozen Crazy Eddie outlets, half of which had opened since the beginning of 1984. Leases had already been signed for eleven more stores, which would be opening through 1987. The company now saturated the five boroughs and suburbs and was opening a store in Enfield, north of Hartford in the far reaches of Connecticut.

Eddie kept away from the press, and rarely let himself be photographed, but he treated analysts like long-lost buddies. With Colloton's prodding, Eddie opened his doors to "manager meetings" for the benefit of analysts. In truth, Eddie was seeing less of his store managers than in the past. Longtime employees were finding that they had scant access to Eddie, who used to get together with store managers on Friday nights. He could do that in the past, but now he was spreading himself thin. There were new territories to open, new analysts to meet and con. There were inventories that had to be padded, comp-store sales that had to be fabricated, and an ex-wife who had to be bullied and kept in line.

On top of all that, in 1986 there was a new challenge for Eddie. Something without precedent was happening, something that was inconceivable just a few years before. Eddie was being beaten by the competition.

CHAPTER SIXTEEN

THE INCESSANT DRUMBEAT OF JERRY CARROLL COMMERCIALS WAS AS PO-
tent as ever—but now it was working against Crazy Eddie. All the "insanely
low prices" propaganda, all the Blowout Blitzes, all the spoofs, all the sales
that weren't sales, all the arm waving and fast talking repeated endlessly on
the airwaves, were motivating other electronics chains to slash their own
prices. The Wiz, Newmark & Lewis, Trader Horn, and a host of humble
upstarts were now bragging that they were the ones that *really* had insanely
low prices. By the summer of 1986, Crazy Eddie was mired in a full-blown
price war.

Newmark & Lewis, Eddie's most aggressive and best-financed competitor, went at him hard in 1986. To counter the obnoxious Carroll commercials, its gray-haired, fatherly founder, Richard Lewis, appeared in TV
commercials, projecting integrity and personal involvement. "Dick Lewis
is watching" went the slogan, which was set to music in his commercials
and which Lewis placed prominently in his newspaper ads. They were illustrated with a close-up of his trustworthy, watchful eyes. "We beat the
competition every day," the commercials and print ads bragged. "I personally guarantee it," said Lewis, looking straight into the camera.

The big chains were a problem, but it was the upstarts, grungy stores
with super-low prices, that set the tone for the market. Compact disk players selling for $330 at Bamberger's, an upscale department store, would go
for $259 at Crazy Eddie. A newcomer on Canal Street called Uncle Steve
was selling the same CD player for $200, close to manufacturer's cost,
forcing everyone else to cut their prices. Eddie's screamer commercials had

conditioned consumers to expect price-cutting; only now he was picking up the tab.

Crazy Eddie's competitors, large and small, had a major advantage: they were not mired in accounting fraud. They did not have a beast to feed. The newer ones were not public companies, didn't report their financial results, and didn't have to worry about satisfying analysts or keeping shareholders happy. They did not have to fret over comp-store sales, stock prices, or inventory audits. Eddie did. Comp-store sales in particular were being severely dented by the competition. And unlike the 1970s, Eddie could no longer steal sales tax to undercut other retailers. Sales tax thievery was well worth sacrificing in 1984, but now it was sorely missed. To make matters even more irritating, Sammy was convinced that some of their competitors were using Eddie's old technique. He couldn't prove it—it was just a suspicion—but he was certain they were.

Going back to that old scam was out of the question. Crazy Eddie had grown too large to pocket sales tax, not on a big-enough scale to make a difference. But thanks to Zazy, Eddie was able to keep the analysts happy. In the second quarter of the 1987 fiscal year (June through August 1986), comparable store sales slowed considerably and were on track to gain just 6.8 percent over the same period a year before. No good. Eddie didn't want to report a crummy number like that. He wanted 15 percent, and that's what he got. The ever-reliable Zazy provided $3.2 million in checks that were deposited in store accounts. Sam M. toasted the superlative numbers in September 1986 by dumping 25,000 shares at a grossly inflated price of $33.75, netting $843,750.

The numbers in the third quarter, September through November 1986, were even worse. The price war was killing everybody. Sales were fading, not just for Crazy Eddie but for all electronics retailers, and Eddie was hit worse than the others. Comp-store sales were now on the decline and were expected to fall somewhere between 5 and 10 percent. To push those intensely watched figures into the positive would take about $6 million stuffed into the older stores' cash registers.

Eddie, meanwhile, was itching to sell stock. His timing was terrible. Sammy later explained why doing so was a bad idea: "Now, you issue financial statements. You go and you meet analysts and you talk to people. Okay? You give them a sense that everything is fine, everything is going very fine, growth is going to continue. You sell all of this stock. You raise all of this money. Then all of a sudden, six months later, your comp store sales drop to negative numbers the first time in—who knows? Ten years? And there is going to be litigation." Lawsuits are a nuisance for a normal company, but can spell disaster for one whose very existence depends upon fraud. Litigation means pretrial discovery, an investigative process under court supervision. That could easily yield evidence of fraud that plaintiff attorneys would happily pass on to the SEC and FBI.

Sammy was elevated to chief financial officer in August 1986, and he took his position seriously. He needed good legal advice, so he set up an appointment with Jim Purcell of Paul, Weiss. Purcell was not a "name" partner, not a "rainmaker," but he was a prestigious lawyer of impeccable reputation, fifty-six years old and twenty-two years with the firm. His many achievements included representing the Las Vegas Sands when it went public and acting as lead counsel to the Department of Transportation when Conrail was founded. A little thing like the problem Sammy brought to him must have seemed minor indeed. The young, nervous, newly elevated CFO was like a lot of rookie corporate managers, worrying about nothing.

Purcell was a straight arrow and thoroughly ethical, which meant that telling him the truth was out of the question. Sammy chose his words carefully as he talked about what was bothering him, describing the terrible comp-store numbers without, of course, disclosing all the creative ways Crazy Eddie was boosting them. Purcell came up with a smart solution, which Sammy implemented at once.

On October 21, 1986, Chief Financial Officer and Executive Vice President Sam E. Antar issued the following memo to all officers and directors of the company: "Please take notice that no sales of stock of Crazy Eddie, Inc. shall be made by any officer of this corporation after the date hereof until same has been specifically cleared in writing by our Securities Counsel, James Purcell, Esquire." To drive the point home, the memo added: "You are hereby required to personally acknowledge receipt of this memo by signing and returning a copy hereof."

The reaction was immediate. Sam M. demanded that he rescind the memo. Eddie called to scream at Sammy, telling him that other people selling stock was none of his business. He summoned Sammy and Mitchell to a meeting at his old office on Coney Island Avenue, which he preferred to the new one in New Jersey. When they arrived, Eddie reamed him out. He forced Sammy to get on the phone with Purcell, right there in his office. "Maybe I'm being a little bit too pessimistic," Sammy told the lawyer. "Maybe I'm overreacting. There's a few weeks left. I got some additional figures and maybe I was overreacting. I'm just going to withdraw that memo." Purcell did not object.

Sammy and Eddie had an opportunity to spin the comp-store sales numbers in just a few days. At the end of October, Morgan Stanley was hosting its twelfth annual Retail Forum at the Plaza hotel. Walter Loeb, Morgan's ace retail analyst, presided over a much-anticipated event that brought together the crème de la crème of Wall Street analysts with the crème de la crème of retail-company executives. The theme of the conference that year was "Global Growth Companies in Retailing—What Will the Nineties Bring?" The next Sam Walton was of course on the program. He and Sammy made a formal presentation and then mingled with the crowd, taking questions and expounding upon their agenda.

They acknowledged that comp-store sales were shaping up poorly. Not down. No, not down! Of course not, but they were expected to be in the "mid-single digits," or about 5 percent. Sammy figured that was about the best he would be able to puff them up and also the least that would be acceptable to analysts. Still, he pulled the number out of thin air. "I didn't even know if I could do that," Sammy explained years later.

The idea was to let down the Street easy and to reduce expectations, following Ed Colloton's "no surprises" dictum. After the conference, feeling that everything was under control, Sammy went with his family to Disney World. He was unhappy that the Purcell memo was rescinded but relieved by the Morgan Stanley meeting. Analysts liked Crazy Eddie. They *wanted* to like Crazy Eddie. It was in their interests to like Crazy Eddie. All Sammy and Eddie had to do was give them a reason, and they were satisfied.

On November 10, while Sammy was in Florida with his wife and kids, Ed Colloton issued a stunning press release. Eddie had just sold 1.5 million shares at $13.88 a share, netting $20.8 million. That was one-third of his remaining holdings, an immense and grotesquely irresponsible share dump. He still owned about 10 percent of the stock, but a child could see that Eddie was ridding himself of the company's shares just as competition was heating up. He did it at a great price thanks to all the frauds he had been committing. Crazy Eddie had already "split" the stock twice. In a stock split, if you own one share at $2, a stock split meant you now own two shares worth $1 each. As a result of the two stock splits, the $13.88 a share Eddie got in this sale was the equivalent of $55.52 before the splits. That was almost seven times the IPO price of $8.

Sammy hadn't been told about it in advance. He called his cousin. He wasn't going to pick a fight with him. No point. Instead, Sammy began the conversation blandly: "You know, you sold the stock."

"Better that you didn't know," said Eddie. "We have a lot of work to do when you get back." Sammy knew what that meant.

■ ■ ■

Like the dedicated public relations professional that he was, Ed Colloton accentuated the positive news coming out of his client. He liked to keep a running count of store openings, so that reporters for the local papers, who always picked up on those things, could easily and accurately describe how Crazy Eddie was growing. And then there was big, exciting news that was attracting nationwide attention: Crazy Eddie was starting its own home shopping network! Colloton worked that one doggedly, milking it to the hilt, generating press release after press release on every minor development in the Crazy Eddie World of Home Entertainment Shopping Network. His hard work paid off, and he garnered a nice feature in the *New York Times* business section at the end of July 1986. "The move would give Crazy Eddie, which is among the largest electronics retailers in the New York City area, a national presence without the expense of building stores all over the country," the newspaper observed.

Announcing insider stock sales was always a painful duty, but Colloton would put on his investor relations hat and do the job. Such releases would just state the facts, using language that was passed through the lawyers. Like the one he issued on November 10, 1986, shortly after that excellent Morgan Stanley Retail Forum at the Plaza.

His release was brief and crisp. In two paragraphs, Colloton disclosed that Eddie had sold 1.5 million shares "solely in anticipation of significant changes in the Internal Revenue Code which will take effect on January 1, 1987 when the federal capital gains rate will go from its present 20% to 28%. The Company also was informed by Mr. Antar that he has no present intention to make any further sales of the Company's common stock in the present calendar year."

Eddie had broken yet another promise not to sell his stock, but no one in the press seemed to care. Eddie's stock dump even led off a *Wall Street Journal* article on tax-motivated insider stock sales a few weeks later. Eddie's timing, the *Journal* reported, came "straight from a tax-planner's manual." His motives were not questioned. CEO motives were rarely questioned. Why should they be? Most were honest. Most.

Yet another retailing conference was about to commence, and Eddie was expected. This was an annual event organized by Salomon Brothers, and—warm climes were preferred this time of year—it was set for Laguna Beach, California, just three days after the stock sale announcement. Questions would be asked about Eddie unloading all that stock. No doubt about it. The analysts and portfolio managers in attendance might not buy the tax code excuse. Colloton wasn't worried. Eddie aced events like this. He always did well in Q&As and one-on-ones. No reason he wouldn't do well this time. It would be a great opportunity to calm fears about the stock sale.

Eddie arrived at the hotel hosting the conference. Colloton was there, ready to go. Eddie wasn't ready to go. In fact, he wasn't going to the conference. Shortly after arriving, he had second thoughts about the whole thing. Without a word to Colloton, Eddie went back to John Wayne Airport, got on a plane, and flew away.

Allen Street—"the street of perpetual shadow"—was the center of Syrian Jewish life in New York City during the early twentieth century. Despite formidable obstacles, the community prospered.

(Berenice Abbott, Federal Art Project)

Murad and Tera Antar, the revered elders of the Antar family, immigrated from Aleppo, Syria, in 1920. Murad became a prosperous merchant, though his fortunes had ebbed by 1970, when they posed for this photo.

(Courtesy Sam E. Antar)

Salim Chera, shown with his second wife, Celia Chippon, in the 1920s, was known as "El Maz"—"The Golden"—because he was the sole survivor of his family, which was wiped out by disease in Aleppo. Misfortune haunted him in the United States as well.

(Courtesy Sam E. Antar)

Salim and Celia Chera in 1970. The Chera family was thriving now, but tragedy would loom in the future.

(Courtesy Sam E. Antar)

Sam M. Antar and his wife Rose sharing a lighthearted moment with nephew Sammy at his bar mitzvah in 1970.

(Courtesy Sam E. Antar)

Irving "Zookie" Antar and his wife, Margie. Like Sam M., he violated one of the community's cardinal rules. Unlike Sam M., he shrugged it off.

(Courtesy Sam E. Antar)

Sammy's soft-spoken father Eddy Antar managed the *nehkdi*—the cash skim—and kept Crazy Eddie's two sets of books in the early days.

(Courtesy Sam E. Antar)

Eddie Antar must have really liked the cover of Robert Crumb's *Zap Comix* No. 2 when it came out in 1968...

(Copyright 2022 by R. Crumb)

... because he stole it. A slightly modified version of the "crazy man" was registered as Crazy Eddie's trademark...

(US Patent and Trademark Office)

... and Eddie plastered the purloined "crazy man" everywhere—in advertisements, on Crazy Eddie stock certificates, and on thousands of souvenir giveaways such as this T-shirt.

Crazy SAM ANTAR

By the time he graduated from Brooklyn's Lafayette High School in 1975, Sammy had been working for Eddie for four years. "Crazy" was penned by a smart-aleck classmate.

(Courtesy Sam E. Antar)

Sammy (bottom center) was interested in business long before it was fashionable. This was noticed by his classmates, who called him "Sam Capitalist" in the yearbook photo of his Advanced Placement History class.

(Courtesy Sam E. Antar)

CLAUDIO
MARY ANN R.
STEVEN
DANNY
SAM CAPITALIST

View of the Greenwich Village store from across Sixth Avenue, November 1980. Eddie grasped the commercial potential of the Village long before it was gentrified.

(Courtesy Mary Conte)

Vinnie Badalamenti began in the stockroom of the Greenwich Village store and moved up through the ranks. In later years he put on weight and achieved considerable success. But the U.S. government, which took this candid photo, did not care for his new line of work.

(U.S. Government photo, via Wikimedia Commons)

CE 0948

2688330

INCORPORATED UNDER THE LAWS OF THE STATE OF DELAWARE

2,688,330

SEE REVERSE FOR
CERTAIN DEFINITIONS

CUSIP 225227 10 7

This Is
To Certify
that

EDDIE ANTAR
2845 CONEY ISLAND AVENUE
BROOKLYN, NEW YORK 11235

Is the
owner of

TWO MILLION SIX HUNDRED EIGHTY EIGHT THOUSAND THREE HUNDRED THRITY

FULLY PAID AND NON-ASSESSABLE SHARES OF THE COMMON STOCK OF THE PAR VALUE OF $.01 EACH OF

CRAZY EDDIE, INC.

(hereinafter called the "Corporation"), transferable on the books of the Corporation by the holder hereof in person or by duly authorized attorney, upon surrender of this certificate properly endorsed. This certificate and the shares represented hereby are issued and be held subject to all of the provisions of the Certificate of Incorporation of the Corporation and all amendments thereto, to all of which the holder of this certificate assents by his acceptance hereof.
This certificate is not valid unless countersigned by the Transfer Agent and registered by the Registrar.
WITNESS the facsimile seal of the Corporation and the facsimile signatures of its duly authorized officers.

Dated: 09/20/84

SECRETARY

PRESIDENT

COUNTERSIGNED AND REGISTERED,
BANK LEUMI TRUST COMPANY OF NEW YORK
TRANSFER AGENT
AND REGISTRAR

BY

AUTHORIZED SIGNATURE

CRAZY EDDIE INC
CORPORATE
SEAL
1983
DELAWARE

Crazy Eddie became a Wall Street darling after it went public in September 1984. The stock price rose nearly elevenfold by August 1986. Here's some of the stock Eddie received in the initial public offering, the certificate bearing the "crazy man" character stolen from R. Crumb.

(Courtesy Paul Hayes)

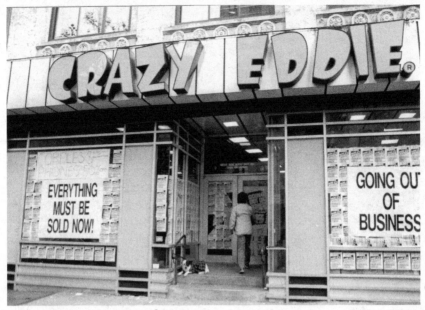

New management took over Crazy Eddie in November 1987, but in two years it was all over. All the stores held Going Out of Business sales, including this one on Broadway in Manhattan.

(Courtesy Sam E. Antar)

Crazy Eddie bids farewell to Greenwich Village late in 1989.

(Courtesy Sam E. Antar)

When Eddie didn't show for a February 1990 court appearance, the U.S. Marshals Service released to the newspapers this unflattering mug shot.

(Courtesy Paul Hayes)

Eddie didn't like to be photographed, but he was happy to sit for this picture. He wore eyeglasses for the occasion.

(Courtesy Paul Hayes)

The Secretary of State
of the United States of America
hereby requests all whom it may concern to permit the citizen/
national of the United States named herein to pass
without delay or hindrance and in case of need to
give all lawful aid and and protection.

Le Secrétaire d'Etat
des Etats-Unis d'Amérique
prie par les présentes toutes autorités compétentes, de laisser passer
le citoyen ou resortissant des Etats-Unis titulaire du présent passeport,
sans délai ni difficulté et, en cas de besoin, de lui accorder
toute aide et protection légitimes.

SIGNATURE OF BEARER/SIGNATURE DU TITULAIRE

NOT VALID UNTIL SIGNED

UNITED STATES OF AMERICA

| PASSPORT PASSEPORT | Type/Caté-gorie P | Code d'issuing / code du pays State USA émetteur | PASSPORT NO./NO. DU PASSPORT 110193512 |

Surname / Nom
SHALOM
Given name / Prénoms
HARRY PAGE
Nationality / Nationalité
UNITED STATES OF AMERICA
Date of birth / Date de naissance
25 APR/AVR 48
Sex / Sexe M   Place of birth / Lieu de naissance NEW YORK, U.S.A.
Date of issue / Date de délivrance 24 APR/AVR 89   Date of expiration / Date d'expiration 23 NOV/NOV 90
Authority / Autorité
PASSPORT AGENCY
NEW YORK
Amendments/ Modifications SEE PAGE 24

P<USASHALOM<<HARRY<PAGE<<<<<<<<<<<<<<<<<<<<<<
1101935127USA4804251M9011230<<<<<<<<<<<<<<4

Eddie used that photo to obtain this passport using a stolen identity, and fled the country.

(Courtesy Paul Hayes)

U.S. Department of Justice
United States Marshals Service

WANTED
BY U.S. MARSHALS

NOTICE TO ARRESTING AGENCY: Before arrest, validate warrant through National Crime Information Center (NCIC). United States Marshals Service NCIC entry number: (NIC/ W575089283).

NAME: ANTAR, Eddie

ALIAS: STEWART, Alexander; ALEXANDER, Stewart; LEVY, Joseph; LEVY, Yosef; SHLOMO, Ezra Ben; "KELSO"; "CRAZY EDDIE"

DESCRIPTION:

Sex	MALE
Race	WHITE
Place of Birth	BROOKLYN, NEW YORK
Date(s) of Birth	DECEMBER 18, 1947
Height	5'6"
Weight	165 LBS
Eyes	BROWN
Hair	BROWN *(small scars on scalp re: hair transplant)*
Skintone	MEDIUM
Scars, Marks, Tattoos	10" VERTICAL SCAR ON ABDOMEN
Social Security Number	120-38-5665, 120-38-5565
NCIC Fingerprint Classification	PO 04 03 15 11 17 05 09 15 12

FBI 927 459 59

LEFT THUMB PRINT   RIGHT THUMB PRINT

WANTED FOR: CRIMINAL CONTEMPT OF COURT
Warrant Issued: District of New Jersey
Warrant Number: 9050-0228-0111-F
DATE WARRANT ISSUED: February 27, 1990

MISCELLANEOUS INFORMATION: ANTAR is a wealthy man and frequent international traveller. ANTAR speaks fluent English, French and possibly Hebrew. He has been described as a heavy drinker. ANTAR may be using an Israeli passport.

If arrested or whereabouts known, notify the local United States Marshals Office, (Telephone: (201) 645-2404).

If no answer, call United States Marshals Service Communications Center in Arlington, Virginia. Telephone (800) 336-0102: (24 hour telephone contact or (800) 423-0719 (TDD). NLETS access code is VAUSMOOOO.

PRIOR EDITIONS ARE OBSOLETE AND NOT TO BE USED.

Form USM-132
(Rev. 4/90)

The wanted poster issued while Eddie was on the lam. The handwritten notations were by one of his pursuers.

(Courtesy Paul Hayes)

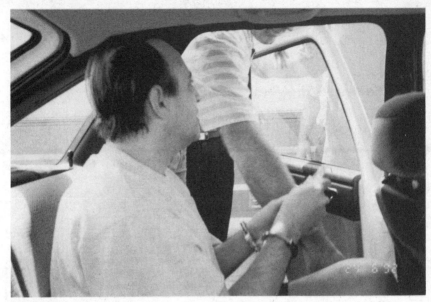

Eddie was arrested by Israeli police in June 1992, and taken to his new home: a maximum-security prison.

(Courtesy Paul Hayes)

A morose Eddie after his capture.

(Courtesy Paul Hayes)

Eddie's principal pursuer in Israel was Yossef Zamory, an Israeli police superintendent of formidable stature. He is shown here with Jayne Blumberg, a federal prosecutor who had come to Israel to aid in compelling Eddie's return to the United States.

(Courtesy Paul Weissman)

U.S. Department of Justice
United States Marshals Service

WANTED
BY U.S. MARSHALS

NOTICE TO ARRESTING AGENCY: Before arrest, validate warrant through National Crime Information Center (NCIC). United States Marshals Service NCIC entry number: (NIC/ W575089283).

NAME: ANTAR, Eddie

ALIAS: STEWART, Alexander; ALEXANDER, Stewart; LEVY, Joseph; LEVY, Yosef; SHLOMO, Ezra Ben; "KELSO"; "CRAZY EDDIE"

DESCRIPTION:

Sex	MALE
Race	WHITE
Place of Birth	BROOKLYN, NEW YORK
Date(s) of Birth	DECEMBER 18, 1947
Height	5'6"
Weight	165 LBS
Eyes	BROWN
Hair	BROWN
Skintone	MEDIUM
Scars, Marks, Tattoos	10" VERTICAL SCAR ON ABDOMEN
Social Security Number	120-38-5665, 120-38-5565
NCIC Fingerprint Classification	PO 04 03 15 11 17 05 09 15 12

LEFT THUMB PRINT   RIGHT THUMB PRINT

WANTED FOR: CRIMINAL CONTEMPT OF COURT
Warrant Issued: District of New Jersey
Warrant Number: 9050-0228-0111-F
DATE WARRANT ISSUED: February 27, 1990

MISCELLANEOUS INFORMATION: ANTAR is a wealthy man and frequent international traveller. ANTAR speaks fluent English, French and possibly Hebrew. He has been described as a heavy drinker. ANTAR may be using an Israeli passport.

If arrested or whereabouts known, notify the local United States Marshals Office, (Telephone:).

If no answer, call United States Marshals Service Communications Center in Arlington, Virginia.
Telephone (800) 336-0102: (24 hour telephone contact or (800) 423-0719 (TDD). NLETS access code is VAUSMOOOO.

PRIOR EDITIONS ARE OBSOLETE AND NOT TO BE USED.

Form USM-132
(Rev. 4/90)

The wanted poster issued after Eddie fled, marked to show that he was safely behind bars.

(Courtesy Paul Weissman)

Both sides in Eddie's extradition fight posing for a photo in Israel. Eddie's wife "Debbie II" is on the far left. Prosecutor Jayne Blumberg is fourth from the left. Eddie's criminal defense lawyer Jack Arsenault (with mustache) is at the far right in the rear, with Paul Weissman to his left. The others are Israeli lawyers.

(Courtesy Paul Weissman)

Prosecutor Paul Weissman and U.S. Attorney Michael Chertoff in 1994.

(Courtesy Paul Weissman)

Sam E. Antar across from the site of the Greenwich Village store, 2021.

Eddie Antar died in 2016 and was buried at a Staten Island cemetery. The stones were placed there by visitors to his grave in memory of the deceased. Despite all that had happened, he remains an object of affection and nostalgia. But there are exceptions.

CHAPTER SEVENTEEN

TO PEOPLE ON THE OUTSIDE, IT SEEMED AS IF CRAZY EDDIE WAS SOARING, blessed with unstoppable prosperity and limitless prospects. Sure, there were more competitors, but Eddie was hanging in there. Stores were opening at a rapid clip. Nine were added during 1986, bringing the roster to thirty-two. CRZY stock hit an all-time high during the summer, as Ed Colloton trumpeted the company's soaring profits and splendid comparable store sales. And of course, there was the home shopping network, which received far more "ink" than it warranted thanks to Colloton's yeoman efforts.

Anything that didn't fit the media narrative went unnoticed or ignored. Reneging on stock sales? Quickly forgotten. A no-show at an important conference in Laguna Beach? Overlooked. The marketing machine coasted ahead on the screamer commercials and free publicity. In the box-office sensation *Peggy Sue Got Married*, released that fall, the Nicolas Cage character was "a philandering sort of 'Crazy Eddie' television huckster." When a five-album set from Bruce Springsteen's E Street Band sold out everywhere in November 1986, the mobs at the Greenwich Village store were so enormous that they were mentioned in the *Daily News*.

In reality, Crazy Eddie was like a volcanic island, with gentle breezes and palm trees on the surface and magma bubbling below, ready to explode like Krakatoa. Down beneath the sand and mud, the inventory and comp-store sales frauds were becoming difficult to sustain. The more they grew, the more they had to grow just to break even. And then there was Debbie I, still fed a diet of lies by Eddie and growing increasingly restive.

If Debbie had seen the *Daily News* article on "Springsteenmania"—it was on page 4 and hard to miss—she had every right to be furious. The Crazy Eddie Record and Tape Asylums were run by Benel Distributors. Eddie had promised Debbie repeatedly that Benel was going to be taken public or acquired and that the result was to be that she'd finally get the wealth he had promised her—half the marital assets. She could see with her own two eyes that Benel was doing just fine. Weren't customers crowding into the Record and Tape Asylums? Wasn't Eddie doing spectacularly well?

In the two years since their marriage went bust after the New Year's Eve Massacre, Eddie had tried to mollify Debbie with one empty promise after another, one lie after another, one manipulation after another. He tried everything, wheedling, cajoling, to get her off his back. Sometime in late 1985 or early 1986, he tried a new ploy, begging her to go back with him. He had married Debbie II immediately after the divorce, but no matter. He wanted to go back with Debbie I. For once, Debbie saw through it as just more empty talk.

"I will give you everything. I will sign over everything I own if you go back with me," Eddie pleaded.

"You never gave me what you promised in the first place," she told him. "Give me my money."

Eddie was ready for that.

"I will give you everything I own," he told her. "I will sign over everything I own, lock, stock and barrel."

"No. You didn't live up to your first promise yet," she reminded him. She hadn't seen a cent of the $8 million–$9 million he had promised her. Now, all of a sudden, he was going to give her all his wealth? She had swallowed a lot of his lies in the past, but this was too much. That con game never played out, but he continued to barge into her life, taking advantage of her weakness and loneliness.

Throughout the summer of 1986, Eddie still treated their old summer retreat on the Jersey Shore as if they were still married. On weekends that summer he came to the house three or four times a month and entertained his friends, cooking for them, a picture of domestic bliss. Debbie never objected. Every time he visited she hammered at him, still chasing the fantasy that she'd receive the money he promised her from the supposed Benel deal. She even approached Ben Kuszer. Benel was his company, after all. But he refused to get involved. The fighting continued.

As summer gave way to fall, there was a change in Eddie's response to Debbie's constant pleas for her fair share of the marital assets. Perhaps he just grew tired of telling the same lies. The elaborate excuses tapered off. Then came another blowup. It happened sometime in late November or early December 1986. It was different from the ones that preceded it, not in what Eddie did but in how Debbie reacted.

He came by the Brooklyn house at night to pick up the children for a visit. As usual, an argument about money commenced. As the fight dragged on, Eddie decided to use his daughters as pawns, saying he wouldn't take them and then backpedaling. It went back and forth like that a few times. The girls started crying, and the older ones argued with him. That was enough for Eddie. He left.

After returning briefly, he left again and called the house. Debbie recounted: "He got into a fight with me, and called me a piece of shit, and I don't know what I am talking about with the money, and I must be crazy like the rest of my family, and I am crazy, and he doesn't know what I am talking about, and he is coming to get the kids."

Eddie came over, took his daughters, and drove away. Then he called. And called. And called. He called again and again until five thirty in the morning, getting more furious each time. The maid fielded the calls. "Put the piece of shit on the phone," he screamed. Debbie could hear him. She did not take his calls.

That night, while Eddie was calling and screaming and cursing, something inside Debbie seemed to snap. She finally saw the truth. If she wanted the money that was coming to her, she would have to fight for it.

■ ■ ■

Eddie's November 1986 stock sale didn't get much public attention, but it created a serious problem. If the stock price declined in the weeks after the shares were dumped, it would look bad for Eddie and probably prompt shareholder lawsuits. And sure enough, comp-store sales were shaping up poorly yet again. If those numbers could not be adequately phonied up, the stock would tumble when quarterly financial numbers came out in early December. Sam Cohen was glad to pitch in and do whatever he was asked, but he couldn't generate enough buying to reverse the comp-store sale decline. He just didn't have the money.

Sammy had an idea. "So I thought to myself that maybe the way to go is to borrow Zazy's checks. In other words, ask Zazy as follows: 'Give us $5 million. Give us $6 million. Whatever that number was. Give us $5 million or $6 million worth of checks. I know you can't take the merchandise and I know you can't pay for it. But we'll not deposit those checks. We'll hold onto your checks. When we ship you that merchandise, that is when we'll deposit them.'"

Sam Cohen was happy to cooperate, as usual, and loaned Crazy Eddie the requisite undated checks, which reached Sammy through Allen and the new hire Abe Grinberg. Sammy made sure that the bookkeeper put them in the ledgers for the month of November and recorded them before Eddie's stock dump. Ironically, one of the store accounts that benefited from the borrowed-check scam was in the corporate name of "Debbie Audio"—affectionately named after his ex-wife, who, needless to say, never got a nickel from that store.

The check-loan scheme was a success. Actual comp-store sales in the September-November quarter declined 8 percent to 8.2 percent when compared to the year before. Thanks to the Zazy checks, Colloton was able to announce on December 4, 1986, that comp-store sales were up 5 percent over the same period in 1985, sparing Eddie from shareholder litigation—and all that came with it—for the time being.

All these machinations inflated Crazy Eddie profits, but were not enough. With a price war slamming profits, more and more fraud was required just to keep afloat. Comp-store sales, the real number, were down 16 percent in the fourth quarter (December 1986 through February 1987). That was too big for Zazy to reverse. Eddie had no choice. After winding up the check-borrowing scheme, he stopped trying to manipulate comp-store sales. "We gave up hope. There was really nothing that could be done," Sammy recalled.

As 1986 staggered to a close, Sammy had a new problem on top of all the old ones. In the past he would have loved a promotion and all the prestige that came with it. Not now, not with the frauds piling up like leaky bags of garbage, their stench threatening to attract attention. The last thing he needed was a fancier title than he already had. And he got just that on December 19, 1986. Eddie put him on the board of directors, and three days later he was promoted yet again. He now shared the title of president with two other "lucky" people. Sammy wasn't the only one shoved up the corporate ladder.

Eddie could always count on Dave Panoff, whether it was committing warranty fraud or inflating the reeps inventory. Sometime in mid-December Panoff learned just how much Eddie valued his loyalty. He was called into the office of Solomon Antar, general counsel, who "informed me that Eddie had decided that I, along with some other people who were executives in the company, were to be placed on the board of directors." This meant that Panoff would now theoretically be at the very pinnacle of Crazy Eddie. Boards of directors are the top decision-making body of public companies, responsible for ensuring that they are run in the best interests of shareholders. Eddie was chairman of the board as well as CEO, and naming Panoff to this high body was the highest accolade he could bestow.

"David V. Panoff, Senior Vice President, Service and Support Systems" (as he was described in the 1987 annual report) wasn't on the board to provide oversight. He was there to do as he was told. Although Eddie didn't drop by the office very much, "all of his wishes should still be followed. That he, meaning Solomon, and Sammy were the people who were going to be giving me directions." Solomon produced a Bible. "He asked me to place my hand on a Bible and swear to continue to follow the orders of Eddie Antar." Panoff did just that.

Eddie needed a loyal, obedient board of directors because he wanted out.

As the fraud became an all-consuming monster, it dawned on Eddie that he needed an exit plan. While it wasn't certain that the company was a goner, he didn't want to be there if it collapsed. He needed to put distance between himself and Crazy Eddie. He devised a plan to quit as CEO, but he also wanted to keep control of the frauds until the last possible moment, like the pilot of a mortally wounded aircraft in an old war movie, holding onto the controls until just before bailing out.

To carry out this mission, Eddie needed to create the facade of a change in management, meaning he needed the assent of Crazy Eddie's board of directors. So he added people he could depend upon: Sammy, his old friend and medical school administrator Ike Kairey, Dave Panoff, Solomon Antar, and two other Crazy Eddie managers. All were trusted Eddie loyalists.

There was only one board member who was not on a leash, but he was no threat. James H. Scott Jr., a Columbia University finance professor, joined in 1984 at the behest of Oppenheimer to provide an independent voice on the board at the IPO. But Scott lacked a retail background and was out of his depth. At board meetings, Scott "asked stupid questions that Eddie would shoot down," Sammy recalled. That made him a perfect outside board member as far as the Antars were concerned, a WASP presence who made them look legitimate to outsiders and could do the insiders no harm. They derisively called him the "fall goy." "We ran rings around him," said Sammy.

With his lapdog board in place, Eddie was ready to watch Crazy Eddie recede into his rearview mirror. First he had to surmount a formidable obstacle: Jim Purcell, the annoying outside counsel. That was the problem when you brought in prestigious names to create the artifice of legitimacy—sometimes they did their jobs. Unlike Scott, Eddie couldn't run rings around the Paul, Weiss partner, who torpedoed the idea of his resigning as CEO. His reason was sound. Quitting a few weeks after dumping all that stock would look terrible. So he proposed a compromise. Aside from being CEO, he held the title of president. Purcell recommended that Eddie step down from that post while staying on as CEO. Eddie reluctantly agreed.

Eddie wanted Mitchell to replace him as president, but his brother turned him down. Mitchell told Sammy privately that "he didn't want to pick up the pieces"—the fraud, that is. "Eddie wasn't around. He would not carry the load." Eddie came up with another idea—three top executives constituting an "Office of the President." Mitchell would be "chief operating officer," in charge of purchasing and marketing. Sammy would continue as CFO, and the third would be Ike Kairey, overseeing store operations. Eddie would float above the three as CEO. That solution was agreeable to all, and it was executed on December 22. Partly because of the holiday, and partly because Eddie was still CEO, the announcement received little attention.

Then Eddie had second thoughts. "He said, 'Fuck Jim Purcell,'" Sammy recalled. He was getting out. Two weeks later, on January 8, 1987, Eddie stepped down as CEO "for personal reasons." The board (that is, Eddie) turned over the "powers and responsibilities" of CEO to the Office of the President that Eddie had created just before Christmas, and he stayed on as chairman of the board of directors. As a cover story for his departure, Eddie spread a rumor that he was seriously ill, figuring that would be viewed as plausible "personal reasons" when the actual reason was "separating himself from an ongoing fraud." Eddie's nonexistent "serious illness" became a regular feature of press accounts that quoted anonymous "sources in the company"—the "sources" being Sammy.

Eddie was the star of the Crazy Eddie Story, so even though the Office of the President received little attention, the same could not be said for his departure as CEO. It was considered a blow to the company, much as when a diva leaves the Metropolitan Opera. "Eddie was the real entrepreneurial spirit of the company," said an analyst quoted in the *New York Times*. It may have reassured him if he had known that Eddie had not actually stepped down. He was still exuding his entrepreneurial spirit by phone and by meeting his top people in and near his Manhattan apartment. He was channeling his entrepreneurial spirit by working behind the scenes to manufacture phony profits.

■ ■ ■

Comp-store sales inflation was a lost cause, but the fraud wasn't over. Toward the end of 1986, Eddie and his fraud brain trust worked out a scheme involving invoices to manufacturers, known in the trade as "debit memos." They were essentially bills claiming that the company was owed money. Vendors would be socked for volume discounts Crazy Eddie hadn't earned, unwarranted co-op advertising credits, and other sums the manufacturers didn't actually owe. Every dollar stated on them was a dollar in phony profits, even if they were ignored by the people getting the debit memos and Crazy Eddie didn't actually get a cent from them.

At Eddie's direction, a slew of bogus debit memos was generated to offset sums legitimately owed by the company. As later recounted by Sammy, the debit memos were written up by Abe Grinberg and Arnie Spindler under Mitchell's supervision. Sammy also pressured their old friends at Wren Distributors to ship $5 million–$6 million in merchandise, inflating inventories just before the end of the fiscal year in March 1987, billing the company at the start of the new fiscal year.

After all, Eddie had to do something, anything, now that the comp-store fraud could no longer be sustained. On January 6, two days before he stepped down, Crazy Eddie reported that comp-store sales fell 9 percent in December 1986 compared to the year before. The stock tumbled, and the Antars' smooth-talking emissary to Wall Street was not around to provide the requisite spin. Sammy was fed up with Colloton's picky and stupid questions, and fired him right after Colloton cranked out a press release announcing the "Office of the President" artifice.

In retrospect, the firing proved to be poorly timed, as Crazy Eddie needed all the flackery it could muster. Shareholders had been losing patience, and when the bad comp-store sales numbers were released, the reaction was fierce. "People were losing faith in the management of the company. Investors were calling up cursing us out, yelling and screaming." They were mad about the comp-store sales decline. They were mad about Eddie dumping stock and quitting. The first shareholder class-action lawsuit came like clockwork on January 7, a day after the poor numbers were released. The suit alleged that Eddie's November stock dump was illegal because he was exploiting inside information on the company's sluggish comp-store sales. That was of course correct, though the plaintiffs were making only an educated guess. If the class action survived—they were often tossed out before trial—plaintiff lawyers would be in a position to turn their litigation into an inquisition, thanks to pretrial discovery.

There was every reason to expect more lawsuits. Share prices, which peaked at $21.625 in August 1986 ($86.50, adjusted for stock splits), fell to $13 in December and then $8 when the bad comp-store sales numbers were released in early January 1987. The puff pieces of 1986 abruptly gave way to skepticism fueled by Eddie's stock dump and sudden departure, "serious illness" notwithstanding. "No one has seen or heard from Eddie since the middle of November," a "Wall Street source" told *Newsday* in an article on the December comp-store sales decline.

Though the press soured on Crazy Eddie, brokerage house analysts remained upbeat, very much as their employers' economic interests required. After all, they were in the business of selling stock, usually shares of companies owned by the brokerages. In 2002 a scandal would erupt over analyst conflicts of interest, stemming from rosy reports cranked out by the large brokerage firms. But in the 1980s analysts were not expected to deviate from the company line and they rarely did, benefiting Crazy Eddie. So even though the Christmas season was "shockingly poor" for Crazy Eddie, as the *Philadelphia Inquirer* reported on January 26, 1987, the newspaper went on to note that analysts "remain enthusiastic about the company's long-term prospects." Bruce Missett of Salomon Brothers told the *Wall Street Journal* that Crazy Eddie was a "fundamentally sound company with tremendous opportunities."

Sammy would have burst out laughing when he read stuff like that, but he was too depressed. He had recalculated the accumulated fraud. As a result of the bogus debit memos, all the fakery to date was now considerably more than he had expected. He figured it totaled $35 million. Only a sudden reversal of fortunes—*real* fortunes, not analyst fantasies—would allow all that fraud to dissolve into the past. It was increasingly clear that just wasn't happening. Since sales were bleak and not improving, they had to either commit more fabrications to keep their heads above water or give up, as they had done with comp-store sales. And they could not give up.

Sammy's struggle to manage the frauds was hampered by strife within the family. With Crazy Eddie beginning to founder, and Eddie in the midst of exiting, Allen and Mitchell grew bitter. Mitchell, Sammy recalled, "felt entitled to a larger share of the business. He only got stock from his father. He never got stock from his brother. His brother always promised him stock but never delivered. He basically delivered only on stock options." Allen felt the same resentment and was upset that he never had become an officer of the company. Rather than quell their frustrations, Sam M. sided with Eddie's brothers.

Even more galling to Eddie, his father and brothers were on Debbie's side in her quest to get a fair divorce settlement. They knew that Eddie had shafted her, just as he had failed to share the wealth with his brothers. Eddie was furious at this "disloyalty" and "ingratitude." He told Sammy that "he made them all rich. It's up to the father to take care of his kids." By Eddie's reasoning, Sam M. had the obligation to take care of his "kids" even when they were grown men with families who worked for Eddie in all of his endeavors, legal and otherwise.

Eddie was shrugging off all he had been taught about the meaning of family, everything that Sam M. had tried to drum into his head when he got his son the lease on Kings Highway back in 1969. Eddie didn't care about all that stuff. He never was going to act like an S-Y patriarch. He didn't want to be an S-Y patriarch. He was Eddie. The legend. The genius. His name was on the stores. Crazy Eddie was his achievement and his alone.

Sammy was caught in the middle, the go-between for the brothers and cousin, while taking orders from both Eddie and Sam M. No one was willing to work together, and that created a leadership vacuum. He had to engage in shuttle diplomacy to keep the peace. "I became like a Henry Kissinger going from one faction to the other making sure that certain things got done." Sammy's diplomatic mission took him to all the warring factions—except for the one that was about to go nuclear.

CHAPTER EIGHTEEN

RAOUL LIONEL FELDER WAS THE MOST FEARED LAWYER IN NEW YORK—but only if you were getting divorced and only if he was representing the other side. If he chose to represent you, it was likely that you or your spouse was wealthy, famous, or both and that your case rose above the ordinary muck and mire of matrimonial practice. "You're Rich? Not Boring? He'll Take Your Case," proclaimed a flattering *Newsday* profile in January 1987. He was the "courtier of rich, unhappily wed New Yorkers." He and his law partner and wife, Myrna Felder, represented a host of 1980s celebrities, socialites, and their spouses. Mrs. Carl Sagan, Mrs. Roone Arledge, and Brian De Palma were on his client list. More important than any of them from Debbie Antar's perspective was a non-celebrity. Her name was Nancy Capasso, and she was wife of a mob associate and contractor named Carl "Andy" Capasso.

The Capassos have long since faded into history, but the drama of Andy and Nancy and related rogues and ruffians was a 1980s tabloid sensation. At the pinnacle of this tower of slime was the Miss America for 1945. In the intervening years, Bess Myerson had morphed from symbol of Jewish resilience in the wake of the Holocaust, gaining the beauty pageant crown at the end of World War II, to 1980s object of derision. She attained the latter status during her tenure as cultural affairs commissioner under Mayor Ed Koch. The scandal surrounding Myerson was one of many that beset the latter stages of the Koch administration, but it was easily the most lurid. Myerson had an affair with Capasso, causing his marriage to fall apart. While the divorce was pending, Myerson gave a job to the daughter of the judge who was hearing the case, who then dramatically cut Capasso's alimony and child support. It was as much of a conflict of interest as one could imagine, but in the Koch years such things had a way of being swept under the rug. The Felders were instrumental in sweeping the "Bess Mess" to where it belonged, in the public spotlight, after they were retained by Mrs. Capasso.

Nancy Capasso's plight was strikingly similar to Deborah Antar's—a victimized spouse overwhelmed by a cheating, abusive, deceitful, wealthy husband and ill-served by the judicial system. Still "in shock over his [Eddie's] betrayal," Debbie hired the Felders sometime in January 1987, a few weeks after Eddie's all-night tantrum. By retaining these superstar lawyers, Debbie had taken a step that was intolerable to her ex-husband.

Though Crazy Eddie was as public as a company could be, Eddie himself was averse to publicity. His credo had long been "in obscurity there is security." This meant that as far as Eddie was concerned, the Felders were the lawyers from hell. Raoul Felder was known for using tabloid exposure to extract favorable settlements for his clients. It "might be called the Felder gambit, after its acknowledged master." And Myrna Felder, a scrappy Brooklyn native like Raoul, was an expert in tax law and investments. She was probably the best matrimonial lawyer in the city in dealing with financial skullduggery, which only added to the nightmare posed by her husband.

Shortly after they were hired, the Felders wrote Eddie a letter in which they advised him that they were representing Debbie. Precisely what else they said is not known, but its effect on Eddie was immediate. He reacted by placing a frantic series of threatening phone calls to Mitchell and Ben Kuszer, who were vacationing with their families in Acapulco, and other family members. His message was blunt. Debbie was to be stopped, "or they will all go down." For the first time in his life, Eddie Antar was afraid.

Debbie had chosen the worst possible month in the life of her ex-husband to sic ferocious, determined matrimonial lawyers on him. It is sheer happenstance—just one of those little points of convergence that happen in the universe—that at the very time she inserted that bayonet into his solar plexus, another one was being placed there by the US Attorney for the District of New Jersey. Within a day or so of learning that Debbie had hired the Felders, Eddie was put on notice that Crazy Eddie was the subject of a criminal investigation into an old, reliable moneymaker.

An FBI agent named Terrence Flynn was the bearer of that horrifying news, serving a subpoena on Dave Panoff that demanded he produce all records pertaining to warranty claims. Eddie knew perfectly well that he had authorized Panoff to con the manufacturers when he was hired, and told him "rip their eyes out" after the IPO. Not only was Panoff a key member of the inner circle—not only a newly appointed, Bible-sworn board member—but he ran the reeps warehouse fraud in addition to his warranty thievery. These were things that he had done for Crazy Eddie at Eddie's instructions.

Panoff had every right to feel both terrified and vindicated. He had ordered an end to the warranty fraud only a few months earlier, after Sharp Electronics had gotten wise to the scamming and confronted him. He later recalled: "They came into our repair center. They basically said: 'Look, we know what you're doing with this. We really need you to stop.'" What no one knew at the time was that someone had gotten sloppy. Panoff or one of his people had submitted claims to manufacturers for units that they didn't make.

The Sharp meeting bothered Panoff immensely. "There was something about that whole meeting that got me very nervous. At the time I realized what we were doing was dangerous, and I figured at that point it made sense to stop the whole thing." Panoff immediately "shut the whole thing down." It had been a neat moneymaker, reaping $400,000 a year for the company, but Panoff felt it was far too risky. That was a good call, even though it was too late. Sharp and possibly other manufacturers had already complained to the FBI. It was in the hands of the bureau's satellite office in Hackensack, the North Jersey town where Flynn was based.

Solomon convened a meeting with Office of the President members Sammy, Mitchell, and Ike Kairey. Since the warranty fraud scheme had ceased, it was decided that they would give the feds only recent records. They would use the excuse that "we had the other records in more of a long term storage situation and asked them for more time to present them." The hope was that when the FBI and US Attorney's Office looked at the papers provided, which were innocuous, "they wouldn't proceed with the investigation." That strategy was put into motion, and everybody kept their fingers crossed.

Business was tanking, but Eddie and his lieutenants were too distracted to care. "The profitability of Crazy Eddie was going down the tubes. There was no direction," Sammy recalled a few years later. At the same time, family friction "was making things very, very very difficult. The company was starting to come apart." Sammy felt like he was "talking to the walls" when he tried to get the brothers to cooperate with each other.

Eddie had his own plans. In February or March 1987, he confided to Sammy that he was moving his money out of the country "in case anything happens." He didn't elaborate, but he realized that the frauds they were committing were not enough to turn the company around. Comp-store sales were horrid. In the fiscal year ending on March 1, 1987, they were down 5.3 percent to 6.3 percent compared to the year before, though the company reported only a 2 percent decline thanks to their fakery.

As the fiscal year came to an end, Eddie decided to engage in a last-ditch inventory-enlargement scheme. Unfortunately, the reliable warehouse manager Dave Neiderbach was gone. The chaos and pressure had pushed him out the door, and he was replaced by an employee of unknown reliability. Eddie and Sammy decided to inflate the inventories in the stores instead. All the Crazy Eddie outlets had stockrooms. Now they were going to be stuffed with merchandise, but only on paper. Sammy was joined in that endeavor by his deputy, Eddie Gindi, as well as Mitchell and trusted employees Arnie Spindler and Abe Grinberg. Just before the fiscal year ended on March 1, the group stayed late and altered store inventory numbers, with Spindler and Grinberg advising them on the best products to change on the inventory sheets. Sam M. pitched in as well.

In past inventory padding, Eddie's people had gone to great lengths to watch the auditors. Neiderbach had his guys follow them around, noting what boxes they were counting, and Arnie Spindler had cleverly kept a copy of their test-count list during the year-earlier inventory enlargement. Sammy discovered yet another simple way of keeping track of those nuisances. The auditors kept their paperwork in a locked box at the Crazy

Eddie offices. He noticed they put the key every night in a small box of paper clips. "After the auditors left after doing whatever work they did during the day, I took the key. I opened the box. I saw which items they had supervised on those stores they had supervised and we changed the items they hadn't supervised."

New board member Dave Panoff was reluctant to participate in the scheme, but he had no choice. He had taken an oath on the Bible, after all. Sammy and Kairey implored him to pitch in. Panoff recounted: "I remember him [Kairey] saying, 'Eddie's going to be crossing the goal line with the football. Don't you want to be on the team when that happens?'" Panoff suited up and got in the game.

Team Eddie had successfully boosted inventories by $15 million to $20 million, but their labors weren't over when the fiscal year ended. The auditors hung around for weeks afterward, continuing their work on the year-end numbers, which would be published in an annual report (a "10-K") in late April. Sometime during that month, Sammy overheard a conversation among the accountants in which they expressed concern about the inventories in five stores they hadn't supervised. The numbers reported there seemed awfully high, they grumbled. Sure they were high. The figures on the inventory sheets had been altered.

Something had to be done to prevent the auditor griping from getting out of hand. After consulting Mitchell, Ike, and Abe Grinberg, a decision was reached. Sammy later recounted: "We decided to overship those five stores with merchandise. 'Ship them to the gills,' it was called. Just ship them, ship them, ship them merchandise until the stores were bursting with merchandise in case the auditors wanted to do a recount of those stores." When those stores ran out of space in the stockrooms, store clerks and salesmen piled up boxes of merchandise on the sales floors. Customers could barely squeeze through all the stacks. The stockrooms were so tightly packed that the clerks couldn't go in to pull out products people wanted to buy. But it didn't matter. Eddie ordered still more unwanted merchandise, truckful after truckful, which was crammed into the stores.

All this cramming and falsification kept Crazy Eddie from going under, but just barely. When the financial results were announced for the fiscal year ending March 1, 1987, they showed pretax earnings of $20.6 million when the real number was a loss of somewhere between $20 million and $25 million. Even though they had turned red ink into black, their profits were still abysmal even after they were faked, 22 percent less than the year before. In the fourth quarter, which included the all-important 1986 Christmas season, profits were down 90 percent from 1985. Crazy Eddie was clinging to solvency by its fingernails. Nothing seemed to work anymore. The home shopping network was a flop, even with Jerry Carroll at the helm. His fast-talking patter didn't work in one-hour segments. He couldn't ad-lib that long, so every word had to be scripted.

Just a few months earlier, it had seemed as if Crazy Eddie was surrounded by Teflon. Bad news never seemed to stick. Now it seemed as if Eddie and his company were swathed in flypaper.

■ ■ ■

After hiring the Felders, Debbie retained the services of professional security personnel. She didn't like to call them "bodyguards," but that's precisely what they were. She went for the best, or at least the best-known, people she could find, hiring a private detective firm recently established by Richard "Bo" Dietl, a retired NYPD detective with a long and colorful career. During his fifteen years as a cop, he had made fourteen hundred arrests and received sixty citations for heroism. Among his exploits was helping to catch the perpetrator of the Palm Sunday Massacre, a gruesome 1984 mass murder in which eight children and two women were shot to death in East New York. A tough cop like Dietl could certainly handle the slippery and ill-tempered Eddie Antar. Dietl's firm was hired to serve Eddie with the lawsuit papers and to protect Debbie from any outburst that might result. Debbie would be protected 24/7 by three shifts of Dietl's men, all retired or off-duty police officers.

Dietl's men began work on April 22, 1987. That night, one of his people served the papers on Eddie while he was dining with Sammy and other pals at his favorite restaurant, Lusardi's, on the Upper East Side. Eddie could see at a glance from the papers shoved in his hands that Debbie had gone and done it, all his threats notwithstanding. She wanted the separation agreement quashed. She wanted her "equitable," and she had hired lawyers known for outcomes that were more than equitable.

Retribution came quickly. Just by coincidence, Debbie's mom had come to her daughter's house in Brooklyn that evening. Lillian Rosen had been with Crazy Eddie for years, starting under Uncle Eddy as a clerk, and had since been elevated to supervisor of Crazy Eddie's payroll department. At about one o'clock in the morning, Eddie called Debbie. "What is your mother's number?" he asked. Debbie summoned her mom to the phone, but by the time she got there, Eddie had hung up. Ten minutes later, Sammy got on the phone with Lillian. She directly reported to him. Don't show up at work, he told her. She was fired. "We were both very upset about these actions," Debbie recalled.

Even though it was clear by now that Debbie was no longer willing to be his doormat, Eddie was not about to skulk off in silence. He sought another opportunity to browbeat his ex-wife, a desperate if not delusional attempt to get her to withdraw her lawsuit.

Two days later, Debbie came home at about four in the afternoon accompanied by one of Dietl's men, an off-duty detective. Lillian was there and so was Eddie, standing in the vestibule at the entrance. He had come to pick up the kids. Two or three of the children were already in Eddie's limo. The bodyguard's presence outraged him. After all, he hired guys like this to guard his stores. And here were off-duty cops being used against him! And in the house he had paid for! His house! "He started calling the man that I was with a moron, and he kept saying it over and over, maybe forty-some-odd times, moron, moron, moron."

"Eddie, what is it that you want?" Debbie asked.

"I want you," he said.

"You want to take the children, go with the children. If you want to go take them to eat, take them to eat. If you want them to stay with you, take the children," she replied.

Eddie was stunned that his ex-wife did not seem to care that he "wanted" her. Her sales resistance was infuriating.

"It is you that I want. It is you I want to talk to. I want to talk to you," he kept repeating, while interjecting his opinion that the stone-faced plainclothes officer standing next to her was a moron. Ostensibly he had come to take the children with him as allowed by his unlimited visitation rights, but that was now inoperative. Eddie kept repeating, "I don't want to take the children. I want you, you, you."

"How can you do this?" he whined before shifting to a threat. "You are going to be sorry."

During this colloquy, Debbie's mom quietly called Dietl's office, whose number was conveniently located near the telephone. The ex-NYPD star swiftly arrived at the house with a colleague, a moonlighting cop, and told Eddie to take it easy. Eddie was not used to people talking to him like that. He was not about to take it easy, and he was unimpressed by the caliber of security personnel Debbie had hired. "I know who you are," Eddie told Dietl. He was not intimidated by a bunch of rent-a-cops, no matter how many massacres they had solved. The two men argued.

"There is going to be fuckin' trouble, and you all are going to be sorry. She is going to be sorry," Eddie grumbled.

As the argument escalated, someone called the local precinct, and before long a squad car pulled up in front of the house. Two cops emerged. One was a captain, an insanely high rank to deal with a minor and thus far non-violent domestic dispute, but this involved a VIP. Actually two VIPs, Eddie and the well-publicized retired detective Debbie had hired. Eddie was no more impressed by the arrival of police brass than he had been by Dietl's men. By now the kids in the limo had gone back into the house. Eddie didn't want to visit with them anymore.

One of the cops advised Eddie that if he didn't calm down, he would arrest him for harassment. Eddie responded rudely, telling the officer that he was part owner of the house and had every right to be there to see his children. While one of the cops asked Eddie if he had ever learned manners, the other one, the captain, noticed the presence of the children. He took them aside and asked if Eddie had harassed them. The younger girls said no, but one of the older girls answered in the affirmative and signed a complaint, pressing charges against her father. Despite that, Eddie wasn't arrested. The cops left.

"How can you bring this garbage into the house?" Eddie asked, referring to Dietl's men.

"Look at the garbage that you live with," one of his older daughters replied. Debbie told her to shut up.

Three days after the confrontation with Dietl and New York's Finest, Debbie sought an order of protection to prohibit Eddie from coming into her houses. His attorneys pledged that he would no longer do so. The petition was withdrawn, but Eddie was furious about it, furious about the promise his lawyer had to make, furious about Dietl. His manhood had been challenged, and not ineffectively. He was determined to exact retribution no matter the consequences, no matter how self-destructive it would be.

■ ■ ■

Lillian's firing was the beginning of a purge. People in the upper ranks of the company had to go if they were insufficiently loyal or too close to Debbie. Getting rid of her mother was actually Sammy's idea—she had given herself a raise and bonus without asking him—but the rest were a product of Eddie's suspicions and paranoia. Eddie's father and brothers were on the hit list. He was certain that they had egged on Debbie, manipulating her to sue him. It was irrational behavior. The family needed to stick together. But Eddie didn't care. He had been humiliated *in his own home*. He didn't live there anymore, but that didn't matter.

Ousting Sam M. was sticky. He quit the board but wouldn't budge beyond that. He was on the payroll as executive vice president, a position with no defined responsibilities that paid $196,000 a year. This was nowhere near the $600,000 Eddie paid himself, thanks to the doubling of his pay the board generously approved the previous September and continued after he stepped down as CEO. Still, $196,000 (about $500,000 in 2022 dollars) was good money, and Sam M. wasn't getting off that gravy train without a fight.

If Sam M. believed Eddie wouldn't fire his own father, he had underestimated his son. He was an officer of the company, so Eddie couldn't dump him unless he obtained board approval. Surely Eddie wouldn't wash the family's dirty laundry in public, would he? Yes, he would. He created a special "executive committee" of the board to do his bidding. Taking no chances, he named himself chairman. The other two members were newly elected board member William H. Saltzman, who had been Eddie's divorce lawyer, and the ever-somnolent James Scott. They met, thought hard about it, and did what Eddie wanted, eliminating Sam M.'s position on May 4, 1987. The full board upheld that decision, unanimous except for Mitchell, who opposed his dad's discharge, and Eddy, who had a board seat and was still on the payroll as treasurer. He abstained.

Mitchell could see that he was a goner himself. He tried a boardroom maneuver to stave off the inevitable. Sometime in May he met with outside director Jim Scott at a diner in Paramus, an atypical location for a corporate tête-à-tête. It must have seemed to Scott as if he was meeting with a Columbia student afraid of flunking out and not a top official of a company. Mitchell floated several ideas. Perhaps he could become CEO? That was one. Scott expressed regret that he could not be of any help, and the meeting ended inconclusively.

Eddie proceeded to fire Allen without severance. Bouncing Mitchell presented a problem because of all the empty titles he held, but his brother saved him the trouble and quit. He had now lawyered up. When Mitchell resigned at the June 5 board meeting, he came with his lawyer and dropped off a letter outlining his grievances against Eddie. The letter said, "Eddie's relationship with my family has been acrimonious and has resulted in a series of very disturbing developments involving the company." He didn't specify what those "disturbing developments" were. He went on to complain that he had not been consulted about major decisions despite being a member of the Office of the President. Then Mitchell got to the crux of the matter: money. Eddie had denied him severance, just as he had done with Allen. "I am sure that the board will consider my long association with the company in dealing with issues of severance, compensation, and the like. My resignation is without prejudice to any rights I may have had vis a vis the company," Mitchell's missive concluded, ending on an unpleasantly lawyerly note.

His youngest brother's threatening letter enraged Eddie, who now had no qualms at all about targeting Mitchell's close friend Ben Kuszer and his wife, Ellen, their sister. Eddie had never forgiven Ellen for siding with Debbie in the New Year's Eve Massacre and questioned Ben's loyalty for the same reason. They were all in cahoots as far as he was concerned. He terminated their company's contracts to operate in Crazy Eddie stores, forcing Benel into bankruptcy.

Behind the anger was fear. That was evident in a letter Eddie wrote to Bank Leumi on May 13, 1987, while all these firings and boardroom machinations were underway. He was writing about the $8 million he had transferred to the Caymans two years earlier after getting Lillian to sign Debbie's name on account documents. Eddie said he was "concerned that my former wife may attempt to utilize the accounts, make withdrawals therefrom, or seek to move them to a different depository." He warned that "if any such transactions are permitted, I would be required, in duty to my children, to hold your bank strictly accountable and liable therefor."

Eddie had kept the transfer a secret from Debbie, but still he was worried. For the first time in their relationship, she was fighting back. But even the Debbie threat paled in comparison to another danger that loomed. They were being closely watched by people who could solve all their problems—or put them in a penitentiary.

CHAPTER NINETEEN

CRAZY EDDIE WAS LIKE A WOUNDED BLUE JAY, SQUAWKING LOUDLY IN THE grass while the red-tailed hawks circled overhead. It had three of the qualities that made a company a takeover target: an established franchise, chaotic management, and, above all, a depressed stock price that give the appearance (in this case the illusion) of being undervalued. The possibility of a corporate raider gobbling up the company had been apparent since late 1986. Eddie didn't focus on it at first, but Sammy grasped how the potential chain of events might go. First the fraud fails. Then the stock price collapses. Then somebody buys up all that low-price stock, and the company gets taken over. Then the fraud is discovered. Then they go to prison.

That scenario was plausible in an unfriendly takeover, in which the pursuer took control and then ousted management. But Eddie could turn takeover mania to his advantage by acquiring the company himself. That was known as a management buyout, also known as a "leveraged buyout," or LBO. "Leverage" is financial jargon for "debt." He'd borrow money, buy up the stock, and revert to being a private company. Since Crazy Eddie would no longer have to file financial reports with the SEC, Eddie reasoned, their crimes would remain concealed. The inventory puffery, checks from Zazy, debit memos, and so on would be tucked away, just another Antar family secret like Sam M.'s first wife and abandoned son. Eddie believed that "no one would suspect management of trying to buy back a company that was engaged in financial fraud." Then they'd be able to start over, "repackage the company and take it public again" after cleaning up the books.

Eddie needed to act quickly to get on top of the takeover menace. Early in the year, the Antars got word that a number of fat cats were considering a bid. One of the most worrisome was from Newmark & Lewis, which was giving them fierce competition with its "Dick Lewis is watching" ad campaign. These potential bidders scared the hell out of Eddie. But outside interest could prove useful if Eddie and his people were able to put together a management buyout. Then the Antars could claim that their actions were defensive, a way of fending off unwanted interest. Sammy had a tape recorder hooked up to his phone, and he taped calls concerning potential buyers of the company in case he ever needed proof.

Early in January, not long after Eddie stepped down, a takeover feeler came from someone they had never expected would want to come anywhere near Crazy Eddie. It was from an elderly gent who lived on the Upper East Side and played whist in his spare time. Milton Petrie was one of the corporate titans who were regaled in the media not because of what they plundered but what they built. He was a canny investor, a philanthropist, and a decent man who gave money to hundreds of ordinary people suffering misfortune. He was everything the Antars wanted to be—successful, revered for his good deeds, and ridiculously rich.

The meeting went as well as they could have hoped. The old man did indeed ask if they wanted him to take over Crazy Eddie and leave them in place. It was what they wanted to hear, but the response of the three Office of the President members was noncommittal. Eddie would make the decision. Even if they were going to say yes, they weren't planning to do so right there at the Regency Whist Club.

The lunch shook up Sammy. For one thing, he admired the guy. Hell, *everyone* admired the guy. Did they really want to take Milton Petrie to the cleaners? It would have been like pulling a bait and switch on Abe Lincoln. The idea of turning Petrie into yet another victim, having to tell him elaborate lies, having to con him, made Sammy feel queasy. Besides, they might not be able to trick him into buying the company the way they wanted. They had moved into a different galaxy. They weren't a gnat on the rump of the manufacturers anymore, mavericks who could beat the big guys by buying merchandise from numbers bankers in the Bronx. They were dealing with people who could crush them. They needed to tread carefully.

Eddie didn't see Petrie as a potential savior, but as a threat. He didn't care one bit about how many widows and orphans the old man had helped out. He'd have lied like hell to him without hesitation. But he didn't believe that Petrie actually would have kept management intact if he took over the company. One way or the other, they would be out. So that was that. Sammy politely declined Petrie's offer.

One silver lining, and it was a very big one, was that word of Petrie's interest did not leak. If it had, it would have resulted in a barrage of offers, perhaps from well-financed vultures who'd have sought to take over Crazy Eddie and toss them out. They needed the company to be acquired *their* way, so that everything they had done could forever be consigned to the memory hole. They needed someone who was too greedy for his own good. Help of that nature soon arrived.

Not long after meeting with Petrie, word of a new possible suitor came from Bill Finneran, a managing director at Oppenheimer. Sammy's conversation with Finneran was brief. The Oppenheimer banker was ambiguous. "The Belzbergs are interested in your company," he said. "You better speak to them." The Belzbergs were a Canadian clan of corporate raiders, and they were interested in accumulating the stock or might have already begun doing so. Sammy needed to get on the phone with Sam Belzberg, chairman of the family's financial vehicle, First City Financial.

Sam Belzberg was the polar opposite of Petrie, though their backgrounds were similar. Both were the sons of hardworking Jewish immigrants in the hinterlands, in Belzberg's case Vancouver. Both had worked their way up from the bottom. Both were philanthropists. That was about it for similarities. Belzberg had a cutthroat reputation. He was not a retailer or engaged in any other pursuit beneficial to society. His stock in trade was squeezing money out of companies by buying up their stock and threatening to take them over, a tactic known as "greenmail" that was widely despised. "I would rather die than be in the same boardroom with Sam Belzberg," remarked Harry A. Jacobs Jr., CEO of an investment bank targeted by Belzberg. "You don't like me because I'm Jewish," said Belzberg. "That's not true. I just don't like you," Jacobs responded.

In the wake of the Belzbergs' latest greenmail gambit, in which they extracted $134 million to drop a 1986 bid for Ashland Oil, the SEC alleged that they skirted SEC rules to avoid disclosing a stake in Ashland. The Belzbergs denied wrongdoing, but maybe they were trying the same tactic and already owned a lot of Crazy Eddie stock? Sammy did not go into this with even the slightest respect for Sam Belzberg. He would have no compunction whatsoever about cheating people he viewed as richer, more successful versions of the Antars.

"Meet with the Belzbergs," Eddie instructed. "See what's on their minds." Sammy's orders were to be a "sponge," to listen and say nothing of substance. Maybe these were guys they could deal with? Sammy's research suggested that these Canadians the world regarded as reptilian might work out just fine for Crazy Eddie. "After discussions with Eddie and the people at Bear Stearns, we believed we could make a deal with the Belzbergs, we could work things out. It might be appropriate for us." Sure, Sam Belzberg was a greenmailer. So what? They weren't planning a testimonial dinner for him.

Sammy and Eddie were worried the Belzbergs would find out about the inventory fraud right away and blow the whistle. They made inquiries into the family's methods and were pleasantly surprised by what they heard: the Canadians were unlikely to uncover the fraud if they kept the Antars at the helm. They decided to try to get them to back a management bid. But they would have to move fast. The company's financial health was deteriorating, as was consumer electronics in general. Sammy recalled being "scared somebody would buy the company out from under us." One bid might lead to others. They had no control over who might make an offer, and they couldn't necessarily stave off takeover efforts they didn't want. There could even be a war between multiple bidders, each of whom would want to dismantle the company and throw them on the street.

After all, they were a great company! Hadn't Ed Colloton been making that point repeatedly (before Sammy fired him)? Hadn't Crazy Eddie become a cultural icon? In January, when the queries started to arrive, they thought it was possible that somebody would come after them. By May 1987 it seemed more like a probability.

There were meetings. "Me and the Belzbergs, Eddie and the Belzbergs. The Belzbergs and Bear Stearns. Eddie and Bear Stearns. Me and Bear Stearns and Eddie and me with Bear Stearns." Sammy had expected Sam Belzberg to be a cold fish. He was surprised to find that he liked him. Belzberg had an earthy sense of humor and was the Canadian version of a street guy. In their meetings with the Belzbergs, Sammy and Eddie hinted that they had been deliberately understating earnings to depress the stock price so they could take it over themselves. "I said we were being 'conservative.' Sam Belzberg knew what I meant," said Sammy.

The con worked. The Belzbergs were hooked. They were prepared to join Eddie in a deal to take over the company. They were not interested in managing Crazy Eddie. That was what they said, which didn't mean anything. The Antars were certain that they would actually do it. They would be left alone, and senior management, including Sammy, would be divvying up 10 to 20 percent of the company for their trouble. Since the size of the buyout might have been as high as $250 million, that was to be a nice wad of cash.

On May 20, 1987, Crazy Eddie's new flacks at Kekst & Co. announced the news in a press release. It was one paragraph in length and crafted so as to make it seem as if the buyout proposal had dropped out of nowhere on an unsuspecting company. The board of directors announced that "it has appointed a Committee consisting of its outside directors to consider and evaluate the offer received earlier today from its Chairman, Eddie Antar, and First City Capital Corp. [the Belzbergs] to acquire all of the Company's outstanding stock at a price of $7.00 a share." The committee would now engage in a ritualistic hiring of "investment bankers and other advisors" to determine if this was a good deal for the shareholders.

The resulting press coverage was harsh. The media, which had served as Eddie's eager publicists only a few months earlier, was now suggesting that Eddie was up to no good. In the *New York Times*, veteran retailing reporter Isadore Barmash noted that Eddie's sudden resurfacing "raised many questions." An analyst quoted in the *Wall Street Journal* said that investors "question Eddie's integrity in this thing." Ed Colloton was sorely needed at a time like this, but it's not clear he would have done much good. How could he have possibly explained that, as Barmash pointed out, Eddie was reported seriously ill after quitting as CEO yet "appeared at a Crazy Eddie board meeting yesterday morning and informed the company's directors of the offer"?

Even worse than the media pokes was the favorable reaction of the stock market. Crazy Eddie shares rose sharply on the news and traded higher than the $7 offered by Eddie. That was the market's way of saying that there would be more buyout offers. Eddie didn't want more buyout offers. He wanted the Belzbergs, not some unknown quantity. Now the Antars were not merely in play, as they had been since the beginning of the year. They were a bona fide takeover target. And cheapskates. The seven-buck offer was widely derided, "opportunism at the expense of shareholders."

Since this was obviously an effort to steal a jewel of a company, a competing bid was soon in coming. On June 1, 1987, a Texas businessman named Elias Zinn announced his offer. He was pudgy, thirty-two years old, and little known outside of his home state. This was his opportunity to get into the big leagues of retailing, which he executed by offering a buck more than Eddie. The interest of this potential adversary was as welcome to the Antars as a baseball bat to the skull, but what else did they expect? Eddie had put his company on the market. It was like opening a store and expecting only your friends to come through the entrance. And Zinn was no friend.

■ ■ ■

Elias Zinn was young enough to be Sam Belzberg's son and Milton Petrie's grandson, but his background had curious points of similarity to the other two suitors as well as to Eddie. He came from a Jewish family out west and started out young in retailing. He dropped out of the University of Texas thirteen years earlier to operate a stereo supply store on campus, and over time it had grown into a chain of eighty Custom Hi Fi discount stereo stores in the Houston area. That went bust, and Zinn went on to start a company called Entertainment Marketing, which by 1987 was a distributor of closeout electronics, selling discontinued merchandise at a discount.

Zinn's company had gone public two years earlier and "earned accolades from Wall Street," just as Crazy Eddie had been doing not long before. Zinn held pep talks for his staff every morning in his "scroungy, makeshift offices, wedged between a tire distributor and a beauty shop in a mall beside a highway." The air-conditioning "is set too low," a visitor from *Texas Monthly* pointed out. Add the beard and the dog, and it was hard to tell the difference from Eddie. Enough had emerged publicly on Eddie by this time that the parallels were obvious: two iconoclastic, somewhat eccentric electronics discounters. Since out-of-the-ordinary CEOs were good copy, Zinn's Crazy Eddie bid got a lot of attention. "Entertainment Marketing and Crazy Eddie share some cultural affinity," the *Journal* observed shortly after he commenced his bid.

The differences between the two made the press tilt in favor of Zinn. The latter was cherubic and outgoing and happy to talk to the news media, unlike the tight-lipped Antars and their no-comment flacks at Kekst. Zinn ("call me E. Z.," he told reporters) was bombastic and quotable, churning out pithy statements like "Money heals everything." Thanks to his big mouth, the Antars immediately read in the newspapers what might have taken days of research to uncover: Zinn would not keep them on. He wanted to run the company. He was much more capable than they were, and he said so. "Mr. Zinn's obsession with hands-on management was reflected in his decision to act as chief financial officer as recently as 14 months ago," the *Wall Street Journal* reported in its second-day story on Zinn. Sammy read those words as if they were his own obituary.

Everything that came out of the Texan's mouth was a lasso around their necks. "I want to run Crazy Eddie. I think it's a gold mine," he told the *Journal*. He repeated those same words, like a mantra, in the *Texas Monthly* profile. Rubbing salt in the wounded egos of the Antars, Zinn told the *Journal* condescendingly that when Eddie was "active, he ran the best sales force in the business." But now they didn't do a good job selling. He could see that with his own two eyes. "Mr. Zinn added that when he visited three Crazy Eddie stores a few days ago, 'the salesmen were rude.'"

Perhaps Zinn was trying to tee off the Antars by attacking the very core of their identity as S-Y tradesmen. He may have been trying to psyche them out, as prizefighters do before matches. But if he thought he was Muhammad Ali in this Thrilla in Manila, Zinn didn't know that these Joe Fraziers hit below the belt, and only below the belt.

CHAPTER TWENTY

EDDIE'S AND ZINN'S COMPETING TAKEOVER BIDS SPUTTERED ALONG INTO the summer of 1987. Zinn, voluble as ever, found an apartment in New Jersey near the Crazy Eddie corporate headquarters, buying up stock while giving interviews to the press and wrangling with Eddie to release financial information. The stock price was falling because the financial results were lousy. That was intentional. Sammy and Eddie wanted them to be lousy.

They had decided to understate earnings after March 1987 to deal with the accumulated ballast of the previous quarters' frauds. It was like letting air out of a balloon so it did not pop if you stuck in a pin. Understating the earnings also might allow the Antars "to take over the company at a much, much cheaper price as these numbers got worse." The thinking was that dreary numbers might undercut financing for Zinn's bid and discourage other suitors. If the company was only worth, say, five dollars, only a fool would bid eight for it.

With the company now in a free fall, the shareholder lawsuits came in earnest. Sixteen were filed within the first few days of Eddie's buyout offer on May 20. All seized on Eddie's reckless November 1986 stock dump. Like the suits that were filed in January, they alleged Eddie sold the shares with inside information that revenues were ebbing. The new lawsuits, taking a quick stab at the circumstantial evidence, also contended that Eddie conspired to depress the share price so he could buy the company on the cheap. This procession of litigants woke up the SEC, which began an inquiry within days of the Belzberg-Eddie takeover bid.

The inquiry was aimed at the allegations in the suits, which were piddling compared to what really happened at Crazy Eddie, so it didn't bother
Eddie very much. "We didn't consider it anything. We were advised it was
nothing. They do this all the time. They ask a couple of questions and it's
over," Sammy later said. SEC inquiries are far more rudimentary than investigations. An inquiry is like a cop pulling you over for a broken tail-
light and telling you to get it fixed. An investigation is when your car is
impounded.

Meanwhile, Eddie's bankers were losing patience. In mid-June 1987,
shortly before the SEC inquiry was made public, Chemical Bank cut off a
$52 million line of credit. The impact on day-to-day operations was man-
ageable, but it was a sign of how the finance establishment was turning on
Crazy Eddie. So was an entire branch of the family. In July Ben and Ellen
Kuszer aired the Antars' sordid underside in the Benel bankruptcy proceedings, blaming Eddie for their troubles. On August 1 there was a long piece
in *Newsday*, prominently placed on page 2, that laid out the family drama in
excruciating detail, quoting extensively from the Benel litigation as well as
Debbie's lawsuit.

Eddie handled the bad press with uncharacteristic good humor. To
squeeze lemonade out of those lemons, he ordered up full-page newspaper
ads promoting "Crazy Eddie's Family Feud Blowout Blitz." His lighthearted
attitude was not shared by Manufacturers Hanover Trust, which was financing
the Belzberg-Eddie takeover. MHT bailed as a direct result of the *Newsday* piece, dooming it. Eddie's initial fears had come to fruition. Debbie's
lawsuit was a threat—but only because of his overwrought, vindictive reaction to it.

Eddie's obsession with Debbie had become sick. He moved next door to
her in Oakhurst and pointed listening devices he had acquired from an Israeli security firm at her house. They enabled him to eavesdrop on whatever
was said in her home. Sammy never discovered whether anything of value
was ever picked up by Eddie's electronic stalking of his ex-wife, which was
financed by the company.

Eddie may have been paranoid, but he was right to suspect that his family was plotting against him. During the summer of 1987, brother Mitchell

seized an opportunity for payback. His meeting with Jim Scott a few months earlier had been a flop, but now he raised the ante. Early in August, accompanied by his lawyer Marvin Gersten, Mitchell flew to Houston and met with Eddie's archenemy Elias Zinn and the would-be takeover artist's father, Julius. Mitchell "offered to help Mr. Zinn if he took over the business and suggested to him that he'd like to work at Crazy Eddie again." He added that Sam M. and disaffected in-law Ben Kuszer would be willing to pitch in by voting their shares in favor of his bid.

Mitchell's offer of help was rare good news for Zinn, who had been beaten down by Eddie's stonewalling. He had dropped out at the end of July, blaming Eddie for not sharing financial information, but he left the door open for a proxy fight, in which rival managements compete for control of a company by offering separate slates of directors to shareholders at the annual meeting. Zinn, bubbly as usual, suggested to Mitchell that he might put the disgruntled Antar sibling on his slate. That would have put Mitchell in a position to personally shaft his older brother, and must have been mighty pleasing to hear.

Word of the meeting got back to Sammy, who heard that Sam M. had met separately with Zinn. The stakes were far higher than was typical in a takeover battle. It wasn't often in one of those fights that the loser was not only ejected from the company but thrown in the clink—and that was entirely possible in this one. Sammy later recounted: "The Antar family was positioning itself with Elias Zinn because they were afraid that if the frauds were uncovered that we would blame them." The family was at war with itself—Sammy and Eddie versus Sam M. and the other brothers—and Zinn had become a pawn in their fight.

One of the secondary players in this battle was Arnie Spindler. He had started working for Crazy Eddie in 1971, got fed up with Eddie's broken promises and mercurial ways, and left for a few years. He came back after the company went public, but he was much closer to Mitchell and Allen than he was to the boss. Eddie grandly offered him a $75,000 bonus when he got married. He received the money, but Eddie had him sign a promissory note, turning the bonus into a loan. Eddie promised him a chance to manage a store in New Jersey. Nothing came of that either.

After the purge, Arnie caught the paranoia bug. Mitchell and Allen were gone, and he was now nervous as well as resentful. He felt that his position at the company was tenuous. He and Sammy had a meeting at a restaurant near the New Jersey offices. It did not go well.

Sammy later recalled: "Arnie came to me perceiving that they were trying to get rid of him. He came to me threatening, saying listen, Eddie is trying to get rid of me, take me out. Give me some severance and take me out of the company, and I'll leave the company peaceably." He was still being paid, but he didn't care. "I want out anyway," he told Sammy. "'My time is limited. They really want me out.' He wanted to work out a deal." There would be consequences if Arnie didn't get a satisfactory severance package: "He was threatening to go to the government," Sammy later testified. He viewed it as blackmail. "He threatened to spill the beans." The price of his silence was cancellation of the $75,000 loan and one year's pay as severance. Sammy and Arnie went back to Crazy Eddie's offices, and things got even uglier. Sammy was afraid of Arnie now and refused to let him back in the building. Eddie did not react well to Sammy's account of their conversation. "Fuck him," he said.

Sammy did not fire Arnie. Instead, he decided to let things cool down. He wasn't trying to be nice. "I felt that since Arnie was not a family member, if you push him too hard he might rat us out."

Things calmed down until a week or two later, when Arnie came into his office in a rage. His pay and benefits had been cut off. Sammy wasn't to blame for that, so the order had to have come from Eddie. "Spindler says 'I'm walking out,'" which he proceeded to do. Thanks to Eddie's pettiness, Arnie Spindler had made the transition from resentful, fearful current employee to dissatisfied former employee—who could, if he so desired, dish the dirt on his old employers. Sammy didn't see Arnie again until a few weeks later, toward the end of June. He was meeting Allen Antar at his house in New Jersey, "trying to make peace," and Arnie was there. "He didn't say anything to me, but he was firmly in their camp from what I could see."

The consequences of pushing out Arnie Spindler became apparent late one afternoon in August. A fax came in from the Paul, Weiss lawyer Jim Purcell. It was a copy of a letter Purcell had just received, and when Sammy read it he "shat bricks." It was from Leo F. Orenstein, an attorney with the SEC, and it was obviously the opening salvo in a formal investigation of Crazy Eddie. This time the SEC was aiming accurately. As was typical, the letter did not disclose the reason for the investigation, but the focus of the probe was clear enough. Orenstein was requesting documents relating to debit memos and inventories. Clearly someone had talked. The SEC letter concerned things that Arnie knew about. Just as significantly, it did not address things that Arnie did *not* know about, such as the Panama Pump. Arnie wasn't the only one who knew about the inventory inflating and debit memos, but the list of suspects was small.

A few weeks later, Crazy Eddie was officially notified that it was the subject of an investigation. Targets of SEC probes are courteously advised when they are put under the microscope, and the agency disclosed that it was probing not only their bloating of financial statements but possible insider trading. That last part was deeply disturbing. The SEC put a high priority on pursuing suspicious trades, and cases were sometimes referred to federal prosecutors.

Sammy and Eddie proceeded to misjudge the situation. Though they suspected Arnie had talked to the SEC, they didn't view him as a "major threat" because he would have to bring down the rest of the family if he told all he knew. Also he would have no corroboration unless one of the Antars testified, and they would have no reason to do that. Sammy viewed Arnie "as an irritant, not with fear because I didn't look at him making the SEC's case against us." Eddie agreed. What they didn't realize was that Arnie wasn't going to tell all he knew. He wasn't going to rat out the people he liked, people like Mitchell, Allen, and Sam M. Only the people he didn't like—Sammy and Eddie.

Arnie told the SEC under oath that "I told both of them [Mitchell and Allen] that I was going to the SEC and telling them everything that I knew about what we're doing to the company for the last two years. Everybody at that point was very curious as to what I had been doing to the company for two years." The reason they were curious, according to Arnie, was that they were completely in the dark. They were as innocent as baby lambs and had no idea what was going on in their own company. "I think I shocked both of them," he said of Allen and Mitchell. Likewise, he admitted to the SEC that he wrote up phony debit memos, but said that he did so under Sammy's direction and knew of no one else's involvement.

Arnie's testimony came to light months later. But even if Sammy and Eddie had known the details, it would not have affected the strategy Eddie ordered as soon as the SEC fax came in from Purcell: "Destroy everything and anything as quickly as possible."

Sammy had already been shredding incriminating documents like inventory sheets, but now the shredders at the New Jersey headquarters were really cooking. He shredded. His subordinates shredded. Eddie Gindi, Sammy's deputy, had six tractor trailers filled with warehouse documents sent to the shredder. Sammy, however, did not shred everything that was potentially incriminating. He made a point of not destroying debit memos that contained Abe Grinberg's signature and Mitchell's handwriting. He also did not shred copies he had made of bank drafts generated by the Panama Pump. He had no specific use in mind for the material he retained, but he had a sense he might need them someday.

The SEC began taking sworn testimony from Crazy Eddie staffers within weeks. Sammy recalled: "They came and I lied under oath. And I had Kathy Morin, my head of accounts payable, lie under oath." Kathy had spent her entire career at Crazy Eddie, rising from clerk to the accounts payable post, which put her at the center of the frantic frauds of early 1987. She was a follower, not a leader, an obedient subordinate who took orders from Eddie, Sammy, and Sammy's assistant Eddie Gindi. Her role in the fraud was to write up $20 million in fictitious debit memos to inflate profits. Like Dave Neiderbach she was basically honest, but was snared by loyalty to the people who paid her salary.

The SEC interrogated Kathy under oath in the Crazy Eddie offices. Sammy recalled: "They actually came on premises because they thought we were destroying documents"—which of course they were. "I told them we're not. Hey, come look and see. There's documents all over the place." All the while, "we had the shredding machines running full steam."

Elias Zinn knew only what Crazy Eddie chose to say about the SEC probes. The inquiry was disclosed in mid-June of 1987. The full-blown SEC investigation and the warranty probe were not disclosed by the company until the end of October. Zinn did notice anomalies, however. For one thing, the company hadn't held an annual meeting. That was a violation of the law in Delaware, where Crazy Eddie was incorporated. Zinn had to file a lawsuit to force Eddie to schedule the yearly conclave, and Eddie promptly gave the Texan what he wanted, slating the annual dog-and-pony show for November 6. Eddie then figured the time was ripe to unload a nice chunk of his stock. On September 15, he sold half his remaining stake—1.4 million shares—which netted him $6.1 million.

Eddie's stock dumps gave Zinn qualms about going through with a proxy fight. He told the *Wall Street Journal* that "it gives a bad feeling in your stomach when the chairman and previous bidder is selling his stock." But Zinn chose to ignore the wise counsel being offered by his intestines and remained in pursuit of this dog's breakfast of a company. After all, he was the solution to the company's problems. In one interview he likened Crazy Eddie to "a big bicycle, and a few spokes are out of order right now." All it needed was "direction," and "I'm the best day-to-day operator in the business."

Just as the latest Eddie stock sale was made public, another player emerged in the quest for Crazy Eddie—a distinguished financier, "turnaround expert," and former diplomat by the name of Victor Palmieri. On September 17, a regulatory filing disclosed that a partnership run by Palmieri was joining Zinn in his effort to take over the company. Oppenheimer & Co., which had handled Crazy Eddie's IPO three years earlier, was now involved in this effort to chuck the Antars out of the company. Right around the time Eddie was selling shares, Palmieri was buying.

In its September 17 filing, the Oppenheimer-Palmieri Fund LP disclosed that it had acquired 1.8 million shares, 5.6 percent of the company. Either the chairman and founder, dumping stock like it was radioactive, knew something Palmieri didn't know, or Palmieri knew something Eddie didn't know. The smart money wagered on Palmieri.

■ ■ ■

If Zinn was young and iconoclastic, Palmieri was staid and established, but with a career that had more than its share of detours and strange interludes.

He was fifty-six years old, the son of a prominent Italian-born engineer. He grew up in Beverly Hills, graduated from Stanford Law School with high honors, and then spent five years at a large, boring Los Angeles law firm before moving into real-estate development. Big-time development. Ski resorts. Mammoth residential communities. When Palmieri had enough money to go on his own, he pulled his first career U-turn by joining the National Advisory Commission on Civil Disorders in 1967 as deputy director. The commission famously concluded, "Our nation is moving toward two societies, one black, one white—separate and unequal," and made bold recommendations that President Johnson ignored. Palmieri went back into business until Jimmy Carter named him coordinator of refugee affairs in 1979. Then he did another career backflip.

Palmieri went from helping Cambodian boat people to rescuing corporations in distress. His specialty was turning around companies that were suffering for one reason or another. He managed to find value in the non-train subsidiaries of Penn Central when it collapsed. In 1983 he was hired by the bankruptcy trustee of Baldwin-United, a piano company that had tried to keep the wolf from its door by branching into finance and insurance. He aced all those jobs and earned big fees. The press swooned. This was a magician of big business, a man who could turn junk into treasure, setting wayward companies onto the path of success. Crazy Eddie was not doing well, but how could it be worse than a piano company that sold insurance?

The Houston discount magnate and the Los Angeles statesman–turnaround artist exuded optimism in the most tangible way possible, by buying up Crazy Eddie shares as if they were scandalously undervalued by the market. On September 25, 1987, the Palmieri-Zinn group disclosed that it had raised its stake in the company from 11.6 percent to 14.6 percent. It was by far the biggest shareholder. Zinn and Palmieri were rolling to victory like Marshal Zhukov in 1945, and now they summoned the vanquished Antars to discuss unconditional surrender. Or as the press release put it, Palmieri and Zinn met with representatives of Crazy Eddie "to discuss the possibility of avoiding the cost to Crazy Eddie shareholders of an unfriendly proxy solicitation."

Palmieri convened the meeting at his New York apartment. Eddie didn't come. Sammy was accompanied by Ike Kairey and David Panoff. During their meeting, Palmieri made a vague reference to Crazy Eddie as a "black hole," which Sammy interpreted to mean that "he knew he was buying into a fraud, but he didn't know the extent of it." That meeting did not accomplish anything. If the purpose was to persuade Eddie to capitulate, it didn't work. Neither did a second meeting that Sammy attended, held at a lawyer's offices in Manhattan. This time Eddie decided to stop by.

Palmieri was no Zinn. He didn't bluster, but he stared at his bearded adversary with determination. "This company is going to be mine," he told the assembled Antars. "I want my company."

Eddie couldn't resist.

"Mr. Palmieri, you don't know what you're getting into."

PART FOUR
"THERE WERE NO FILES"

CHAPTER TWENTY-ONE

ROBERT A. MARMON WAS NOT A MAN TO BE FOOLED. EVEN TO TRY WOULD have been deeply unwise. Crazy Eddie's newly appointed chief financial officer had an MBA from Columbia University, worked for Standard Oil in the 1960s, and served in the Army in data processing when computers were as big as Mack trucks and used spools of tape the size of hubcaps. He had been with Victor Palmieri since 1973 and had worked with him on whipping into shape some of the biggest corporate disasters of the century. Marmon's specialty was finance and computers. He knew both backward and forward. He was not easily intimidated. One of his projects was the Teamsters. One did not screw around with Bob Marmon. He was tough, cocky, maybe a little arrogant.

When Palmieri tasked him to Crazy Eddie late in October 1987, he thought it was strange that his astute and seasoned boss was taking on a company without first performing a "due diligence"—the thorough examination that Zofnass and Berman had carried out before the IPO. But that was not his call. He did as he was told, coming up with a plan to belatedly give Crazy Eddie a good going-over. The first step would be, of course, an inventory. "We learned in the military that before you accept responsibility for somebody else's assets, you better agree what you are taking responsibility for."

The Palmieri team went straight to work on November 6, right after the annual meeting at the Meadowlands Hilton, when the Zinn-Palmieri group won control of the company. The outcome of the proxy battle became a foregone conclusion on October 19—coincidentally the day of the Black

Monday stock market crash—when Eddie Antar announced he was not contesting the takeover. Every possible effort to thwart the Zinn-Palmieri threat had already been explored, including putting Crazy Eddie into bankruptcy, which Sammy mulled in October and then abandoned.

Eddie's cozy board of cronies and relatives was replaced at the annual meeting with fresh faces from the heartland. The stewards of Crazy Eddie's fate could not have been more responsible, more independent, more trustworthy, or more colorless. The new board members included a former CEO of Halliburton and a vice chairman of Con Edison. There were former senior executives of Dresser Industries and W. R. Grace. Palmieri was named chairman. Except for Zinn, the new CEO, not a single one had ever worked in retail, and neither had Marmon.

November 6 was a Friday, but no one was leaving for an early weekend. The new board met immediately after the annual meeting, right there at the Meadowlands Hilton. All former top executives were fired, and the inventory was to be conducted forthwith. All forty-two stores would be closed on Monday for that purpose. The plan was to send CPAs to every one "to observe and validate the count." It was expensive and not standard procedure, but he felt more comfortable doing it that way.

After the board meeting, Marmon went immediately to the Crazy Eddie headquarters in Edison. Just outside the CFO's office he encountered Sammy, who had just been fired but had known since October 19 that he was a goner. Marmon recalled that he "took me into an office just outside of his office. He put his arm around me and he said that the creditors will only get 50 cents in a bankruptcy, so blank them." (In recounting the conversation, Marmon tastefully omitted an obscenity.) Marmon's encounter with his predecessor left him "speechless. I really didn't know what to say."

Marmon went into Sammy's office, expecting to find mounds of paperwork: "Files that would contain information about the company. Cash flow. Budgets. Plans. Status of SEC matters. Status of cash and credit with banks and status of relationship with vendors and computer runs and analysis of where the company is and what the plans were. What are you going to do tomorrow morning?" Instead, he "found nothing. There were no files." There were plenty of file cabinets containing green hanging folders, but they were empty. Not only were the folders gone, but so were the tabs that showed what was in the folders. The desk was bare except for a single file envelope. It contained the employment contract of Sam E. Antar.

The company-wide inventory commenced as scheduled on Monday. Everything went according to plan. The contents of all warehouses and stockrooms were laboriously counted by hand. It took considerable time and effort, but the work was satisfactorily completed under the steady gaze of independent auditors and the resulting numbers fed into a computer. Six days later, on November 15, the computer spat out the total value of all merchandise held in Crazy Eddie's stores and warehouses: $75 million.

Impossible. There had to have been a mistake. Crazy Eddie recorded total inventory at *$126.7 million* on August 30, when the company filed its last quarterly report before the takeover. Marmon was expecting the new inventory numbers would be about $118 million–$120 million. He went to the original inventory sheets. He double-checked and triple-checked. He and his people spent three days going through the paperwork, and they still came up with the same number, which meant that there was a $45 million inventory shortfall.

In the weeks that followed, they tore through the data and found numerous discrepancies, bringing the inventory deficiency to $65 million. Then Marmon and his people dug further. They found more and more numbers that did not jibe with what they had expected. Despite the work Sammy and Eddie had done to ease the air out of the fraud balloon, it now popped like an H-bomb.

After uncovering the initial $45 million gap, Marmon had no choice but to issue a press release announcing the dispiriting news. Zinn was quoted in the newspaper coverage as saying that he was "surprised" and "shocked" by the inventory shortfall and that "we have no indication now what caused this." He did not raise the possibility of chicanery, at least not publicly. Analysts and experts quoted in the press suggested "poor management, inaccurate bookkeeping or theft of merchandise." The word "fraud" had not yet crept into the public's perception of Crazy Eddie.

■ ■ ■

Sammy was expecting an inventory shortfall, since he and Eddie had created it with the help of their colleagues. But $45 million? He was certain that the Antars hadn't swollen the company's inventory by more than about *$28 million*, tops. It might have been just $22 million, and in subsequent years he never wavered from that calculation. He had no idea how Palmieri's people came up with that bigger number. He speculated that new management might have been creating a "rainy day fund" that could be used in the future to offset bad results. When the updated $65 million number was announced a few weeks later, his mystification grew, but he no longer cared. He was out of a job for the first time since he was twelve.

Still, Sammy had a job to do—for Eddie. His cousin expected him to be his eyes and ears within the new regime at Crazy Eddie. Sammy was to use the court system for that purpose. Before the Zinn-Palmieri team took over, Sammy and four other top people had signed generous employment contracts. New management tore them up. No problem. In fact, it was expected. Sammy and the others sued. They did so not to win a courtroom victory, but to use pretrial discovery to monitor the investigators sorting through the mess at Crazy Eddie.

New management commenced litigation of its own, joining shareholders in suing the old regime. Sammy was sued by Lillian Rosen over her firing, and he and Eddie tried without success to criminally prosecute her for the unauthorized compensation. Eddie's divorce litigation was heating up as well. Subpoenas were flying in every direction, mostly theirs. The warranty fraud probe, the SEC investigation—the list went on and on. All had to be thwarted. Clearly, the battling, feuding Antars needed to stop their squabbling and work together to fend off the onslaught of investigations, lawsuits, and, quite possibly, criminal prosecutions.

Sammy's affable, quiet father took the lead. A few weeks after the takeover, Eddy brought Eddie and Sam M. together for a peace meeting at Tera's house on Ocean Parkway. The revered family matriarch had been a widow since Murad died in 1977. She was increasingly frail, but her house was still the center of the family, still the site of gatherings on Jewish holidays. It was neutral territory, and Eddy expected that everyone would be on their best behavior out of respect for Tera, the last of the Aleppo generation of Antars.

Sammy and his father both showed up. "My father said, 'I want to make peace between the sons,'" Sammy recalled. Allen and Mitchell weren't there, but their presence wasn't necessary. Sam M. would be speaking for their faction of the family.

There were few preliminaries before the acrimony began. Sam M. was not in a mood for reconciliation. His attitude was demeaning and antagonistic. He was still bitter at how he had been treated by Eddie, and he would not let it go. In response to his barbs, Eddie said to Sam M., "I'm your son." Sammy recalled that his uncle "was very sarcastic. He said in front of my grandmother, 'You're the load I should never have dropped.' I never saw Eddie ever turn white in his life as he did then. Sam M. said, 'Maybe I made you with a finger.' My grandmother heard that, and she went away crying." Tera passed a few days later, on December 1, 1987. Eddy blamed Sam M. for their mother's death, breaking into tears when recalling it a few years later.

Now the hatred between the Antars was worse than ever. Sammy believes that what happened next was instigated by Sam M.: a few days after Tera's death, Mitchell's attorney Marvin Gersten talked to investigators retained by Palmieri and Zinn, who had commenced an internal probe of the Antars' management of Crazy Eddie. The lawyer provided a mix of fact and fantasy to Akin Gump, the prominent Houston law firm conducting the probe along with the accounting firm Touche Ross. Gersten blamed Sammy and Eddie for the inventory fraud while not mentioning other members of the family. He also falsely accused Eddie of being a cocaine addict, and shared rumors of Sammy bribing a partner of the auditing firm. "He was making wild accusations," Sammy recalled. "The accountants were incompetent, but we never paid them off."

The SEC had two whistleblowers now. In addition to the much-reneged-upon Arnie Spindler, there was Abe Grinberg, who had performed the valuable service of bringing Zazy to the Antars. Both were viewed by the agency as well informed and credible. In Spindler's first meeting with the SEC he had not even come with an attorney. That was a point in his favor. Spindler and Grinberg were the agency's tour guides into the morass at Crazy Eddie, in which the perpetrators were Eddie Antar, his chief accomplice

Sam E. Antar, and pretty much nobody else of any consequence. Certainly not Mitchell, Allen, and Sam M.

"At the time, even though they may have had their doubts, they thought it was basically Eddie and me. They threw out the other factions of the family because they were legitimate," Sammy recalled. The SEC's stance was not unreasonable, since Sammy's fingerprints were all over the fraud. He and Eddie Gindi were the only trained accountants in the family. Asked by an SEC lawyer at a November 1987 deposition if he "had any reason to believe that his [Eddie's] brothers were involved" in the early 1986 inventory inflation, Spindler replied, "I have no knowledge of their involvement in any of this stuff." He made a point of implicating Sammy, saying that Eddie's cousin "directly invited" him to participate in boosting the store inventory counts in early 1987.

With Spindler and Grinberg as their principal truth-tellers, the SEC began to gather evidence by issuing subpoenas and taking testimony. Sammy testified for five straight days in Washington in May 1988. His strategy was simple: he lied about everything. "I basically said, 'I'll tell you the truth, it didn't happen. There was no fraud at Crazy Eddie. If this happened, it was a mistake. If that happened, it was poor controls. It was poor communications'" or, perhaps, wrongdoing by new management. Everyone lied—if they testified. Eddie never did. He didn't have to, since he successfully ducked the SEC's process servers.

The SEC not only had Spindler and Grinberg, ostensibly honest and well-informed whistleblowers, but also had something just as important pushing the probe forward—the media. Nothing greased the sometimes atrophied wheels of the SEC as much as news coverage. "Filings by Crazy Eddie Suggest Founder Led Scheme to Inflate Company's Value" was the headline of a *Wall Street Journal* article on May 31, 1988. Two weeks later, *Barron's* weighed in with a long, scathing article by the acerbic Joe Queenan. The piece was illustrated in the usual fashion with the ubiquitous Jerry Carroll, only this time he was up to his neck in water. The former wunderkind Zinn was portrayed as a hapless rube.

Eddie wasn't around to discuss the vagaries of press coverage. He wasn't around for anything. After the horrible meeting at Tera's house in November

1987, Eddie pretty much vanished. Sammy saw little of his cousin until May 1988, when he reappeared before evaporating again. The two were in touch only when it benefited Eddie to do so; otherwise Sammy had no way of reaching him. On the rare occasions they talked on the phone, he never said where he was.

Whenever they did meet, always at Eddie's behest, Sammy's cousin took extreme precautions because he was afraid of being followed. Debbie II's brother would call him from a pay phone at three or four in the morning. He would pick up Sammy and drive him to Manhattan to meet Eddie. It could be anywhere. They'd meet under the FDR Drive, in Greenwich Village, on Park Avenue at Fiftieth Street. The topics of conversation were always the same. They'd talk about how to coordinate testimony and how to get Sammy's former subordinates to lie. They'd chew over what "the government had on us and didn't have on us."

It would have been logical and reasonable for Eddie to go out of his way to keep Sammy on his side by sparing him undue financial hardship, but Eddie was not a logical and reasonable person. Even though Sammy was doing as asked and using the employment contract litigation to gather information for Eddie, his cousin wouldn't pay any portion of his lawyer bills. All he was willing to do was to loan $175,000 to Sammy and the four other plaintiffs, to be split five ways. He even had them sign a promissory note. Sammy's one-fifth share of the loan was hardly any help at all. Meanwhile, Eddie kept him off-balance by talking about moving his money overseas and acquiring phony passports.

While he wouldn't help with Sammy's legal fees, Eddie was generous with free advice. He repeatedly told his cousin to lie to their lawyers, claiming that if he told the truth they would not fight hard for him. "So I would go to his lawyers and act like nothing happened. We didn't do anything wrong."

Crazy Eddie's fame now was working against the Antars. Its cult status fed the media coverage and gave regulators added motivation. Sammy was well aware that SEC probes had been known to blossom into criminal investigations. That didn't happen very often, but high-profile cases like Crazy Eddie had a way of beating the odds. Those famous Jerry Carroll commercials, still being aired by the new management, were screaming them right into jail. The pressure from the feds put Sammy's home life in turmoil. He vividly recalls returning from his five days of lying to the SEC in Washington, and one of his toddler sons asking, "Daddy, when are you coming home?" He said everything was fine, but it wasn't. "I was beginning to feel at the time that I wasn't going to be a father to my sons. That I would be away for a long time."

Eddie's absence nagged at him. He felt unmoored. Sammy was not only out of a job but had also lost the mentor and friend he had known all his life. His cousin's tightfistedness depressed him, as it did that Eddie did not trust him with his phone number or his whereabouts. Was he being paranoid or was he really about to vanish for good?

CHAPTER TWENTY-TWO

AS THE PRESSURE MOUNTED, SAMMY ANTAR FOUND REFUGE IN RELIGION. He started going to the synagogue twice a day, and every day he read from *Tehilim*—the Book of Psalms—in the original Hebrew. In a week he would read the whole thing. He couldn't understand it, but it made no difference—"God understands Hebrew." During one especially difficult period, his kindly uncle Al Cohen loaned him a Torah scroll for comfort. God would not forsake him. Eddie already had.

Just a year and a half before he had occupied a lucrative position, easily providing for his family. He was prosperous and successful, running the financial affairs of a growing retail chain. Now he was unemployed and under investigation. He was turning thirty-two in February 1989, and he had a wife and three young sons, the oldest not yet seven. What did he have to show for all his hard work? He was named in twenty lawsuits by shareholders. He was being sued by Eddie's ex-mother-in-law and former management. He was under investigation by the SEC. The US Attorney's Office in Newark was also picking through the shattered remnants of the company. As a result of the inventory shortfall uncovered by Marmon, the FBI's narrow warranty probe had expanded into an examination of the entire Crazy Eddie morass. The SEC's whistleblowers, Spindler and Grinberg, were now guiding federal prosecutors as well.

All the litigating and investigating meant Sammy's lawyer bills were climbing toward $400,000. His highest compensation at Crazy Eddie had been $237,500, but he didn't earn it for very long and his living expenses were high. He had no money stashed away in Israel, as he knew Eddie did.

Their interests had diverged, and now they were widening. Debts were the wedge. Sammy owed $100,000 in credit card bills alone. That put him in the humiliating position of having to ask Robin's father for money.

Sammy spoke with Eddie rarely now. Whenever they talked, he pressed Eddie for money. The responses were always the same, always promises and more promises. Excuses and more excuses. Eddie's lawyer said he couldn't help. He wasn't able to come up with the cash. Stalling and more stalling. Eddie was becoming increasingly hostile. He never showed a shred of sympathy for what Sammy was going through, even though he knew damn well that his cousin didn't have a fraction of his wealth.

"Sometimes he would threaten me and say, 'Sammy, if you don't listen to me and do exactly what I say, I'm outta here, and you'll be left holding the bag alone.' He'd say, 'I don't need this shit. My family hates me anyway. I'm outta here.'" He took no responsibility for anything. "I remember in one conversation I said, 'Eddie, I did this for you.' He said, 'No, you did it for yourself.'" Sammy had become just another relative asking for money, and Eddie had only one way of dealing with that.

In February or early March 1989, they had a phone conversation that was still ringing through Sammy's ears decades later. "I asked him about the money, and he says, 'What are you complaining about?' Didn't I do this for you, didn't I do that for you? 'I made you. Anything you became came from me. I did everything for you. You're nothing but a piece of shit. You're on your own.'" Then Eddie slammed down the phone. "At that point I never felt more betrayed in my entire life."

It was almost as if Eddie was replaying his blowups with Debbie. The same rage-induced spasms of honesty and even the same foul language. There was something else that Sammy shared with Debbie: The same reaction. The same feeling of despair. The same desire to strike back.

The following day Sammy went to see his father, who lived a couple of blocks away. Eddy had been involved in the skimming and was part of Eddie's inner circle, so he had exposure in both the SEC investigation and the criminal probe. Anything Sammy might do to protect himself would impact directly on Eddy, who had suffered a heart attack in 1978 and was turning sixty-four that year. Sammy expressed concern that his father would lose his house and go to prison. Eddy replied, "Don't worry about anything having to do with me. Take care of yourself."

Sammy proceeded to do just that. "I figured I was hanging anyway. The only way to hang less than the others was to hang them all." He would cut a deal with prosecutors.

After carefully weighing which lawyer he was prepared to trust, he set up a meeting with Michael Nolan, who represented him in the suit by Eddie's former mother-in-law. Sammy spent five or six hours in Nolan's office, telling him the whole story of Crazy Eddie, the true one. Nolan pointed out that Sammy shouldn't go to the feds with Bruce Kaplan, who had represented him when he was lying to the SEC. But Nolan couldn't represent him because his firm represented Sony in some legal squabble with Crazy Eddie.

Sammy had to act quickly. Just a couple of days earlier, Nolan had stopped by the US Attorney in Newark and saw his old friend Dan Gibbons, who was in charge of the Crazy Eddie case. Gibbons seemed well along in his work. His desk was covered with documents related to Crazy Eddie. "Gibbons indicated that I'm in a lot of shitty-ass trouble and that I'm going to jail for ten or fifteen years. 'He's guilty. We have a big case against him.'" Though it might have been posturing, Sammy was alarmed. Nolan recommended that Sammy see an experienced criminal defense lawyer named Anthony Mautone.

Nolan walked to his office window. "You see this window over here?" He pointed to it. "You're going to have to trust Mautone that if he tells you to jump out this window here on the fifth floor, and he's going to catch you on the ground—he's going to catch you." No more lies. Now, for the very first time, Sammy would have to put his life in the hands of people outside of his family.

Sammy went to see Mautone a day or two later. His office was not impressive. It was in a converted private home in East Orange, New Jersey. Mautone was a towering, beefy man in his midforties with a confident, no-nonsense air. He was a former prosecutor in Newark and was chief of the homicide squad for six years during the 1970s crime wave. He'd been in private practice for eight years, mainly civil litigation but also handling serious criminal cases, like the one involving a young man named Kalman Pentek Jr. In 1981 Pentek shot to death a youth who was terrorizing his family, stealing his car and setting their house on fire. It was a tough case; Pentek had taken the law into his own hands. Mautone put Pentek on the stand, which was always a gamble, but in the end it paid off. Pentek was acquitted. Totally cleared—not even a gun charge.

Sammy saw clippings about the Pentek case on the wall as he was ushered into Mautone's office. Yes, this is the lawyer he wanted. Would Mautone want him? Sammy brought him up to speed, explaining why he couldn't be represented by Bruce Kaplan. He had lied to Kaplan, and Kaplan relayed those lies to the SEC. He needed a new lawyer, one who could credibly represent him now that he was committed to telling the truth.

"Let me tell you something now, Sam," Mautone said, rising from his desk and walking over to where Sammy was sitting, towering over him, pointing in his face. He was genuinely teed off. "You bullshit me like you bullshitted Bruce Kaplan, I'll fucking slam you out of this office on your ass."

Sammy spent the rest of the day in Mautone's office, giving him all the details of the Crazy Eddie scams, leaving out nothing. Mautone took the case. He called Gibbons, and they set up a meeting in Mautone's office for March 8, 1989.

Sammy was filled with optimism and hope as he drove to West Orange. "I got this great lawyer now. I think I got it made, right? I'm going to be the hero now, right? I'm going to walk away with immunity." Sure he had lied in the past, but now he was going to tell the truth. Gibbons would see that, and now everything would go well. This terrible chapter in his life would end. The lawsuits would end. The threat of prison would no longer be dangling over his head.

Dan Gibbons was already there, as were two agents from the FBI and one from the Postal Inspection Service. For two or three hours, Mautone and Sammy laid out the case, the true story of Crazy Eddie just as it really happened—all of the crimes, who had committed them, and who was at fault. Sammy was portrayed as the "nerdy cousin they needed to help make all these people fit together and how to do it." It was all off the record, part of a ritual called a "proffer session," informally known as "queen for a day."

Potential cooperators lay out all the facts in the hope that they will be able to get a deal from prosecutors. Gibbons sat impassively. When he finally spoke, he made it clear that he didn't believe a word Mautone and Sammy had said. The Panama Pump? Fiction. The pre-IPO reduction in skimming to manipulate earnings? Didn't happen. Gibbons already had the true story from witnesses who hadn't mentioned any of that stuff. They had provided him with hard facts, not the fairy tales Sammy was trying to feed him.

"Gibbons says, 'My witnesses don't lie. I have a case with or without you. I don't need you.'" Then he turned to Mautone: "I want from your client three five-year counts, and he's going to jail for five to seven years."

"Dan, you have the case all wrong," Mautone protested. Gibbons shook his head. The meeting ended.

Sammy left Mautone's office in a daze. He had parked his car—where? It had to be somewhere. Sammy had trouble remembering. "At that point, I was ready to commit suicide." He was in no shape to drive back. He called a relative of Robin's, who sent over a guy who drove Sammy back to Brooklyn. He went home and cried.

Sitting at home, feeling depression wash over him, Sammy remembered something. He fished a business card out of the pocket of his suit jacket. As he left the meeting, one of the FBI agents had come over to him. He was young and tall, dressed in a sharply tailored suit, looking more like a business executive than a fed. "When you have a chance," the agent had said softy, pressing the card in his hand. Sammy put it back in his pocket. He was in no state to call anybody or do anything. He was being set up by Gibbons's star witnesses, and he knew who they were—Spindler and Grinberg. They knew enough to entice the SEC and prosecutors. But they knew nothing about the skimming, nothing about how money was funneled to the company from overseas, through Panama, to boost comp-store sales. They were protecting Sam M., Mitchell, and Allen.

A week or two later, Mautone scheduled another meeting with Gibbons, this time at the US Attorney in downtown Newark. Again he tried to make the case for Sammy as a prosecution witness. Again Gibbons was adamant. Mautone, furious, walked out. Sammy was startled. His lawyer walked out of a meeting?

Mautone was putting on an act, trying to startle Gibbons, but Sammy didn't appreciate it at the time. He started having doubts about his hot new lawyer. He went to see his father-in-law, who went down to see Gibbons. Why had he spoken to Sammy this way? Gibbons was imperious and rude, just as he had been during his meetings with Sammy. He reduced the old man to tears. Mautone was angry that Mr. Betesh had seen Gibbons, as it was not appropriate for third parties to do that kind of thing, but what he suggested next had nothing to do with that.

Mautone instructed Sammy to "call this guy and plead your case with him" and gave him a business card. The name sounded familiar. Then he remembered the tall, soft-spoken FBI agent.

CHAPTER TWENTY-THREE

SOMETHING MORE CAPRICIOUS THAN FATE—THE FICKLE FINGER OF THE federal bureaucracy—brought Crazy Eddie to an overworked FBI agent in his midthirties named Paul Hayes.

The warranty fraud probe had been creaking along for nine months before the inventory shortfall was uncovered by new management. Now it was obvious that stealing from manufacturers was just a curtain-raiser. The main event was complex, sprawling, and greatly unappetizing. It was too big, too much of a conundrum for the tiny FBI satellite office in Hackensack, even if the agent handling the case had accounting training, and he did not. So it was assigned to Newark, where a small but experienced squad handled white-collar crime, including corporate fraud, the most difficult kind to crack. "This case is going to be a real mess," a veteran agent grumbled after the case landed on his lap. Since the agent had seniority, in fact the power to assign cases, he tossed the case to Hayes.

It was not a bad move. Corporate crime was a Paul Hayes specialty. When he was assigned to Crazy Eddie he already had a real bear of a case on his hands. Hayes was working undercover in an elaborate sting operation involving stolen pharmaceutical company trade secrets, playing a "business broker from Atlanta." That assignment was as easy as swimming in quicksand. At one point his cover was almost blown due to an FBI clerical error. Wading through the detritus left by the Antars was going to be hideously time-consuming. But FBI resources were not unlimited, especially when it came to white-collar calamities, so Crazy Eddie was shifted over to Hayes in February 1988, while he was still immersed in his undercover role.

Just as Raoul and Myrna Felder were the divorce lawyers from hell for Eddie, much the same could have been said for Hayes, though his plainspoken, ordinary-guy demeanor was the polar opposite of the Felders' publicity-seeking flamboyance. He was one of the unheralded workhorses of the FBI, patiently unwinding snarled and mangled white-collar crimes for impatient, equally overworked federal prosecutors. In addition to possessing the steely nerves required for undercover assignments, he was noted for his facility at interrogating, vetting, and winning over cooperating witnesses. That was a delicate art requiring diplomacy and finesse, as well as deep knowledge of the crimes involved.

Hayes had movie G-man good looks and was physically imposing, at six-foot-two and a muscular two hundred pounds. He rode motorcycles and overhauled auto engines in his spare time. He first started working on cars when he was twelve and fished an outboard motor out of the bottom of a lake. Using his father's tools and no manual, he figured out how to get it running. An old car's bum engine or creaky suspension system was very much like a fraud—it might look hopeless at first glance, but there was always some way of making sense of it, and there was never a manual.

There wasn't much crime in Hayes's hometown of Whitesboro, a hamlet of forty-eight hundred souls in New York's Mohawk Valley. The same could not be said for its neighbor to the east. Utica was a crime-ridden stinkhole, known as the "Sin City of the East" due to its rampant vice and corruption, with a small but violent Mafia crew and unsolved murders that included the slaying of a crusading prosecutor in 1960. Hayes found himself in the belly of that small-city ogre after graduating from Utica College with a degree in accounting and financial management. He found employment in downtown Utica at Oneida National Bank and Trust as a management trainee. As a junior banker he displayed insight into human nature and a knack for numbers, which served him well because, for some reason, he found himself handling headaches. There were many. The Mohawk Valley had seen better days, and its banks had to cope with the detritus of industrial decay.

Hayes was eventually put in charge of overseeing delinquencies in the consumer loan portfolio, a kind of Migraine Central for the bank's forty-two branches. None throbbed more acutely than the one that faced him when he came back from vacation one day. While he was away, the FBI had learned that one of the branches had been defrauded by a loansharking and gambling ring with the connivance of the branch manager. It seemed that Sin City had intruded on one of the outlying areas where organized crime was rarely seen. His job was to wade through the mess and clean it up, as well as comply with document requests from the feds. By the time the red ink dried, it was found that $750,000 had been siphoned off, thirteen people were arrested, and, in the best traditions of Utica, there were murders. Three bodies dropped into ravines. Hayes's performance as the bank's liaison and mess-cleaner-upper impressed the local FBI, whose busy office was just a few doors down the street. He was encouraged to apply to the bureau, which he did. He was taken on in 1982.

As it turned out, there were overlaps in the skills that made for good bankers and federal agents. Successful bankers, especially in woebegone towns like Utica, learned to look into the souls of people. The customer had fallen behind on his loan payments. Was he a good person down on his luck, who just needed a little time, or a deadbeat? Those character traits did always not scream out from credit agency reports. Insight into what drove people was an essential quality for FBI agents too, whether they were infiltrating a criminal enterprise, penetrating the Ku Klux Klan, or attempting to make sense of a white-collar crime. One needed to know why very nice people, and very bad people, did things they shouldn't do. One needed to tell when someone was telling the truth or lying to your face.

As a banker, Hayes had found that arrogance was a flaw, not an asset. He got the most from people when he talked to them decently, "so that they see you more as a friend instead of as an adversary." At the FBI he used the same approach in dealing with suspects. "A lot of them, everybody they've been working with, their family even—there's no one they can trust. So you have to develop trust, and make sure that if you say you're going to call at two o'clock, you call at two o'clock. You treat them with respect and they know you're an honest guy and you're treating them well, and after a while they know 'This is somebody I can trust versus most of my friends and guys in my neighborhood who I can't.'"

This approach was more Dale Carnegie than Dirty Harry. "You don't try to be tougher than them. You let them be the tough guy. Then you ask them questions. You ask them for advice. 'You know, I'm looking at this thing here . . .' Even if you know the answer." You get them to relax their guard and try to build rapport. If they wanted to be abusive, fine. They could be abusive. Hayes didn't mind. "I can tolerate a lot of abuse," he says. In his Utica days he was threatened while cleaning up after that loansharking ring. Someone visited him at his home and made gangster-movie threats about bullet holes in his suit. Hayes shrugged it off, responding nonchalantly. He didn't get mad, but he got even. He "cranked up the heat"—making extra efforts to seize cars that were left as collateral by the bad guys.

Patiently courting potential cooperators was time-consuming, and would have exhausted the patience of some agents, but Hayes found that it tended to pay off. Not long before Crazy Eddie was dropped on his lap, this technique worked exceedingly well with Gilbert C. Schulman, who presided over one of the biggest corporate disasters in New Jersey history, the 1985 collapse of the state's largest brokerage house, Bevill, Bresler & Schulman. Schulman and other top execs had made off with $15 million of the firm's money, which they used to finance their lavish lifestyles. After he was convicted and incarcerated, Schulman thought things over in the federal pen and decided to talk about a deal with the prosecutors and FBI agents who had put him in the can.

Hayes had the former mogul brought to Newark for a talk. After a while it was getting close to lunchtime. Schulman had a request. "Is it okay if my friend Paul Hayes can go down to get me a bagel and lox with cream cheese?" The other two agents in the room were amazed. Hayes had been instrumental in sending him to federal prison for eight years. This was a friend? Yes, it was. Hayes had always treated Schulman and his attorney courteously and with respect. Schulman got his bagel and lox, and Hayes got a cooperator.

Schulman went on to rat out a fellow New Jersey banker named Robert Rough. He was a member of the Board of Governors of the Federal Reserve Bank of New York, and he was leaking market-sensitive information to other bankers. He was president of a reputable bank in the rural highlands of Sussex County, New Jersey. He had wealth and status. He didn't need money. He didn't personally profit by blabbing in such an obviously improper manner. Why did he do it?

The only motive that made sense was ego fulfillment. Leaking that information solidified Rough's standing among banker friends like Schulman, who executed a $900 million trade in government securities based on information from the Fed that Rough had provided. They were all part of the establishment in northwest New Jersey. Pals help pals. Rough was the leader. "He was kind of like the king of Branchville," the village where Rough resided. There was a culture of crime in his little corner of rural New Jersey, just as there used to be among the moonshiners of the Ozarks and the slums of old New York.

Crazy Eddie had a culture of crime as well, and Sammy was an insider who could walk Hayes through the thickets, a cooperative chap who didn't have to be persuaded to talk. Indeed, Sammy was anxious to help. *Desperate* to help. He had no choice but to put his life into the hands of this laid-back FBI agent with the Upstate New York accent. Sammy took Mautone's advice and began the long process of telling Hayes everything he knew about Crazy Eddie. One part of his approach was irritating to Sammy, though he accepted it: After their second meeting with Gibbons, Mautone would not take his calls for months at a time. And when he did talk to him, he would say "Talk to Paul Hayes," and hang up. Sammy had his instructions. There was nothing else he needed to know.

Mautone's strategy was as risky as putting Kalman Pentek on the stand. Perhaps more so, because he would not be present to monitor their conversations and there was no quid pro quo, no cooperation agreement. Indeed, the prosecutor in charge of the case was downright hostile. Mautone was shooting the dice, but he felt that Hayes would deal fairly with his client and that this approach would be the best way to keep a terribly exposed corporate criminal out of prison. Sammy would be at Hayes's mercy, but his options were otherwise bleak. "Mautone said, 'Listen, you're not going to have immunity if you're talking to these guys, but they can only hang you once.'"

As part of this strategy, Sammy would hire new lawyers for the civil suits that were plaguing him. This did not go unnoticed by Eddie's lawyers. One of them called Mautone late in March 1989, after Sammy started signing the paperwork firing his former attorneys. He later told Sammy about their conversation.

"Is Sammy still in the loop, or is Sammy out of the loop?" the lawyer asked Mautone.

"Sammy's not in anybody's loop," Mautone replied.

■ ■ ■

As in a murder case, a fraud investigation begins by conducting an autopsy. The Crazy Eddie cadaver was composed of paper—stacks and stacks of it, requiring a forensic examination. Paul Hayes, still juggling a high-stakes undercover assignment, began by poring over records of stock sales by Eddie and family members. He pulled the company's financial disclosures, which were mainly corporate filings with the SEC. He read through the reams of testimony taken by SEC lawyers. This was largely useless. "My impression, kind of across the board, was that nobody knew nuthin' about nuthin'. A lot of questions were answered with vague answers and 'I don't know.' Nobody wanted to give up a family member."

Hayes was too busy undercover to spend much time on Crazy Eddie in 1988. Meanwhile, the Sam M.–Mitchell-Allen faction of the Antar family was jockeying for advantage with Dan Gibbons. Mitchell's lawyer Marvin Gersten "kept running in and talking to the prosecutors, trying to sell the fact that Mitchell didn't know anything and he was just as much a victim as everybody else." Hayes was not invited.

Gibbons is described in one account as a "harsh, unbending prosecutor," but Hayes had a less positive opinion. He was nonplussed when he learned that Gersten's and Gibbons's girlfriends (in Gibbons's case, later his wife) were close friends. He recalls that at this early stage of the investigation, there were "concerns expressed that Mitchell's going to get a pass and Mitchell might have been the key guy."*

---

* Gibbons, now retired from the US Attorney's Office, says that he and Gersten, who is now deceased, "were friendly as lawyers are friendly with each other." He says that they "weren't adversarial adversaries. We were polite with each other" and that it was "a professional relationship."

And now here was the CFO Gibbons had rejected as a liar, young, nervous, talkative, and anxious to prove his veracity. Mautone worked hard to persuade Hayes that Sammy wouldn't dare to lie as he had in the past, and related a crude anecdote he said he had told Sammy about prison rape. Hayes didn't know whether Sammy was actually "scared straight" by the rape anecdote and never asked. It didn't matter. Hayes was willing to listen. Sammy was more than willing to tell his story.

Rather than needing to coax his "extremely hyper and nervous" would-be cooperator to tell the whole story, Hayes's task was to calm him down, slow him down, and get him to differentiate between the things he knew from his personal knowledge and information he had picked up from others. His undercover assignment was slackening off, and by the summer of 1989 he was working on Crazy Eddie full-time. Much of that involved taking Sammy's calls and checking out his account.

Sammy's instructions were to call with anything he remembered or encountered. So he called. And called. And called. Over the next three years, he would call the FBI in Newark, mainly Hayes, 1,820 times—Sammy kept a count—talking to his patient interlocutor two to three times a week, daily at first. Much of the time he would simply report Eddie's whereabouts, which Hayes specifically requested at their first meeting. Even though Sammy would call at all hours, Hayes would stop what he was doing and take his call. "I didn't want him to think I was putting him off." Gibbons, however, was not impressed. The interplay between the sympathetic Hayes and the unbelieving, cold Gibbons may have seemed like a good-guy, bad-guy routine. It wasn't. Hayes had no use for that kind of game playing. He found Sammy helpful and told him so. He never once caught Sammy in a lie. "He went 180 degrees and stayed there."

At Mautone's suggestion, beginning in May 1989 Sammy kept a detailed record of his information sharing with Hayes and prosecutors. It recounted, in real time, the degree of his anxiety and the obstacles he encountered, making his case that he was the truth teller and Spindler and Grinberg were the liars. Sammy was at the mercy of a hostile US Attorney's Office that was in no hurry to cut a plea deal with him, even though he was telling Hayes everything he knew. As he was well aware, everything he said could have been used against him.

A recurrent challenge was keeping Sammy's cooperation secret. If discovered, it wouldn't have put him in physical danger but might have induced Eddie to follow his money out of the country. In the very first entry in his notes, dated May 14, 1989, Sammy recounts lamenting to Hayes that one of his former lawyers had met with the other former Crazy Eddie execs that were suing the company over their employment contracts. He heard that the lawyer "told them he couldn't represent them anymore because of a conflict of interest with SEA [Sammy] but he couldn't reveal to them what the conflict was." He told Hayes that one of the participants in the meeting "reported the problem to Eddie." Sammy also "expressed alarm that EA [Eddie] probably feels [Sammy] is going to cooperate & that EA will flee." Because of that possibility, he warned Hayes, "gov't must move fast!" He reminded Hayes that he told prosecutors only the previous week about "Eddie moving all his money out of the U.S.A. during Feb/Mar 87 with his express representation to [Sammy] that he didn't want to have his money around in case anything happens (possible gov't investigations, lawsuits etc.)."

On May 23 Sammy met again with Gibbons and went into detail on inflation of the comp-store sales. He also described the cash skimming and secret foreign bank accounts. Three days later he delivered documents to the FBI and told Hayes about the systematic insurance fraud. No sale. At a meeting with the stone-faced prosecutor in mid-July 1989 that he recounted to Hayes, Gibbons "played down my importance as a witness." Hayes "reassured me of my importance & seemed surprised." He told Sammy that he should have been at the meeting and recommended that Sammy "not worry about 'lawyer talk.'"

"I told him it's my life at stake," Sammy added.

While Sammy was wrestling with the immovable Dan Gibbons, another threat arose: the SEC's investigation. Like Gibbons, SEC lawyers had Spindler and Grinberg, and they were planning to plunge ahead with a civil action no matter what the US Attorney might or might not do. This was understandable; many criminal investigations of securities fraud fizzle out. And of course, such a headline case would have done no harm at all to the careers of the SEC officials involved. But the agency did not seem to know, or care, that Eddie was a flight risk. Their apparent eagerness to act—and reliance on Spindler and Grinberg—ramped up Sammy's anxiety.

Sammy constantly warned Hayes about Eddie imminently absconding, but as spring gave way to summer of 1989 his cousin was still around. Sammy even ran into him at the Jersey Shore house of a mutual friend, Harry Shalom, on Labor Day. Eddie, paranoid as ever, insisted that Sammy change into a bathing suit and go into the swimming pool to show that he wasn't wired. Eddie was probably aware Sammy was talking to the feds, but he didn't let on. He went out of his way to calm down his cousin. Sammy, he said, "has nothing to worry about."

Actually, he had a lot to worry about. The SEC struck two days later. Eddie and Sammy were the principal targets. The other defendants were Mitchell, Ike Kairey, Eddie Gindi, Kathy Morin, and David Panoff. All were charged with committing or abetting securities fraud and the Antars and Panoff were accused of insider trading. Kairey, Gindi, and Morin quickly settled with the SEC without admitting or denying liability, consenting to permanent injunctions against them. The case was proceeding against everyone else. Sammy told Hayes with disgust that the SEC case was riddled with omissions, making no reference to Sam M., Allen Antar, Ben Kuszer, or Zazy. Comp-store sales inflation wasn't mentioned. And although Mitchell was named, his role was minimized.

Sammy's fear and anger escalated the following day. There had been a leak to the press, obviously from the US Attorney's Office in Newark. Articles in both the *New York Times* and the *Daily News* revealed that Sammy was cooperating with the government. The *Times*, citing "people close to the grand jury," said Sammy "has been cooperating with the federal authorities." That was odd, because Sammy hadn't testified before a grand jury. The US Attorney's Office had not impaneled one in order to facilitate its cooperation with the SEC, because information obtained via that legal mechanism could not have been shared because of grand jury secrecy rules.

The *Daily News* went one step further than the *Times*, reporting that "sources familiar with the investigation" were saying that Sammy "is cooperating with the government and providing information about Eddie."

About Eddie. Eddie now had another reason to flee, and Sammy was furious that the feds were treating him simultaneously as a cooperator and a target. Gibbons, he complained to Hayes, "wants to fry me."

In the weeks to come, Sammy highlighted to Hayes all the many things that the SEC downplayed and omitted from its complaint. Since Sam M. was among the omissions, his uncle was breathing easy. Sammy learned from a family member that Eddie's father "is not sweating [the] situation." Sam M. was up to his neck in the frauds, yet SEC lawyers weren't even suing him. Why would they? Their star witnesses, Spindler and Grinberg, had both excluded Sam M. from their accounts of the frauds, and had only nice things to say about him. On October 19, 1989, Sammy mused in his notes: "I was puzzled how the SEC could elevate me so high when I walked away from large trading profits in stock . . . and in fact lost $10,000 selling all my stock while other Antar family members made over $100 million in stock sales."

■ ■ ■

While the SEC and FBI investigated Crazy Eddie's sordid past, the company's public image remained remarkably resilient despite press barbs about the Antars. There were forty-three stores as 1989 began—one opened in Hamden, Connecticut, in November 1988—and the Jerry Carroll commercials were bellowing out of TV sets from Pennsylvania to Massachusetts. When a Soviet hockey team visited Long Island, the *Washington Post* reported, "They seemed more interested in a shopping trip to Crazy Eddie than in the game itself." Wall Street analysts and portfolio managers were still supping on the Crazy Eddie Kool-Aid. Even when the chain announced at the end of March 1989 that seventeen stores were shutting down, the president of an investment company called it "a sound survival strategy that might save the company."

It wasn't and it didn't. Closing those stores did not reverse the chain's downward spiral and may have made it worse. A $50 million loss was recorded for the fiscal year ending on February 26, 1989. When the miserable results were announced, the stock traded at just 32 cents, a 98.5 percent decline from its all-time high in August 1986. On June 6, five creditors tried to force Crazy Eddie into involuntary bankruptcy in a desperate effort to extract payment. That backfired, resulting in banks cutting off the credit that was the company's financial lifeline. Crazy Eddie applied for protection under Chapter 11 of the bankruptcy code on June 20, 1989. Chapter 11 is a kind of legal lifeboat, designed to keep companies operating while they fight to stay alive, but it was too late to do any good. Eight more stores closed in August, bringing the total down to eighteen. That was where the store roster remained until the end, which was soon in coming.

Songwriter-turned-marketer Harry Spero had survived both Eddie's purge and the post-acquisition bloodletting, making him one of the few longtime top-level people at Crazy Eddie's morose corporate headquarters in 1989. Zinn certainly tried to keep the company alive, but "he had a major bogie to overcome," Harry noted. Such concerns were above his pay grade. His job was to pitch Crazy Eddie. The new owners had not tampered with marketing, staying with Jerry Carroll and his screamers, so Harry just kept on doing what he was doing when Eddie was in charge. He became friendly with Zinn, visiting him at an apartment he kept in Manhattan, and they got to know each other. "He was a Texan, spoke like a Texan, loved being in New York, loved being the head of Crazy Eddie, gregarious, friendly. I never got a bad vibe from that guy." Zinn "wanted to do the right thing. He just went into the wrong company."

Zinn quit as CEO and went back to Texas in early February 1989, replaced by a Palmieri aide. His departure was apparently amicable, and his outlook remained rosy even as he cleaned out his desk. "I believe we made tremendous progress and we are now postured toward a much better future," Zinn told the *New York Times.*

Crazy Eddie's new bosses were indeed "postured toward a better future"—somewhere else. Anywhere would have been better because the company was about to fold. Harry got the word two weeks in advance, as he and his team had to prepare the advertising ("The greatest going out of business sale ever!"). He was told not to tell anyone, though by then word of Crazy Eddie's closing would have surprised no one because bankruptcy had been in the cards most of the year. CRZY stock was ousted from the Nasdaq marketplace on September 5, one day before the SEC enforcement action.

It was now trading on the "pink sheets," a kind of skid row for stocks where the tiniest and least solvent companies were relegated.

On October 2, 1989, Crazy Eddie's blue-ribbon board pulled the plug. All the stores were ordered closed. The Chapter 11 reorganization was converted into a Chapter 7 liquidation. New management neglected to put out a timely press release, so word of Crazy Eddie's death emerged from a supplier, a small record company in Albany. Nothing was working anymore, not even the hype machine. Crazy Eddie wasn't even waiting for the Christmas season to help recoup its losses. It was bleeding so badly that the most merciful course was to put the company out of its misery.

The Edison headquarters building was stripped to the walls. Everything was put up for auction. Just before Thanksgiving, six hundred bargain hunters swarmed over the building, paying fifteen dollars for "wood-grain tables" and thirty-five dollars for "swivel armchairs." All of Crazy Eddie's worldly goods were on sale, every stapler and pencil sharpener, even file cabinets filled with papers that had missed a date with the shredder. Among the items sold off were two company cars, a Jaguar and a BMW Eddie had bought for use by his loyalists.

Jerry Carroll's last commercial went out over the airwaves in mid-November. No Blowout Blitz this time, no Christmas in August. This time, Jerry Carroll was somber: "Crazy Eddie, may he rest in peace."

CHAPTER TWENTY-FOUR

CRAZY EDDIE WAS DEAD, BUT EDDIE ANTAR WAS VERY MUCH ALIVE AND READY to abscond if given the right impetus. And impetus kept piling up throughout 1989. As the year began, Debbie was blowing the whistle on Eddie shuttling money overseas. During divorce case depositions in December 1988 and January 1989, she testified that Eddie's salary was put in Israeli bank accounts in her name, and that he took cash to Israel strapped to his body. Eddie could hardly complain. After all, getting her to testify was his lawyers' idea, not hers.

While it's not known if that revelation reached the FBI or SEC, Eddie surely knew about it. Then came the SEC suit in September 1989 and public disclosure of Sammy's cooperation that followed. Then worse.

A week after the SEC's post–Labor Day lawsuit, the lead story in *Crain's New York Business* reported that Eddie would be criminally charged "within the next two months" under the Racketeer Influenced and Corrupt Organizations Act. RICO was designed as a nuclear weapon in the war against organized crime, reserved for major criminals, and conviction could mean immense prison terms, as much as twenty years per count. By the mid-1980s it was being used to prosecute white-collar offenders as well as mob bosses. Infamous financier and "Junk Bond King" Michael Milken had just been indicted on ninety-eight federal charges, two of them RICO.

Brother Mitchell, however, didn't have much to worry about, according to *Crain's*. He "is not expected to be charged, according to sources familiar with the investigation." Sammy was another matter. He "figures prominently in the SEC complaint," unlike Mitchell, who "is not expected to be charged." There was no reason to charge Eddie's brother, not with someone far worse walking the streets. "Sources say the government could find it hard to prosecute Mitchell if it strikes a deal with the more culpable Sam E."

Sammy's blood pressure practically burst from his ears as he read the article, since he had no doubt that the "sources" were Marvin Gersten. The lawyer was trying to pull Mitchell off the prosecutors' target list by planting spin in the press. The *Wall Street Journal* picked up on the possible RICO charge in an article on October 27. The *Journal* did not continue with the Mitchell Antar Innocence Project, but reported that prosecutors had warned Eddie "that they may soon seek an indictment on racketeering and securities fraud charges." That was like giving Eddie a set of Michelin guides. Sammy complained bitterly to Hayes that "someone in government doesn't want EA [Eddie] hanging around!"

The RICO news was followed by two other developments that Sammy viewed as the last straw for Eddie. If they couldn't propel him out of the country, nothing could. One was publicized, the other not, but Eddie was acutely aware of both of them.

On January 23, 1990, US District Court judge Nicholas H. Politan gave the SEC what it wanted, agreeing that evidence was strong that Eddie had reaped $60 million by trading on inside information—knowledge that fraud was elevating the stock. Politan ordered Eddie to repatriate to the United States $52 million he had sent to Israel. The money would be placed in the custody of a trustee, so that it would be available in case he lost the SEC case and was subject to a restitution order. Ironically, Sammy was responsible for Politan's order. The SEC disclosed years later that it had been put on the money trail to Israel by Sammy's lawyer Jonathon Warner in a July 1989 proffer session. Sammy received no deal for this crucial information, but the SEC jumped on it and Politan's ruling was the result.

Sammy learned of the second development a week after it happened. On January 24, one day after Politan's ruling, New York State Supreme Court justice Barry Hurowitz gave Debbie a decisive court victory. In a sixteen-page, furiously worded decision, Hurowitz spared no adjective in ripping Eddie and Solomon to shreds. Divorce cases are sealed in New York, and the Felders for some reason decided not to leak to the tabloids that Eddie had been drawn and quartered.

The decision began on a compassionate note: "Deborah Antar and Eddie Antar were the American Dream," Hurowitz wrote. He flattered Eddie as "a financial genius; a super-businessman who can sell anything or anyone; he is the ultimate financial survivor; no one will ever best Eddie Antar financially." That was the last nice thing he had to say about any of the parties. Debbie, he wrote, was an "emotionally upset person who had, on many occasions, acted in so immature and naïve a manner as to verge on the ridiculous." From then on the judge could not have been more favorable to Debbie if her own lawyers had drafted the ruling.

Hurowitz threw out the "shockingly bizarre" separation agreement and agreed with Debbie that she had been coerced into signing it. He described that document as "a coldly calculated scheme to commit civil theft," a product of "Fraud, Duress, Overreaching and Coercion," using capital letters for dramatic effect, and excoriated Eddie for his "lies and deceit to fool Deborah Antar out of any money to which she was entitled."

Solomon had asserted his Fifth Amendment right against self-incrimination when he was called as a witness at the trial of the suit, but he gave sworn testimony in a pretrial deposition that the judge admitted into evidence. Solomon had contradicted Debbie on pretty much everything, saying, for instance, that he had come to Debbie's home with the divorce papers in January 1985 and that Eddie wasn't present. But Hurowitz found that he "had no reason to doubt [Debbie's] version of the facts and her story" and asserted that Solomon "is unworthy of belief and not a credit to the legal profession."

The judge observed that Solomon was not only an officer of Crazy Eddie but that in 1984 he had received twenty thousand shares of the company's stock and an interest-free loan of $237,500. Hurowitz agreed with Debbie that she never had a divorce lawyer when she signed the papers and that Solomon was "acting as agent and friend and for the benefit of Eddie Antar at all times." The defense had contended that Solomon had been Debbie's lawyer and entered into evidence a retainer agreement. But the judge found it to be faked. Handwriting experts had testified that the signature was not hers and that the retainer agreement was on stationery showing the office phone number preceded by an area code of 718. That created a problem for

Solomon, because the 718 area code was not created until five months *after* Debbie supposedly signed the retainer.

On and on it went, piling on the opprobrium. The separation agreement was so one-sided that "no attorney could have possibly recommended to a client in good faith" that she sign it and would not have "represented said client under all the surrounding circumstances." The decision did not specify the amount of Debbie's "equitable." That awaited further proceedings, so despite this courtroom victory, Debbie was still not getting a judgment against Eddie that she could cash in. But she was getting there.

Eddie was, of course, infuriated. Even before the decision was handed down, he was stewing over Debbie and whining to everyone in earshot about her. When Sammy ran into Eddie on Labor Day at Harry Shalom's swimming pool, his notes record, Eddie was "bragging how generous he was to Debbie #1." He claimed that he had an "off the books deal with Debbie, himself & SMA [Sam M.] relating to divorce settlement" and that he "dropped off $950K in her house in Bklyn, would send her to bank vault to tell her to take whatever she needed." Given Eddie's propensity to lie, especially when it came to his ex-wife, the chances he was telling the truth don't seem very high (though Sammy, despite his own split with Eddie, tended to believe his cousin).

Sammy feared that Hurowitz's decision guaranteed Eddie's departure from the country. He told Hayes that even if Eddie won the civil and criminal cases, "he will have to give 1/2 of [his] money to Debbie #1 which he'll NEVER do."

By now, Sammy felt as if his one-sided, no-cooperation-agreement information dump on the feds was like trying to claw his way through granite with his fingernails. It was now practically a year since he began feeding the FBI information, yet it seemed as if Gibbons's position was only hardening. On February 4, 1990, Sammy vented his frustration again to Hayes, recounting Gibbons's comments to Sammy's civil-case lawyer that were "implicitly saying I am lying." He implored Hayes "to tell me what can I do to convince [Gibbons] that I am telling the truth."*

* Gibbons says that he can't discuss his interactions with Sammy due to "Justice Department guidelines," which he feels still bind him even though he is retired from the US Attorney's

There wasn't much Hayes could suggest. Sammy was already telling all he knew. Eddie, meanwhile, devoted his energies to fighting Politan's restitution order. His lawyers claimed that if Eddie had to admit the $52 million existed it would violate his Fifth Amendment right to not incriminate himself. Politan, irritated that the Constitution had been flung in his face, ruled that Eddie could only make a Fifth Amendment claim in person. He would have to show up in court, and Politan ordered him to do so. When he didn't, the irate judge ordered his arrest for contempt of court. Eddie surrendered to the marshals on February 13 and was fingerprinted and photographed. He then was taken before Judge Alfred J. Lechner, who stayed the proceedings until February 27, when Eddie would appear before Politan on the contempt charge. Eddie walked out of the courthouse that day a free man.

Sammy called Hayes frantically, "concerned that [the] gov't did not get the judge to hold [Eddie's] passport or give an account of what he was doing or where he was." Eddie had not even been ordered to post a bond, which was astonishing since he was an obvious flight risk. Indeed, that was why Politan held him in contempt in the first place: he had millions of dollars overseas that he was refusing to return to the United States and refusing to even appear in court to discuss. Sammy urged the FBI to "keep [Eddie] under surveillance because he will flee rather than pay up."

After leaving the Newark courthouse on February 13, Eddie let it be known to the US government that he had no intention to abscond. He transmitted that message cleverly. The normally phone-averse Eddie called Harry Shalom to say that he wasn't fazed by the court proceedings and invited Harry to come to Florida with him. It's not known if that conversation was wiretapped, but Eddie may have thought it was. He certainly knew that Harry was friends with Sammy. Sure enough, Harry told Sammy about Eddie's total absence of concern, and Sammy conveyed that insight to Hayes.

The carefree, relaxed Eddie Antar did not appear in court on February 27.

That same day the US Marshals Service provided Eddie's February 13 mug shot to the media, which was published in newspapers across the

Office. He describes Sammy's assertions that Gibbons didn't believe him, and instead gave credence to Spindler and Grinberg, as "speculation as to my state of mind."

country and abroad. It depicted a balding, scowling Eddie, in front and side view, holding up an identifying plaque and standing against a ruler showing that he was five feet, six inches tall.

Eddie Antar was a fugitive.

■ ■ ■

After the stores closed and the last display case and chair were auctioned off, all that was left of Crazy Eddie were corporate records stored in "transfiles," cardboard file boxes that had drawers that pulled out rather than lids on top. They were under subpoena, and Hayes and other investigators had free rein to peruse them in the old Crazy Eddie New Jersey warehouse, now emptied of merchandise. To say that they were not kept in good order would be an understatement. Hayes's first encounter with a Crazy Eddie file box was not propitious. "I forget what it was supposed to be. Accounts payable, something like that. I open the drawer, and the contents don't match. We tried some other boxes, and it was the same. The boxes labeled 'Accounts Payable' were sales records. I said, 'What the heck is going on here?'"

There were sixty-five hundred transfiles in the warehouse, and they were all just as disorganized. Hayes went to Sammy, "and he says, 'Oh, yeah, we had a whole team shuffling all the documents, so anybody trying to come in and figure out what happened would have a nightmare going through these boxes.'" All the file boxes had been mislabeled, making it necessary for Hayes and other agents to laboriously go through every single one of them, putting the right files in the right boxes. Even that time-consuming task did not yield bank statements, which had been shredded by Sammy and his people in the final months of the Antar regime.

Once the files were sorted out, the tedious process began of matching thousands upon thousands of sales slips—old-fashioned carbon copies—to inventories. There were loading dock and shipping records too, providing clues to the people outside Crazy Eddie who had cooperated in the inventory inflation. All the while, Hayes was fielding calls from Sammy. Though Hayes's trust never wavered, it was increasingly apparent that Sammy's Hail Mary pass had not worked. Despite all the information he had given the FBI, Dan Gibbons was still unwilling to sign a cooperation agreement.

It was beginning to look completely hopeless until a day in late spring of 1990 when Sammy and Mautone met with Samuel Alito, the US Attorney for New Jersey. The future Supreme Court justice had already been confirmed by the Senate for a seat on the Third Circuit Court of Appeals, and Sammy's meeting was one of the prosecutor's last as US Attorney.

The purpose of the meeting was to make yet another effort to hammer out a cooperation agreement. Nothing was resolved, but Alito had an open mind. Though he wasn't giving the green light, Sammy was happy with the meeting. He was pleased with Alito's courteous, respectful attitude, which contrasted with the condescending contempt displayed by Gibbons in their previous meetings. Sammy was also relieved by an almost offhand, throwaway remark from Alito, that "we have this guy Weissman on the case."

How, and why, a veteran white-collar crime prosecutor named Paul Weissman replaced Dan Gibbons on the Crazy Eddie case was still a bit murky three decades later. Sammy believes Hayes was responsible, Hayes believes Mautone may have been responsible, and Gibbons maintains that nobody was responsible, that no complaint ever reached him, and that his reassignment was totally routine. According to Gibbons, it was decided to transfer him from the Crazy Eddie case late in 1989, when he was slated for a move to the civil division to handle complicated medical malpractice cases. The US Attorney's Office defends lawsuits brought against federally run medical facilities.

Whatever the reason for Gibbons's departure, there is no question that the case was stalled and that his two star witnesses were nonstarters. Weissman recalled, "The reality was that Spindler gave us almost nothing that was useful, and Grinberg had already lied to the SEC in a deposition." The result was that "we couldn't have even begun to make a case against the Antars based solely on the two of them."

With Weissman running the case, Sammy saw a welcome change in the tone of his contacts with the US Attorney's Office. Weissman was a prosecutor who would listen, who was not openly hostile. Still, it required another year of convincing—more calls to Hayes, more information, more meetings. On August 22, 1991, Mautone's risky gambit finally paid off. Twenty-nine agonizing months after the first meeting with Gibbons, Sammy reached a plea agreement with the US Attorney's Office. He would plead guilty to conspiracy to commit securities fraud and obstruction of justice. He would fully and truthfully cooperate with prosecutors and the SEC. In return, on paper, he did not get much at all.

As was standard in plea agreements, his sentence would be solely at the discretion of the court. No promises were made, except that the prosecutor would disclose the extent and value of his cooperation. Then it would be up to Politan, who would be presiding over the criminal cases. It didn't look like much to nonlawyers who couldn't read between the lines and understand what it meant—that Sammy had his deal. The length of Sammy's sentence would depend on the truthfulness, quality, and impact of his cooperation. Politan was a tough—and temperamental—judge, so nothing was guaranteed. In cooperation agreements, sentence length is never guaranteed.

Sammy's deal with the US Attorney's Office was kept under wraps, but another pact was made public five weeks later. Sammy had convinced yet another key federal official of his truthfulness—Richard Simpson, the chief SEC lawyer handling the Crazy Eddie case. Beginning in March 1991 he had started meeting with Simpson and other SEC lawyers, and gradually his cooperation had won them over. On September 25, 1991, Sammy settled the SEC's lawsuit under terms that were as favorable as he could have expected. He agreed to pay $80,000 in disgorgements and $80,000 in civil penalties, with the penalties and all but $20,000 of the disgorgements waived because Sammy couldn't afford to pay them. Sammy also began working with lawyers for plaintiffs in the civil suits, without formal agreements but with much the same outcome. Because of his cooperation, no damages were ever imposed upon him.

The lenient SEC settlement terms made it abundantly clear to the other Antars that Sammy had become a cooperator. Eddie now knew that he was going to have to face his cousin in court, if he were ever caught. Meanwhile, he engaged in some "bad boy" antics. Hayes picked up reports that Eddie had left the country but would return on a fake passport for brief visits, driving through his old haunts, never leaving the car but making sure that people saw him. It was Eddie's way of thumbing his nose at the government, his way of saying, "You are never going to catch me."

Eddie kept in touch with his lawyer Jack Arsenault via a cell phone, and he had used cloak-and-dagger precautions to set it up. Arsenault had to "get somebody to register it in their name, and then I was to supply somebody else the phone number." As with Sammy a couple of years earlier, it was a "Don't call me, I'll call you" arrangement. The phone was only for incoming calls, and only from Eddie. He would never reveal his location, but it was sometimes apparent that he was calling locally. "He'd make a comment based upon what was happening in the news, to try to indicate that he was not far away."

The FBI wasn't far away either. Hayes learned about the calls to Arsenault, and one day he went unannounced to the lawyer's office. "I said, 'Look, I hear that Eddie has been calling you periodically; you've got a special phone that he calls in on. You know, if he wants to talk to you, maybe he should be talking to us.'" Eddie's lawyer did not react well to the visit. "Arsenault tried to accuse me of trying to intimidate his staff and other types of things. All I could do was smile." Hayes didn't want Eddie to think that he was off the case, that he'd "retired or transferred to some pleasant place," that nobody would pick up on the case and he would go scot-free. "I was sending a message to Arsenault that I wasn't going anywhere."

That was certainly true, but there were no criminal charges pending against Eddie except contempt of court for not appearing before Politan in February 1990. He was not under indictment. Prosecutors were not about to charge Eddie—not until they knew where he was. And who he was.

CHAPTER TWENTY-FIVE

OF ALL THE INNOCENT PEOPLE CAUGHT UP IN THE EDDIE ANTAR SAGA, none was more pathetic than David Jacob Levi Cohen. David was born in Brazil to a wealthy family. He moved to Israel in the late 1980s, and within a few years became entangled in an international banking morass of Kafkaesque dimensions. In October 1991, David wrote an angry, impassioned "Solemn Declaration" that he sent to United Overseas Bank in Geneva, in which he described how his life savings—millions of dollars—were frozen and could not be withdrawn. All because of one incompetent banker, a stupid, little man.

The Declaration was sad, emotional, but thoroughly factual. It began by describing how David's ordeal began in December 1989. At the bar of the Dan Hotel in Tel Aviv, he fell into a conversation with a man named Alexander Stewart, "an investor specializing in real estate in the United States." Stewart lamented the declining market for properties back in the States, and David had an idea. He had inherited some precious gems from his father. Why not buy some of them? Stewart "immediately expressed keen interest."

Obviously, there was something about David that inspired confidence. Stewart was willing to buy gemstones from this total stranger on the spur of the moment. The trusting, kindly Stewart "proposed, in order to show his good faith, to wire transfer to my account 45 million US dollars immediately and before the handing over of the parcel of diamonds." Done. David gave him the diamonds. The sum was wired to David's account. Both men were happy. They looked forward to doing more deals.

Then came the misunderstanding that threatened to ruin David's life. When they first met, Stewart asked David "to do him a favor and to submit to the bank two names which he gave me" as potential clients of United Overseas Bank. David did as requested, only to find months later that a terrible mistake had been made. A bank employee, a man named Fisch, gave those two people power of attorney over David's account! Legal proceedings were pending against them, which resulted in his account being frozen.

David's Solemn Declaration concluded: "Since these accounts have been blocked I feel that I have been unduly and harshly victimized by a bizarre set of circumstances way out of my control. It took a tremendous toll on my life."

David retained a Swiss attorney and offered him $5 million if he could extricate his money from the bumblers at the bank. The lawyer wrote a strong letter pointing out that "the error and negligence on the part of both Mr. Fisch and his office are capable of causing Mr. Cohen serious harm." When the bank did nothing, David traveled to Switzerland and complained in person to the Swiss police. Again, nothing. But it can't be said that nothing was accomplished. He had given a great deal of help to the US authorities hunting Eddie Antar.

One day in 1992, an SEC Enforcement Division lawyer in Washington named Richard Wallace received a two-inch-thick file of papers from the Swiss government. Because he was about to leave for California on a business trip, he didn't have time to go through them in detail. He skimmed them, found nothing that rang a bell, and brought them to Richard Simpson on the floor below. Some of the documents concerned David Jacob Levi Cohen. A familiar birth date—December 18, 1947—was on one of the Cohen documents. Eddie's birth date.

All the pieces fitted together. Eddie had committed a blunder commonly made by fugitives: he had used his real date of birth. The two supposed total strangers who had power of attorney over the account were Eddie's second wife, Deborah Ehrlich Antar, and his mother's brother Murray Tawil. The photograph attached to David Jacob Levi Cohen's Brazilian passport showed Eddie Antar staring placidly at the camera. He had generated that persona to throw off pursuers, but it had left a trail of breadcrumbs that brought the Eddie hunters literally to his doorstep.

Eddie had been thwarted by the devil that lurked within him. He had provided the phony passport as proof of identity in his quest to sandbag the innocent bank officer, Fisch. Had he succeeded, he would have ruined Fisch's career. It was an act of pure evil.

"David Jacob Levi Cohen" was but one of several identities that Eddie created after he decided to abscond. Israel was a logical destination. The Antars had no close family in the Jewish state, but they were frequent visitors and had taken *nehkdi* there for many years. His money went first, then Eddie. In February 1987, Eddie transferred the bulk of his remaining US cash to Israel, wiring $43 million to the Bank Leumi Foreign Resident Tourist Center at 130 Ben Yehuda Street in Tel Aviv. It was no coincidence that Eddie did that after Debbie sicced the Felders on him and the frauds were losing their power to prop up the company.

A year later, Eddie made his overseas financial holdings a convoluted mess that, he hoped, only he could unravel. On February 5, 1988, he transferred $50 million from Bank Leumi in Israel to a numbered account at Bank Leumi in Zurich that he had opened a day earlier. Later that month he transferred $40 million of that money to a bank in Lichtenstein. Then he transferred the remaining $9.8 million to Credit Suisse in Zurich, depositing the money into an account owned by an entity called Conductive Corporation, which was incorporated in Monrovia, Liberia. Then he closed the Bank Leumi Zurich account.

By shuffling around the money, Eddie was trying to conceal its origins while maintaining access to the cash. He had control over the Conductive Corporation account, which was set up in Liberia because of that country's low rate of taxation and loose rules on incorporating businesses. By 1992 Eddie would open at least twenty accounts, "nearly all of them either numbered or in the name of some Liberian or [Gibraltar] corporation."

With his money safely scattered across multiple continents, Eddie made his move. Under Israel's Law of Return, any Jewish person can immigrate and become a citizen. Criminals have exploited this policy over the years, in the hope that Israel would be a refuge not from persecution but from prosecution. Meyer Lansky famously tried to do so in 1970. Like Lansky, Eddie made his move when he was not under indictment but feared danger down the road. Unlike Lansky, Eddie moved to Israel quietly, and his acquisition of Israeli citizenship received no public attention. Lansky was eventually thrown out of Israel, but Eddie was hoping for a better outcome.

Eddie flew to Israel on June 15, 1988, and eleven days later registered as an immigrant, all legally and aboveboard. Debbie II joined him on July 7, 1988, also filing papers to become an immigrant. Five days after immigrating, Eddie took a step to wall off the past. Many immigrants to Israel cast off the names of the Diaspora and substitute Hebrew names. But Eddie did not Hebraize his name; he Scotlandized it. Eddie Antar was officially entered in the records of the Israeli government as "Alexander Stewart"—the "diamond buyer" in Eddie's tall tale to the Swiss authorities. Deborah Antar became "Debbie Stewart." He was able to use the "Stewart" name legally in Israel, but he was still listed in Israeli records, and on his Israeli passport, as Eddie Antar. That wouldn't do much to cover his tracks.

So Eddie went on a passport-buying spree. He acquired six passports in five names. They were in phony names, but were not forgeries. Customs officers could have examined them minutely and they would have passed muster. Like the others, the "David Jacob Levi Cohen" passport was a genuine Brazilian passport, though "Cohen" was an invention. Hayes surmised he "probably paid off someone to get it."

The FBI had been picking up leads on Eddie for quite a while. Agents learned that when he fled the United States in February 1990, he did so using a genuine US passport that stole the identity of his friend Harry Shalom, host of the Labor Day gathering where Sammy had run into a friendly, reassuring (but paranoid) Eddie Antar. The State Department provided Hayes with a passport photo of "Shalom," showing Eddie hardly concealing his identity at all, except for glasses in a Superman-as-Clark Kent fashion. "Now we kind of knew where to start," Hayes recalls.

Eddie had obtained the Shalom passport in April 1989, confirming Sammy's hectoring during that time that he was ready to flee. His cousin started using that passport during 1989 to travel to places that included Israel. But that alone didn't prove he had moved to that country. "David" performed that function.

The Brazilian "David Cohen" passport showed entry and exit stamps from Ben Gurion Airport in Israel. Israeli police ran a computer check and were nauseated to find that this nonexistent person had registered as an immigrant on May 13, 1990. When "Cohen" became a citizen, he gave his address as 3 Kohavit Street in Yavne, a town thirty miles south of Tel Aviv. Israeli police put the house under surveillance, and, sure enough, Eddie was living there. He hadn't moved, a mistake he would soon regret.

Unlike Lansky, who lived a law-abiding life in Israel, Eddie infuriated his hosts by exploiting the Law of Return to register an alias as a citizen. If Eddie Antar could become a citizen of Israel using a fictitious identity, a terrorist or spy could do the same thing. Discovery of his ruse was deeply embarrassing. "Providing false documentation to the Israeli government was not smart. The Israelis were extremely cooperative once they knew that he filed false documents with them," Hayes recalled.

Israel was happy to get rid of Eddie, but US officials needed to take one more step before their quarry could be arrested overseas. An Interpol Red Notice would have to be issued so the Israelis could collar him, and contempt of court was not sufficient to warrant nabbing someone in a different country. He would have to be charged with a more weighty crime than dissing a judge. The US Attorney in Newark, now Michael Chertoff, set the wheels in motion for that as soon as Eddie was located in Israel. On June 11, 1992, a federal grand jury in Newark handed up an eighteen-count indictment charging Eddie with conspiracy to commit securities fraud, filing false and misleading annual reports and false warranty claims, and obstruction of justice. Allen and Mitchell Antar were named in the indictment, as was Sammy's assistant Eddie Gindi. The charges were sealed, to be made public only after Eddie was in custody.

■ ■ ■

The job of apprehending Eddie in Israel was assigned to a six-foot, five-inch colossus of a man by the name of Yossef "Yossi" Zamory, a chief superintendent in the Israeli police. Eddie's carelessness had made locating him easy. But capturing him would require care. Raiding the house where he was harbored was not advisable, lest Eddie destroy evidence while Israeli cops were breaking through the heavily fortified doors. The entrance to his hideout had "big bolts like a battleship." He needed to be grabbed outside.

Kohavit Street was a narrow, quiet, residential street of upscale single-family houses. Unfamiliar vehicles would be quickly spotted, but police somehow were able to watch the house for days without being noticed. Eddie and a companion were driving away from the house the morning of June 24, 1992, when they were stopped by Israeli cops. In future years, word would spread that Eddie was a victim of his libido and was arrested by a female police officer dressed in a tight skirt posing as a motorist in distress. Eddie supposedly stopped to offer assistance and flirted with the woman, only to be placed under arrest. That rather humiliating tidbit, if true, was omitted from the account of Eddie's apprehension that Zamory would later give to an American court.

The beefy Israeli took Eddie back to the house, where his shell-shocked prisoner let him into his messy, sparsely furnished room. Israeli cops seized booty that included credit cards under phony names, "lists of holding companies in Liberia, the Cayman Islands and Gibraltar, identification and passports in four names, a lease on a London flat in the name of David Cohen and travel records for stops at the Eden Roc in Miami, Quatre Saisons in Montreal, Hotel du Rhone in Geneva and Hyatt Regency in Jerusalem." With his passports, millions in cash, and multiple overseas accounts, Eddie was well prepared to go on the run. And sure enough, he was on the verge of absconding yet again.

By the time of his arrest, Eddie had decided to get out of Israel. It's not clear whether he got wind of the surveillance, was tipped off to the sealed indictment, or had simply realized that he had been in one place for too long. Something had made him pack his bags. They were in his tiny room, filled with the phony passports and bank papers the Israelis had found, ready to be taken to Lord knows where.

Visiting his client in an Israeli jail a few days after the arrest, Jack Arsenault found a bitter Eddie who correctly blamed himself for his predicament. "He was on the move again. He was leaving Israel. You know, he had been in and out of Israel. My impression was he had traveled a lot, and he was actually leaving Israel when he was arrested. And therefore he had on him false passports.

He had all of his bank account information for accounts all over the world. It was a pot of gold for the government. He was very, very angry at himself."

The fifty-two-page indictment was unsealed when Eddie was behind bars. He was held at Ayalon Prison, a fortresslike maximum-security penitentiary with a morose history. It was where Adolf Eichmann was executed in 1962, and the Ukrainian Nazi camp guard John Demjanjuk had been confined there in 1986. The prison was in Ramla, a working-class town not far from Yavne, but access to the facility was so restricted that Eddie's niece Rori thought it was on the West Bank when she traveled there with other family members to visit her uncle. Security was tight. At the prison she was strip-searched. She found Eddie to be gaunt—"scary," she says—but he acted like his old self when he saw her. "How ya doing, kid?" She at least had come to see him. His own daughters had not.

While his Israeli lawyers wrangled over extradition, which Arsenault vowed to "fight tooth and nail," US prosecutors turned the screws. On August 10, 1992, a federal grand jury in Newark handed up a superseding indictment, adding another charge under RICO. Two weeks after that, the Ministry of Justice approved the US extradition request. Eddie's lawyers appealed. The case was now in the hands of an Israeli court, and during its deliberations Eddie would be kept under lock and key.

It was almost unheard-of to release a prisoner awaiting extradition—especially one who was found with multiple passports, millions of dollars in overseas accounts, and his bags literally packed when captured. If Eddie could get out of prison, he could—and probably would—find his way out of Israel, so obviously he wasn't going to be sprung. The no-nonsense, security-obsessed Israelis would never do that.

Or would they?

Eddie had a plan. Fakery was his modus operandi, his "franchise," to use a latter-day business term. If anyone could con his way out of an Israeli prison, it was Eddie Antar.

CHAPTER TWENTY-SIX

EDDIE HAD A RELAPSE. THE ILLNESS THAT PLAGUED HIM WHEN HE QUIT AS CEO was back with a vengeance. The man was sick. Very sick. He told anyone who would listen that Ayalon Prison was such an awful place that it was killing him and that the cause of humanity required that he be released.

Within days of his capture, articles began appearing in the American and Israeli press reporting that Eddie's health had suddenly and sharply deteriorated while he was in the hands of a cruel Israeli prison system. Seasoned foreign correspondents, accustomed to reporting on serious political issues and violent conflict, found themselves filing dispatches on Eddie's elaborate malingering and histrionics. Israeli authorities were neither amused nor fooled. A month after his capture, the *New York Post* reported that Eddie was viewed as such a flight risk that his bathroom breaks went on the police radio when he was taken to the hospital with a supposed kidney ailment. The newspaper reported that he was shackled to his hospital bed.

Debbie II flew to Israel to be near her husband and began appearing in press reports. When Eddie made a court appearance in August 1992, "looking weak and sickly," he "had to be supported by police and his wife, Debbie. 'They're treating my husband as if he were a bloodthirsty criminal,' she said."

Actually, Eddie was being treated like a captured fugitive and flight risk, which he was. Israeli prisons were not Club Fed, and his lawyer, Arsenault, realized that when he visited his client shortly after his arrest. He was in a cell that "had a dirt floor. It wasn't heated. It obviously wasn't air-conditioned; it was a pretty dire holding cell." Arsenault complained about Eddie's treatment, and "Yossi kind of basically looked at me and said, 'Jack, it is in our interests that he waive extradition quickly. So this is our way of trying to convince him that it's better for him to waive extradition and go back.'"

Eddie was not convinced. He went on the offensive. Eddie had avoided the press at Crazy Eddie, but now he broke his silence. The result was a series of articles that described in heartbreaking detail how he was being killed by his hellish confinement. None of the coverage mentioned Eddie's "serious illness" when he quit as CEO in January 1987, and that his malady had mysteriously vanished by the time he commenced a buyout bid in May. That anomaly wasn't buried in some obscure newsletter, but was mentioned in *New York Times* coverage of Eddie's buyout bid. Yet apparently he was never asked about it.

"I'M GOING TO DIE!" screamed the headline on page 3 of the *New York Post* on September 25, 1992. "Crazy Eddie Antar is wasting away in the notorious Ramle Prison here," the *Post* reported, referring to Ayalon. "He thinks he is dying." After three months in custody, Eddie talked to an enterprising reporter who tracked him to Ichilov Hospital in Tel Aviv, where he had been sent to treat his terrible illnesses. The reporter conceded that Eddie was a "veteran con man," but said the notion he was "faking excruciating pains seemed absurd after seeing him. His hair was long and neglected, his beard wildly overgrown, and he was bony thin." The story went on like that, piling on the horrendous details.

Eddie was honest about his objective in granting the interview. "I can't stay in that jail," he moaned. When asked about the accusations against him, he grew testy. "Why are you asking me all these complicated questions? Don't you have any mercy?"

Eddie's "condition" steadily worsened as his effort to get out of jail continued. The reports of his declining health coming out of Israel were daunting. By early November 1992, the US media grimly reported that his list of ailments included "liver and kidney disorders, a urinary tract blockage and an undisclosed blood disorder." A "private medical report" commissioned by Eddie's Israeli lawyers recommended that he be removed to a "supportive environment" and claimed that the prison stay was "endangering his life."

Debbie II weighed in with a graphic depiction of Eddie's deplorable state. She told the *Jerusalem Post* that Eddie was a "broken man, hardly recognizing his surroundings, and is deteriorating physically and mentally." Eddie was at death's door, according to his spouse. "He has lost the will to live," she reported. "What do they want, a death certificate? He won't be of use to anyone dead."

Faced with Eddie's legal and press juggernaut, an Israeli court ordered that he be evaluated by a psychiatrist to determine if he was fit to remain locked up during the extradition proceedings. A short time later, Eddie took an overdose of sleeping pills. Israeli police believed Eddie had no intention of killing himself, and that he was trying to con the authorities to cut him loose.

And then, quite abruptly, the curtain came down on Eddie's sick act.

On December 30, 1992, Arsenault and US prosecutors cut a deal in which Eddie would cease fighting extradition in return for not being charged with crimes he committed after he became an Israeli citizen in 1988. That meant he would not be prosecuted for the fake Harry Shalom passport or anything else related to his flight. But the major charges—the securities fraud and racketeering—would remain. Though "deathly ill" just a short time earlier, Eddie was somehow able to withstand the long TWA flight back to the United States, arriving at Kennedy Airport in New York on January 10, 1993. There were no further reports of physical or mental afflictions while he was in federal custody. No suicide attempts. No blood disorders. Eddie had regained the will to live. Apparently, US prisons were a more "supportive environment" than the ones in Israel.

According to Arsenault, the deciding factor in Eddie throwing in the towel was the failing health of one of his daughters. In the fall of 1992, seventeen-year-old Danielle Antar was diagnosed with terminal cancer. "So I flew over, and I had to unfortunately break that news to him. And his reaction was, he immediately wanted to be extradited back. It was the only reason he agreed to come back." However, Weissman points out that "the judge who conducted the [Israeli] hearing seemed disposed against him, and I think Eddie's defense had also found that they weren't getting the support they had hoped for from the Israeli press." Rather than circle the wagons around "this fellow Jew in his hour of need," the feeling "seemed to be more 'Why should we become a haven for unsavory Jewish criminals who are trying to pervert the original intention of the Law of Return?'"

Eddie was let off easy by the Israeli criminal justice system. He had committed multiple violations of Israeli law, yet he wasn't prosecuted. He was spared punishment not because of any doubt about his guilt, but because Israel simply wanted to get rid of him. When he was held in Israel, Eddie contended that he was a victim of Israeli politics. National elections took place the day before he was arrested, with Yitzhak Rabin of the Labor Party defeating the incumbent prime minister, Yitzhak Shamir of Likud. Eddie claimed in his *New York Post* interview that he never would have been arrested if Likud's Menachem Begin was still prime minister.

It was true that Likud depended upon support from Jewish refugees from Arab countries, and there was speculation during his extradition fight that if Eddie stalled the proceedings long enough, he would eventually be freed once Likud regained power. What such theories ignored was that Eddie had made a mockery of the Law of Return by obtaining citizenship under a fake identity. Even if Likud had remained in power, it doesn't seem likely the Israelis would have let bygones be bygones.

■ ■ ■

In the closing days of the hunt for Eddie, Paul Hayes pulled a vanishing act of his own.

The FBI agent was working closely with the prosecutors and marshals tasked with Eddie's case, and his availability was especially important while Eddie was being cornered. Yet suddenly he vanished every afternoon. He refused to disclose the truth to Crazy Eddie prosecutors, which was that he was engaged in a desperate search, a matter of life or death.

On the morning of April 29, 1992, Exxon's chief of international operations, Sidney J. Reso, vanished from his home in Morris Township, New Jersey. A ransom note appeared the following day, purporting to come from an environmental group, demanding $18.5 million. The FBI began an intense hunt for the kidnappers and Reso, using every available agent, including Paul Hayes. Every day at four thirty in the afternoon, after a full day of working on Crazy Eddie, Hayes had to report for an assignment on the Reso case. The kidnapping was cloaked in secrecy, and for days the press was told only that Reso was missing. "As far as I was concerned, I couldn't tell the prosecutors. I didn't have any information to say otherwise. When you get stuff in the hands of the prosecutors, sometime between their clerks and talking to their buddies, before you know it, it leaks out." Hayes wasn't taking any chances with a life at stake.

"So I'm disappearing every day, and Weissman calls me up. I think I had a mobile phone at the time. 'Where are you? What are you doing?' I said, 'I can't tell you.'" Every night was a different stakeout or assignment, as the FBI and police frantically tried to track down the missing executive. This went on for two straight months, with Hayes working a double shift, until the kidnappers were arrested picking up the ransom. The perps turned out to be an ex-cop who had worked in security at Exxon, Arthur Seale, and his wife, Irene. Mrs. Seale was persuaded to cooperate. She led police to the shallow grave where Reso was buried and revealed the grisly details of his confinement in a storage bin. Arthur Seale pleaded guilty, and in November 1992 he was sentenced to ninety-five years in prison. Irene Seale was rewarded for her cooperation with a lighter but still severe sentence of twenty years.

A kidnapping and murder is of course poles apart from a white-collar crime like the Crazy Eddie frauds, but the dynamics of relying on coopera- tors are much the same. Had Arthur Seale gone to trial, his wife would have been the principal witness against him. She would have been ripped apart on the stand by the defense as a perpetrator at least as guilty as her husband. In Eddie's trial, which was coming up in mid-1993, the job of the defense would be to turn Sammy into the worst person in the courtroom. Certainly worse than any of the defendants, including Eddie.

Other cooperators would testify at the trial—Sammy's aide Kathy Mo- rin, Zazy's Sam Cohen, and the inventory inflaters Dave Panoff and Dave Neiderbach among them—but Sammy was the key. If Eddie was to have any chance of freedom, he needed to discredit Sammy or, even better, per- suade him to shut up.

Sammy received a phone call not long before the trial was set to begin. Vinnie Badalamenti was on the line. It was a strange call. By then it was widely known that the decent young kid with the engaging manner and sweet father was "connected." Vinnie said that he was approached by some of the Antars to talk to him. So he did. It was an amicable call, though Vinnie was irritated—and not with Sammy. He was annoyed with whoever approached him. "What do these fucking people want?"

Vinnie was not asking Sammy to do anything or not do anything. He knew better than that. He called mainly to vent. Sammy and Vinnie were friends at Crazy Eddie, and they would be friends in future years, meeting for dinner with other Crazy Eddie alumni on occasion. Vinnie was the same as he'd always been, though he'd put on a bit of weight. They'd chat about the old days. Certain subjects were off-limits. It's not hard to guess what they were.

Sammy told Paul Hayes about the conversation, but emphasized that nothing untoward had happened. Just a conversation between friends.

CHAPTER TWENTY-SEVEN

WHITE-COLLAR CRIME—THE MORE COMPLICATED, THE BETTER—WAS PAUL Weissman's specialty. He had made it his life's work to incarcerate the sophisticated, jail the smug, humble the determined corporate criminal. You might say he was born to do it. Had Eddie Antar fully appreciated the situation, had he known that the worst possible FBI agent was teaming up with the worst possible prosecutor, Ayalon Prison might not have seemed all that bad.

Weissman was in his late forties when Eddie Antar was brought to justice. Though he was not the lead prosecutor—Chertoff bigfooted that privilege a few weeks earlier—he performed the grinding but vital work of overseeing trial preparation. Weissman was neither showy nor theatrical, but no one was more skilled at mastering the details of a real beast of a fraud. The intricacies of a complex white-collar case were like the pieces of a jigsaw puzzle— frustrating, perhaps maddening, but deeply satisfying to resolve because the adversaries were rarely deserving of sympathy. Once he tried a drug case to get trial experience. A young guy, just twenty-two, had been found with a few kilos of cocaine in his car on the New Jersey Turnpike. Weissman won a conviction, and the defendant was sentenced to twelve years in prison. It made Weissman sick to his stomach. He went back to white-collar crime and never looked back.

Weissman was a child of the sixties with an affluent upbringing, the son of a paint company executive in New Jersey. He graduated from Harvard in 1965, alienated and antiestablishment, with a strong social consciousness that would be shaped by opposition to the Vietnam War and the Nixon administration. After Harvard Law he did not immediately find his calling, spending four unsatisfying years in the litigation department of a large law firm, representing big business. When he was offered a job by the US Attorney's Office in Newark in 1982, he felt as if he was being thrown a lifeline. As a federal prosecutor, "I had the incredible luxury of prosecuting only people I was sure were guilty, and who I thought actually deserved prosecution." He could do good for society with the full power of the federal government behind him.

Weissman's ethos flummoxed the silky scoundrels he prosecuted. One of them, a defendant in the Bevill Bresler case named Stuart Gottlieb, put the question to him bluntly one day: "You're a smart guy. Why are you doing this when you could be making a lot more money?" Weissman was not offended. People like that just did not understand.

Over time, Weissman became adept at handling messes, very much like Paul Hayes, so it was no accident that they worked together on Bevill Bresler and then Crazy Eddie. The FBI agent had high regard for Weissman's painstaking attention to detail, which was essential in a case in which the slightest inconsistency could be exploited by the defense. When Hayes found that cash was being added to individual Crazy Eddie store accounts to boost comparable store sales, "I tried to describe to Paul how important it was, and he, like, cross-examined me for a half a day. 'How could it be possibly important?' 'What difference does it make?' I didn't lose my cool because I knew Paul; I knew what he was about. He could get even prosecutors he worked with upset by cross-examining them. But he was very effective."

Weissman's meticulous approach earned Sammy's respect as well. As sometimes happens when cooperators work closely with prosecutors, the nervous young ex-CFO began to identify with the government. In Sammy's case, he literally acted as if he was part of their team, going well beyond what was expected of cooperating witnesses. A good example was the aid he provided to SEC lawyers when they took testimony in pretrial depositions in the SEC's civil litigation. If not handled correctly, unfriendly witnesses tended to say they "didn't know nuthin' about nuthin'," as Paul Hayes had put it. And friendly, supposedly cooperating witnesses sometimes didn't tell the truth. That was a mistake when someone who knew the truth was sitting right there.

Before he settled the SEC suit, Sammy would sit in on depositions, as was his right as a codefendant in a civil case. But he was there to help the people suing him and his fellow defendants, which infuriated defense lawyers. He would give SEC attorneys lines of inquiry to pursue with witnesses. SEC enforcement chief William McLucas wrote that "during breaks in the depositions, Sam E. pointed out the particulars in which certain witnesses—who were supposedly 'cooperating' with the SEC—were lying under oath to protect co-conspirators."

One deposition witness in particular found Sammy's presence to be problematic. On May 28, 1992, the former SEC and Dan Gibbons star witness Abe Grinberg was indicted for committing perjury at two depositions Sammy attended. It was the first criminal case to emerge from the Crazy Eddie fraud. Grinberg pleaded guilty to reduced charges in May 1993. McLucas would later observe that "the perjury to which Grinberg pled guilty was committed in response to questions posed by Sam E.'s attorney" Jonathon Warner. Before there was even a single day of trial, prosecutors had already snared a conviction based entirely on Sammy's cooperation.

Sammy cooperated beyond the call of duty in another way. He agreed to plead guilty to a third felony count in October 1992, "encompassing a more recent time frame," to facilitate the effort in Israel to extradite Eddie. He received nothing in return—except the goodwill of the prosecution team.

The feds reached out to other potential cooperators, including Sammy's deputy, Eddie Gindi. He needed to be approached gingerly for several reasons. Gindi was far less culpable than the other Antars. He was also sick with AIDS. He was a younger brother of Ronnie Gindi, Eddie Antar's cousin and original partner in Sights and Sounds. Sammy suggested approaching Ronnie as a way of getting to the brother, so Hayes paid him a visit early one morning at his home on Long Island. "It's basically a sales pitch. I say 'Look, your brother didn't sell stock, he wasn't the one who orchestrated this. He has some knowledge. We'd like to talk with him. We'll treat him fairly.'" Ronnie relayed the message to Eddie, who was in Florida. He agreed to talk. Not to cooperate, but to talk. Just talk.

It was decided that an Assistant US Attorney named Jayne K. Blumberg would accompany Hayes to Florida. She was a Florida native and Tulane

Law graduate in her midthirties who had once been a professional dancer. At the US Attorney's Office she had handled the usual run of ordinary cases given to junior prosecutors, as well as a headline case involving the Born to Kill gang of young Vietnamese immigrants, several of whom were nabbed in 1991 for selling weapons in Jersey City. It was decided to assign her to Crazy Eddie to round out the prosecution team along with Chertoff and Weissman.

The precarious state of Gindi's health meant the meeting would require a special degree of tact and finesse. Hayes and Blumberg met with him in a conference room at an FBI office in a suburb of Orlando. Gindi was polite but evasive. It went on like that for a frustrating two days. "We really didn't get anywhere after two days sitting there with him. . . . He's sitting in a chair, and so am I. Blumberg stands up and starts screaming at him." Hayes was stunned, as was Gindi, who did not react except to look down. Apparently, it was an effort to shock Gindi into talking, and if so it didn't work.*

There was no deal. But in August 1992, Gindi agreed to cooperate. He could have avoided testifying entirely because he was gravely ill, Weissman recalls, but he chose to testify "because he wanted the truth to come out. He was quite brave about it." Because of his illness he testified via videotaped deposition from Florida, and he could only do that two hours a day, one hour in the morning and one in the afternoon. He would die in January 1994.

With Gindi removed from the case, and plea bargain negotiations that went nowhere, Eddie, Allen, and Mitchell were the sole remaining defendants. On June 15, 1993, they went to trial in Courtroom 5A of the Martin Luther King Courthouse, a newly constructed behemoth in the harshly redeveloped vastness of downtown Newark.

■ ■ ■

From the beginning, *USA v. Eddie Antar et al.* had three top-billed stars. Two were what you'd expect in a major criminal trial: the zealous US Attorney Chertoff, who was personally trying the case, and the dedicated, flamboyant defense counsel Jack Arsenault, a former Marine Corps officer with

* Blumberg did not respond to requests to be interviewed for this book.

a booming voice that "made defense witnesses cower." Eddie had made a savvy choice. Arsenault was a highly regarded criminal defense lawyer, and in 1989 had adroitly handled the first RICO prosecution of a Wall Street defendant. Arsenault's client, a trader named Paul Berkman, was convicted on sixty-three felony counts in a widely publicized case stemming from the prosecutorial jihad against Drexel Burnham's Michael Milken. But he was sentenced to a mere three months in prison. The wrist slap could not have failed to impress Eddie.

Chertoff—"pale, bony and balding, with a soft, almost reedy vocal delivery"—was a Harvard graduate and a native of working-class Elizabeth, New Jersey, where he was the son of a rabbi. He had received considerable attention when he led the prosecution of Sol Wachtler, former chief justice of New York's highest court, for threatening to kidnap his lover's young daughter. He was a quick study who impressed Hayes with his ability to absorb the murky, interwoven details of Crazy Eddie in his relatively short time on the case. Mitchell was represented by the telegenic John R. Ford, who would go on to a career as a broadcaster. Allen's lawyer was Arsenault's former partner, Gerald Krovatin.

And then there was the third star in the courtroom, Judge Nicholas H. Politan. Some judges, like some movie directors, give performers considerable latitude, letting lawyers emote without constraint. That could not be said for Politan. At his death in 2012, a newspaper obituary noted that he was "known for his one-liners." During the Crazy Eddie trial he enjoyed bantering with the lawyers and the jury, whether it was about the excessive air-conditioning, the quirky microphone stand, or a new white-sound machine, designed to keep jurors from overhearing conferences at the bench, which didn't work very well. "Every jury I've ever had in here says it's the most annoying thing they ever heard in their lives except their spouse's voice," he said on the first day of the trial, drawing laughter.

Politan was protective of the jury to an unusual degree and was not a fan of the news media. He sealed all identifying information on the Antar jurors, so reporters could not question them after they reached their verdict. Attempts to interview jurors were routine in major cases, but Politan would have none of it. News organizations appealed, and Politan was reversed by the Third Circuit Court of Appeals—but not until five months after the trial ended, long after the news value of questioning the jurors had faded.

There can be little doubt that the judge had a dim view of Eddie Antar. After all, Eddie had shown him blatant disrespect, failing to appear in court when ordered and then fleeing the country. He probably felt that Eddie was guilty as hell. In fact, he pretty much said so in open court. In January 1990, ordering repatriation of the $52 million held in Israel, Politan said from the bench that there were "strong prima facie showings" of securities fraud. Whether his apparent disdain for Eddie tainted his courtroom conduct is another matter. Some of his exchanges with Arsenault were certainly testy. "Please stop playing to the Third Circuit," Politan snapped at the lawyer a week into the trial. "If you try this case, try it to me. I'm as smart as any judge on the Third Circuit. . . . My decisions are generally upheld."

"I'm not implying anything different," Arsenault responded.

"Forget about the record," Politan went on, still fuming. "I couldn't care tinker's damn about the record. I care about being played to me so that I have an opportunity to judge it based upon what is presented before me. Whatever goes up on the record goes up on the record. But give me a chance."

"You're right, Judge. I apologize," said Arsenault.

"Give me credit for having a modicum of brains here," Politan responded, unmollified.

"I apologize, your Honor," the attorney said again. That seemed to calm down the judge.

"Okay," he said. Politan never had exchanges like this with prosecutors.

In the years since the trial, Politan has been accused of showing gross prejudice against Eddie, a "trial-long impersonation of Judge Roy Bean," as one account put it. Arsenault believes even now, his views undiluted by the passage of time, that his client got a raw deal from the judge and goes one step further. He contends that Politan was so prejudiced that he had heard reliably in recent years that the judge kept a dartboard in his chambers with Eddie's picture as the bull's-eye.

Even if the blustery Politan had adored Eddie, it's not clear it would have affected the outcome. Throughout the trial, it was plain that Crazy Eddie was riddled with fraud. The only question was the identity of the principal fraudster. The prosecutors maintained that it was Eddie aided by his brothers, all of whom sold stock whose price was elevated by their fraud. The defense would claim that Sammy was the true mastermind.

Sammy's testimony began on June 25, 1993, one year almost to the day after Eddie was captured in Israel. As the Joe Valachi of the Antar Crime Family, his job was to walk the jury through the mass of documentation and financial gobbledygook being put into evidence, the debit memos and inflated inventories and checks from Panama. He dissected the family dynamics and the company's lies, many of which he had manufactured. Sammy's dissembling had been considerable; in fact, the basis of the defense case was that Sammy had lied so much that nothing he said at the trial was believable. The defense portrayed Eddie as a substance-abusing henpecked husband who fled the country to avoid the wrath of his ex-wife. Mitchell and Allen were depicted by their lawyers as innocent family members who were dragged into court purely because their names were Antar.

After a little more than two full days of direct examination by Weissman, the defense lawyers, mainly Arsenault, commenced three days of cross-examination aimed at tearing apart Sammy's credibility and showing him to be a despicable crumb who was the real villain of the Crazy Eddie Story. Arsenault got right to the point.

"Mr. Antar, you're an admitted liar, aren't you?" he began.

"That's correct. I've admitted to perjuring myself under oath numerous times and I pled guilty to the crimes."

"You lied thousands of times, correct?"

"That's probably correct. I lied about five days with the SEC. Seven days with the SEC."

"You testified 32 times, correct?"

"I don't know how many, but that's probably correct."

"About 7,793 pages of sworn testimony. Does that sound about right?"

It went on like that. While questions posed in cross-examinations aren't testimony, that point is often lost on juries. "So is it fair to say that we now have to rely on a liar to tell us when he's telling us the truth?" Arsenault asked. He pointed out that Sammy declined an opportunity to speak with him before trial, leading to an exchange that may or may not have gone over well with the jury of eight women and four men.

"Did you give me an opportunity to hear all these things that you had to say in a one-on-one interview?" Arsenault asked.

"I gave your client an opportunity, but he left the country."

"Oh."

"He was involved in the litigation that I was involved in. He had attorneys. He decided to leave the country and run out of the country and he had an opportunity. I made myself available for 21 days under oath in a civil litigation that your client was a defendant in, Mr. Arsenault." Sammy made that point in a raised voice, gesturing with a finger.

That made for good theatrics, but Weissman recalls being unhappy with them. "You don't want to see your star witness fencing with the defense, fighting or being antagonistic. It doesn't typically play well with the jury." Sammy, however, remembers suppressed grins at the prosecution table.

A difficult moment in the trial came on the third day. Eddie's daughter Danielle had died, and Eddie applied through Arsenault to attend the funeral. Meeting in Politan's chambers—apparently the dartboard with Eddie's picture, if it actually existed, was put aside for the occasion—the matter was thrashed out. Debbie I's lawyer agreed after consulting with his client. Despite all that had happened between them, Debbie was not going to deny Eddie an opportunity to bid their daughter farewell.

It turned out that going to the funeral was not enough. Eddie wanted more.

Resuming in open court, an informal hearing began on another item on Eddie's agenda that was not mentioned in chambers. A rabbi told Politan that the wife beater, chronic adulterer, and inveterate liar at the defense table was actually a pious individual. "He's Orthodox. He's very traditional. He practices. . . . His behavior is one of very traditional Jew." Eddie would, of course, be sitting shiva, a traditional Jewish mourning practice held at a family member's house. Precisely which family member was not mentioned, but Debbie I was Danielle's closest relative. Was Eddie trying to use the occasion to barge in on his ex? She had agreed to the funeral, not for Eddie to be her guest for a week.

Arsenault assured the judge that Eddie was willing to "post whatever surety if the issue is an issue of flight." Politan responded that "the surety part doesn't make sense. There is $60 million laying out there. I'm not going to divorce myself from my knowledge." It still grated on Politan that Eddie had skipped out on him in February 1990 after refusing to repatriate $52 million from Israel, the lion's share of $60 million the SEC initially accused Eddie of reaping from his stock sales. (Actually, his share dumps, as toted up by the feds in the indictment, totaled $74.8 million.)

"Does he want to sign the $60 million over?" Politan asked.

"The price of my daughter is $60 million?" sneered Eddie, in the only words he spoke during the trial.

"Please, sir," said the judge.

"'Please, sir,' nothing," Eddie shot back.

It was all for naught. No way Politan was giving him another chance to flee. The episode was later used to demonstrate Politan's supposed bias, which the judge called "a feigned issue designed to create an issue for appeal."

The trial resumed, with the defense relying heavily on reasonable doubt, predicated on poking holes in the testimony of the cooperators, especially Sammy. Only Ford, representing Mitchell, called witnesses, and it was to no effect. An effort to prove that Mitchell was busy at home preparing for a trip to Taiwan in early March 1986, when the inventory was being inflated, crumbled under Chertoff's cross-examination. Ford called board member Jim Scott as a witness, which gave Chertoff an opportunity to show that Eddie was never drunk at board meetings. Arsenault had intimated that Eddie was too addled with booze to commit frauds.

In his summation, Arsenault maintained that Eddie's failure to contest the proxy fight with Zinn and Palmieri to the bitter end was evidence of his innocence. "He would have fought until his last breath and he didn't." Predictably, Arsenault portrayed Sammy as the only truly guilty party, motivated by ambition. He "wanted to be the next Eddie Antar." It was Eddie's diabolical cousin who was the true villain, "laughing hysterically" at the swindle he had perpetrated on a pathetically gullible US Attorney's Office. Arsenault played up the discord in the family and the animosity of Sam M., and asserted that Eddie shifted his assets overseas to escape the Felders' legal juggernaut. Sam M. "supported [Debbie I]. He counseled her. He helped her. All to the detriment, from his perspective, of his own son. All to Eddie's detriment." Though this was all true, Debbie posed just one of the legal threats breathing down his neck when he fled to Israel.

Some players in the Crazy Eddie drama were not included in the courtroom cast of characters. Office of the President member Ike Kairey, the psychologist and would-be medical school administrator, pleaded guilty to one count of securities fraud before the trial began and was not called as a witness by either side. Grinberg obviously wasn't getting anywhere near that courtroom, but what about Arnie Spindler? In his opening statement, Jack Ford, representing Mitchell, dwelled at length on Spindler's sterling qualities. "One witness I want you to listen very carefully to [is] Arnold Spindler. I don't know if the government is going to call Mr. Spindler or not as a witness. But I can guarantee you, I will promise you, if the government doesn't call him, I will. And Mr. Spindler will tell you some things that should be very helpful to you," he said. Spindler was the one who blew the whistle, who went to the SEC first, et cetera, et cetera.

Ford went on like that for quite a while. If the jurors remembered the buildup given Spindler, they might have noticed that Ford broke his promise. Spindler was never called to testify by either side.

While figuring in Arsenault's narrative, Sam M. was kept off the witness stand as well. The volatile family elder had refused to talk to Hayes and was obviously toxic from the defense perspective as well. He was in the courtroom every day, sitting incongruously next to Debbie II—as Sammy took pains to point out during cross-examination by Arsenault. Solomon was absent from the witness list as well. His presence was felt in another way.

For months preceding the trial, some of the lawyers involved in suing Eddie and tracking down his assets had been getting anonymous phone calls from someone with good inside information about Eddie. He called himself "the Shadow." Using voice samples, Hayes (whom the Shadow had called a "skirt-wearing friend of J. Edgar Hoover") was able to determine that the anonymous caller was Solomon Antar. Solomon also taunted Sam M. with faxes, earning the name "the Mad Faxer." Apart from the scolding he received from Judge Hurowitz and Debbie I's quest for her "equitable"—he was named in a suit against Eddie filed by the Felders in early 1987—there were no legal consequences for Solomon Antar. He was never prosecuted or sued by the SEC. Nor was his law license jeopardized by Hurowitz's skewering. Fraud expert Joseph T. Wells observed that Solomon "had found ways to dodge the slings and arrows of the judicial system." The result was that "though he had violated the rules of the Bar, and the judge called Solomon's actions reprehensible, no complaint was filed against Solomon's license to practice law."*

Also absent from the trial were brokerage house analysts. Their crowing about Crazy Eddie had helped elevate the stock, and they were made to look like credulous fools by the company's collapse. They may have seemed to be victims of Eddie's lies, but Paul Weissman found that wasn't so. He learned that when he tried to get testimony from them. Not a single one of Crazy Eddie's former cheerleaders would agree to go on the witness stand. Weissman simply wanted an analyst to say that he was deceived, that he "looked at the profits they were reporting and that's why I was recommending the stock to my clients."

Weissman later recalled: "I was stunned by the fact that I could not find an analyst to give that testimony. You would think it would be like falling off a log, right? I thought it would be the easiest thing in the world. Just stating the obvious. Nobody would say that." They wouldn't say that because "basically it's not true." They recommended Crazy Eddie stock because their brokerage firms underwrote the stock offering or perhaps owned shares. "It was a real education for me in that respect." Instead, a handful of small investors testified that they were deceived.

■ ■ ■

The jury reached its verdict after six days of deliberation, on July 20, 1993. Eddie was convicted on all seventeen counts, Mitchell on six of the eight counts against him. Allen was acquitted on all charges. This was not a great surprise; he was the least culpable of the brothers and did not have an executive position at the company. Reasonable doubt worked in his favor. Allen

* Solomon Antar did not respond to requests to be interviewed for this book.

walked out of the courtroom a free man, but he was not out of the woods. In September 1993 the SEC brought a civil action against Allen, Sam M., and Ben Kuszer, charging all three with participating in the inventory-inflation scheme and selling stock knowing the shares had been jacked up by fraud.

In a bid for leniency at sentencing, in March 1994 Eddie finally repatriated the $52 million in Israeli bank deposits that he had refused to bring back to the United States in 1990. With interest, it was now $53 million. But it didn't do him much good. On April 29, 1994, Politan threw the book at Eddie, sentencing him to the maximum allowable sentence under the guidelines, 151 months in prison, and ordering him to pay $121 million in restitution. Returning the $53 million had cut just one month off his sentence. Mitchell was sentenced to 4 years and 3 months in prison and assessed $3 million in restitution.

Prior to sentencing, Chertoff called Eddie "a kind of Darth Vader of capitalism," a catchy sobriquet that would follow him for the rest of his life. Chertoff contended that Eddie would never have succeeded were it not for fraud. That lead to an out-of-court outburst from Eddie, who told the press that the public flocked to his stores for "the best prices and service" and that "we executed what other people could not do."

Eddie's lawyers launched an appeal, but his chances weren't great. "My decisions are generally upheld," Politan had bragged during the trial. That was true of not just Politan's trials but jury trials in general. Most jury verdicts are upheld on appeal, as it requires gross bias or a major error to overturn a conviction. While Politan had made some barbed comments, it would take more than a few ill-tempered remarks to get the conviction tossed out.

Eddie was taken to the tomb-like Metropolitan Correctional Center in Lower Manhattan, where his principal task would be to keep his mouth shut and not antagonize the Third Circuit Court of Appeals. His chances were dim, but only a damn fool would risk blowing his only hope for freedom. Only a fool—or Eddie Antar.

CHAPTER TWENTY-EIGHT

Eddie had no intention of keeping his mouth shut.

Three weeks after the sentencing, Eddie gave the first of a series of jail-house interviews. It was a bold and deeply stupid thing to do. Public griping could do him no good at all, and it's unlikely the jurists weighing Eddie's fate missed the interview he gave to *New York Post* columnist Cindy Adams on May 18, 1994. Like his press interviews in Israel, Eddie portrayed himself as a tragic figure. The guilty verdict was a miscarriage of justice. He was an innocent man! "For two hours," Adams reported, "he repeated variations of 'I've been charged with a crime I didn't do.'" Sure there was fraud, he said, "but the question is, *who* did the fraud?" Not him. "I was not involved in any fraud." He went on like that, and on and on. He left "a healthy company, a cash machine," he asserted, but it was brought to "bankruptcy level" by new management.

Arsenault's tireless advocacy for Eddie at the trial? Eddie's sharp-witted "price of my daughter is $60 million" exchange with Politan? Well, apparently all this was a figment of everyone's imagination because, according to Eddie, "there was no defense because I was not able to assist myself. I was not focused. I wasn't there. You could put me in front of a train and I wouldn't have cared."

Eddie continued in that phantasmagorical vein in other interviews. Eight days after the Cindy Adams column came an interview with *The Record,* a New Jersey newspaper: "Sure, I'm not perfect, I've done some things that were wrong, and I'm willing to take responsibility for them." He did not specify what those wrong things were. Six months later, now confined to a prison in Otisville, New York, he made much the same points in an interview with the *Philadelphia Inquirer*. This time he admitted that he might have been a bit naughty, conceding that, though innocent, "I was not what you would call, I guess, a model citizen or a model person."

In December 1994, Eddie apparently felt that he had not alienated the judicial system of New Jersey with sufficient gusto. In his *Record* interview he had attacked Politan, and he now raised the ante, telling the *Asbury Park Press* that the judge hearing his case was "a blatant anti-Semite." He made no effort to substantiate that vicious (and patently false) attack on a sitting judge.

Surely the appellate court decision would put an end to the drama, finally bring closure. End the carping. End the lies. It was announced on April 12, 1995.

Paul Weissman had the day off. His wife took the message. First she had him sit down. "Haven't we had a good life together?" she asked. Then she broke the news. Eddie's and Mitchell's convictions had been overturned. A three-judge panel of the appeals court seized on a remark that Politan had made at a 1994 sentencing hearing, while he was engaged in an exchange with Chertoff about restitution. Chertoff suggested a procedure, and Politan replied:

> Because that is a more complex issue, I'd like to get the input from the SEC and experts. . . .
>
> *My object in this case from day one has always been to get back to the public that which was taken from it as a result of the fraudulent activities of this defendant and others.* We will work the best possible formula we can to be as fair as possible to the public. If we can get the 120 million back, we would have accomplished a great deal in this case.

The remarks—italicized in the decision—didn't seem all that noteworthy when Politan made them. Defense lawyers did not object to his comments at the time. It was beyond dispute that investors had been swindled and only natural that Politan would want them made whole. And "this defendant"— Eddie—had just been found guilty.

Eddie's appellate lawyer, John Barry, spouse of Donald Trump's sister Maryanne Trump Barry, seized on those words as evidence that Politan had prejudged Eddie's guilt. The appeals court agreed, saying that "this is a case where the district judge, in stark, plain and unambiguous language, told the parties that his goal in the criminal case, from the beginning, was something other than what it should have been and, indeed, was improper." To buttress its argument, the appellate court pointed to Politan's "$60 million" remarks when Eddie asked to be released to sit shiva. Politan had called it a "feigned issue," but the appellate court didn't look at it that way. Eddie's overreaching had helped get his conviction overturned.

Prosecutors were convinced that the appellate panel had misconstrued Politan's remarks, and Weissman sought to have the case heard by the full appeals court. He argued in a legal brief that the "day one" remark was a reference to the civil case and the 1990 repatriation order, not Eddie's trial. His effort failed. Politan was not only removed from the criminal cases, but also tossed off the civil cases, including the suit the SEC had filed in 1993 against Sam M., Ben Kuszer, and Allen Antar.

Unlike Eddie, who was free to rant and lie from jail, Politan was forced by judicial custom to refrain from commenting on his drubbing. The next development in the case, however, may not have bothered him very much. The fate of the Antars was now in the hands of a judge who was at least as tough as Politan. The criminal and SEC cases were assigned to Judge Harold Ackerman, a former journalist and labor lawyer. He once freed 173 prisoners from the Essex County Jail because of overcrowding, but a bleeding heart he was not. Though quiet, soft-spoken, and, at times, plodding on the bench, he could get good and mad when the occasion demanded. Sentencing a former Atlantic City mayor for extortion in 1985, Ackerman quipped, "You reached for that honey pot and you got stung." Once he trebled the thirty-year sentence called for in the guidelines and sentenced a child molester and pornographer to ninety years in prison. Eddie wisely decided to strike a plea bargain, and Mitchell followed suit.

When defendants plead guilty, court procedures normally require that they admit guilt. They don't have to be sincere, but they have to say the right words. Eddie engaged in that kabuki dance when he appeared before

Ackerman on May 8, 1996. In agreeing to plead guilty to a single count of racketeering conspiracy, both sides stipulated that everything Eddie said publicly up to that point was a lie, that he "was an organizer and leader of the criminal activity" charged in the indictment, and that he "demonstrated a recognition and affirmative acceptance of responsibility for his offence." But words on paper were not enough. Ackerman would have to hear it from Eddie's lips. "We don't accept guilty pleas from innocent people in this court for obvious reasons," the judge explained. He asked him a series of questions.

Beginning since before the IPO in 1984, "did you and others agree on various schemes to falsify the books and records of Crazy Eddie so as to make the company's financial performance appear stronger than it actually was?"

"Yes, your honor," Eddie replied.

On it went, Eddie admitting his guilt to one offense after the other. Everything the government had charged, everything Sammy had described on the witness stand and in his marathon meetings with prosecutors and hundreds of phone calls to Paul Hayes. Everything. No blame shifting, no excuses, no lies. The appeals court decision had been a blow to the prosecution, and it was unjust, but it had accomplished something that the jury verdict had not achieved: it forced Eddie Antar to tell the truth.

EPILOGUE

LATE IN DECEMBER 2006, A MAN WITH A VAGUELY FAMILIAR NAME TRIED without success to leave a comment on a blog I was keeping at the time. He was stymied by a technical glitch, but his thoughts were interesting so I used them in full as a blog post. He had written an open letter to a controversial CEO I'd mentioned in a book on Wall Street fraud. Patrick Byrne of Overstock.com was a stock market conspiracy theorist. He had many enemies who had done all sorts of bad things. They had destroyed fine companies and rigged the financial markets in diabolical ways. Worst of all, they had criticized him. Journalists, myself included, were high on his list. He dispatched an employee to stalk, defame, and harass the "miscreants." In the course of what he called his "jihad," Byrne smeared an innocent Canadian businessman as an al-Qaeda financier, but even the resulting record libel verdict, and condemnation by the judge, could not curb his zeal.

Byrne had uncovered the news media's dirty little secret: intimidation works. That first became evident in 2005, when he accused a female reporter of "giving Goldman [Sachs] traders blowjobs" and continued attacking her online. There was no outcry, no action by his board or press groups, no consequences—except that she stopped covering him. "If the purpose of this was to silence us, it worked," wrote Bloomberg columnist Joe Nocera. In 2006, Nocera warned in the *New York Times* that Byrne was "using the courts, the Internet, his taunting e-mails—and even his conspiracy theory—as part of a thinly disguised effort to squelch any and all criticism of Overstock."

Despite all that, here was someone willing to confront Byrne. Addressing the CEO in his open letter, the blog commenter wrote, "As an ex-felon and admitted fraudster, I really have to admire you and the way you handle yourself. Being that I feel a special bond with you because you remind me of my youth. I hope you can take some of my advice as a person who has 'been there, done that.'" It went on in that vein and was signed "Sam E. Antar (former Crazy Eddie CFO & ex-felon)."

It had been thirteen years since Sammy testified against Eddie in Newark, and since then he had worked to turn his life around. The open letter was one of the ways he did that. Sammy was drawing Byrne's fire, and doing so quite cheerfully. The result was predictable. Sammy was now part of the conspiracy. The attacks went on for years. Byrne and his operatives made Jack Arsenault seem like a pussycat. When Sammy split from Robin, she was contacted for dirt without success. It couldn't have been more vicious, but he kept on slugging, criticizing Overstock's accounting methods in detailed blog posts.

For Sammy, fighting a corporate bully was his way of engaging in *teshuvah*, repentance. He had confessed his sins, forsaken them, and he was seeking to pay back society for the wrongs he had committed at Crazy Eddie. A few months later, Sammy faced off against the man who had brought him to this point in his life. It was the real-life version of what is known in drama as an "obligatory scene"—the confrontation between a story's protagonist and antagonist. Meeting in a Manhattan hotel suite booked for the occasion, Sammy confronted Eddie while CNBC cameras recorded their encounter.

Their face-off lasted hours, but only brief excerpts were aired on June 27, 2007. One exchange that made the cut showed Sammy leaning to within inches of a somber, wan Eddie, gesturing with a pointed finger and shouting, "You brought us up to be crooks, Eddie. Everything I became came from you." Eddie looked helplessly at the interviewer, journalist Herb Greenberg, making a gesture of exasperation as if Sammy was a lunatic.

Eddie turned to Sammy but did not look him in the eye. "You didn't just learn from me," he said softly. "You learned—we learned the culture. So it's not that I taught you. You knew the culture."

That was Eddie. Someone else was always to blame, in this case "the culture." He did not elaborate, but Sammy understood him to mean the culture that their grandparents' generation had brought over from Aleppo. But the Syrian Jewish culture was a culture of endurance, of survival in a harsh environment, not a culture of crime in America. Except for the obligatory recitation at his sentencing, Eddie never acknowledged that he had committed crimes, let alone repented. He never offered a word of remorse, not even once. That's because he felt no remorse. Neither did his father.

Eddie and Sam M. reconciled after Eddie's downfall. Sam M. had won their long rivalry by default. He was no longer jealous of his humbled offspring. He was head of the family again. Now well into his seventies, he carried out his responsibilities as family elder by writing to the people he felt had wronged Eddie. This was the son he had worked so hard to undermine, whose marriage he had tried to wreck, who had humiliated him and forced him out of the company.

One letter he wrote in 1997 to his brother Eddy, who had testified for the government at the trial under a grant of immunity, went as follows:

DEAR BROTHER, HOW? WHY? WHERE? WHO? I AM STILL BEWILDERED. PERHAPS YOU HAD NEVER SEEN OR HEARD OF THE ENCLOSED DOCUMENT. IT MAY HELP PUT 2 + 2 TOGETHER.

YOU & YOUR SON DID A MASTERFUL JOB SAVING SOLOMON'S ASS MEANWHILE DESTROYING YOUR OWN FLESH & BLOOD.

THANK YOU & MAY GOD FORGIVE YOU

Sam M.

The "enclosed document" was Judge Hurowitz's decision in the divorce case, in which Eddy had played no role whatsoever. It did not even mention Sammy, and nothing in the ruling "saved Solomon's ass." Sam M. wrote letters to his nephew that made even less sense. Decades later, Sammy learned that in 2001 Sam M. hired a psychiatrist, Isaac Herschkopf, to create a psychological assessment of his nephew based on his demeanor at a public speaking engagement that Sam M. had on tape. The report was not made public and was apparently prepared for Sam M.'s private enjoyment.*

Unlike Eddie, who was forced to admit guilt in court, Sam M. never confessed to anything or atoned for anything—not for abandoning his firstborn son, Mark Daniel Antar, and not for committing fraud at Crazy Eddie. He was never criminally prosecuted, but he, Allen, and Ben Kuszer lost the SEC civil case on July 16, 1998.

In a harshly worded decision that sided with the SEC on all its claims, Ackerman began with the same flair that he had employed when he dumped on the mob and corrupt politicians: "There is perhaps no more insidious drain on the overall welfare of society than greed unchecked." His ruling recounted the Crazy Eddie frauds in meticulous detail and dwelled at length on the mendacity and inconsistencies that had riddled Sam M.'s sworn testimony. He was happy to lie, and happy to admit that he lied. "I lied, I lied, I lied, I lied, I lied, I lied, but then I rescinded the lies and told them the truth," he testified on one occasion. On another: "If I lied in the past, when I talk about it—you talk about my son, I maybe like to cover things up. You know what I mean?"

Sam M., Allen, and Ben were just one theater of operations in the SEC's worldwide quest to recoup for investors the fruits of the Crazy Eddie fraud. In the late 1980s and early 1990s, the SEC brought court cases in Switzerland, Israel, Canada, Liechtenstein, and Great Britain, pursuing funds that Eddie had secreted in various accounts. The SEC even sued Debbie I and her four surviving daughters, seeking the proceeds from Eddie's sale of the $8 million in stock he had gifted to the girls—money he had transferred to the Cayman Islands in 1985. The SEC did not accuse Debbie or her daughters of wrongdoing; it just wanted to grab that cash as a product of insider trading by Eddie. In the divorce case, Debbie had testified it was all done behind her back, with Eddie getting her mom's signature on account documents. One of her lawyers even called it a "preparatory effort" by Eddie to

---

* Herschkopf lost his license in 2021, and in that year he was the subject of a miniseries, *The Shrink Next Door*, based on a podcast by Joe Nocera.

rob his own daughters. When she was sued by the SEC, Debbie said that her previous account was not the "whole story" and claimed that she, not Eddie, had chosen to sell the shares. Politan was not persuaded and ruled against her in 1993. Shortly before the ruling, the SEC cut a deal with Debbie and settled for about half, $3.9 million.

The SEC is sometimes chided for laxity and even for bumbling, but when it came to Sam M. it resembled Inspector Javert a great deal more than Inspector Clouseau. The agency pursued Eddie's father to the end of his days, at one point threatening him and Rose with criminal contempt for transferring funds to avoid seizure. He died at eighty-three on August 8, 2004, the last buck squeezed out of him—at least as far as the SEC could determine. During the litigation, Richard Wallace, the SEC lawyer, thought it might be useful to explore the space above a ceiling where Sam M. had stored *nehkdi*. A court order was obtained. A camera panned around. An examination of the resulting video showed an odd-looking bundle in the corner. It turned out to be a package of cash, about $100,000, that Sam M. had tucked way, forgotten, just as Murad had neglected to retrieve cash he had left with a stranger so many years before.

By the time the SEC called off its hunt for Antar cash in 2012, about $120 million had been recovered. Some of it was still being found as late as 2009, when the SEC found $158,841.37 in a dormant Israeli bank account in the name of "Caliver Enterprises SA." The "beneficial owner and sole signatory" was Eddie's good friend "David Cohen." It would be no surprise at all if other Antar *nehkdi* were still out there somewhere, in safe-deposit boxes, overseas bank accounts, or even ceilings, gathering dust mites to this day.

After his plea deal, Eddie gave no more spiteful interviews to the press. When Ackerman sentenced him to eighty-two months imprisonment and two years of supervised release in February 1997, he said nothing publicly. He settled into prison routine and worked as a cook. While incarcerated, Eddie finally saw one of his life goals achieved. He had always wanted a son, and in October 1995 he got his wish. Deborah Ehrlich Antar gave birth to a boy they named after Sam M. as tradition required. The blessed event seemed a bit odd because conjugal visits were not allowed. Debbie was mum when asked about it by a reporter, but in vitro fertilization was Eddie's apparent path to fatherhood.

Mitchell was released in September 1998 after serving a year and a half in prison, and Eddie followed on March 15, 1999. He emerged into a different world than the one he left when he was apprehended on a street in Yavne in 1992. The Internet was beginning its inexorable process of draining the life out of consumer electronics chains. In 1998 some members of the Antar family planned to revive Crazy Eddie as brick-and-mortar stores. Jerry Carroll was brought into the venture, with Harry Spero handling the advertising. That did not take off, so another approach was tried in 2001, this time an Internet business. Eddie, in prison during the earlier venture, was hired as "director of marketing and strategic relations." Jerry taped commercials on a "shoestring budget," and Larry Weiss was creative director. It received a smattering of publicity, mostly favorable. A nonfamily member was CEO.

Larry by then had left advertising and was running an interactive pay-per-call telephone company. He hadn't forgotten how Eddie had ripped him off, but he thought he'd give it a shot and work for the new Crazy Eddie—though just part-time, not investing a penny, and retaining his telephone business. "It was moving to see him. When he went off to jail, everyone loved him. I did too. I don't know why," he says with a laugh. During the years Eddie was in jail, Larry would occasionally consider visiting him, but then he would remember how he had been treated and get annoyed "because I couldn't believe what he did." Actually seeing him in the flesh, "I melted. We hugged." Prison had not changed him much. His old boss was thinner, but "he was still Eddie."

"It's a great operation that's going to rise to the top," Eddie was quoted as saying at the time. It did not. The online venture failed. Investors didn't want to go anywhere near Eddie, and the website was taken down by 2004.

Apart from his role in the two abortive Crazy Eddie revivals, Jerry Carroll faded from public view after the chain collapsed. Serving as Eddie's spokesman had never been a full-time job; he did radio and voiceover work, started a small ad agency, and tried his hand at acting, appearing in "three or four TV pilots that never took off." In 2000 he offered his services as a disc jockey specializing in "EuroDance—today's discotheque," creating a website that mentioned Crazy Eddie only in passing. The shyness that Harry Spero observed at store openings never abated, and any doubts on that score were resolved when Jerry died on September 3, 2020, felled by a longstanding heart ailment. He was a few weeks short of his seventy-sixth birthday.

In compliance with his wishes, Jerry was cremated and his ashes were given to his widow, Andrea, who kept them in their Manhattan apartment. There was no funeral, no death notice, no media coverage. Some of his friends didn't learn of his passing until months later. Some never did. The man who had screamed his way into the public's consciousness had left the earth in silence.

Another participant in the post-collapse Crazy Eddie revival had a different encounter with fate. Sam A. Antar, son of Allen, was a driving force behind the 1998 effort to bring back the stores. The 2000 crime anthology *Frankensteins of Fraud* portrayed him sympathetically, noting his "decidedly sweeter disposition than his uncle" and his "lively, curious eyes, without Eddie's grudges and hurt." The Crazy Eddie chapter of the book ended on a hopeful note thanks to new leadership in the form of Sam A.

In January 2013, Sam A. pleaded guilty to investment fraud. He was sentenced to twenty-one months in prison. Six years later he was named in criminal and civil charges alleging another scam, this one targeting the Syrian Jewish community. The SEC alleged that Sam A., now forty-four, "told investors that he would use their funds to buy shares in emerging companies whose stock had not yet begun to trade publicly," but kept their money instead. A criminal complaint lodged by the New Jersey Attorney General put investor losses at $794,000. Both the criminal and the SEC cases were still working their way through the courts in early 2022.

Another member of the new generation of Antars received public attention, but for all the right reasons. In November 2017, Eddie's son, Samuel Alex Antar, and his mom were featured in an ABC News segment on a snack business that gave employment to young people with autism. It was an engaging, uplifting story. Though delving into Sam's background in some detail, his famous father was not mentioned. By then the Antars were no longer in the media spotlight. When Debbie II and Eddie divorced in 2009 it received no attention, and neither did her 2010 remarriage.

■ ■ ■

Several of the people who crossed Eddie's path were in trouble with the law in later years, but only one served a prison term anywhere near as long as Eddie's.

It wasn't Sam Cohen. The agreeable immigrant head of Zazy pleaded guilty in 1997 to tax evasion unrelated to Crazy Eddie and was sentenced to eighteen months in prison. It wasn't Vinnie Badalamenti, the stockroom boy who went on to success in the Bonanno crime family. It wasn't Sam A. or other family members. It wasn't any of the working stiffs Eddie taught to inflate inventories, deceive customers, and hose down merchandise in store basements.

It wasn't Dick Lewis. His reassuring, fatherly integrity lured customers to Newmark & Lewis when it competed with Crazy Eddie. His catchy jingle told the truth. Dick Lewis was watching. He was watching out—for himself. In 1993, Lewis was rounded up with more than a hundred other businessmen, home owners, and insurance adjusters in a crackdown on insurance fraud by federal prosecutors in Brooklyn. No one at Crazy Eddie was implicated, and neither was "Donald," the hose-wielding insurance adjuster, or his firm. No one from the chain was ever charged with spiking claims—or stealing sales tax, that other old standby that happened to be a felony. But Dick Lewis was not so fortunate. He pleaded guilty to one count of mail fraud for exaggerating fire damage to one of his stores. He was fined $20,000 and sentenced to five years' probation.

Lewis got off easy, but that can't be said for an Ivy Leaguer who had limitless prospects for the future when his life intersected with Crazy Eddie.

After the IPO, the young Oppenheimer banker Todd Berman lived up to his early promise. He went on to another prestigious investment bank. He partnered with financier Eli Jacobs to buy the Baltimore Orioles, becoming the team's vice chairman. He founded a private equity firm. He had political connections and was happy to flaunt them, luring George Stephanopoulos and Evan Bayh to the board of his firm. He was a member of the Foreign

Policy Association and the Council on Foreign Relations. He "founded a nonpartisan political action group that meets with political leaders." When the Buffalo Sabres was in distress, he pitched in to help his hometown hockey team. Berman financed a bid to rescue it from the clutches of the indicted corporate villain John Rigas, who would go to prison for looting Adelphia Communications. The bid failed but the Sabres stayed in Buffalo. Berman was a hometown hero, a white knight.

Then he was taken into custody.

On December 6, 2004, Berman pleaded guilty in federal court to stealing $3.6 million from his private equity firm. He didn't need the money. He wasn't a drug addict. He wasn't in hock to hoodlums like the branch manager in Paul Hayes's early banking career. Could it have been what Eddie called "the culture"? Perhaps the culture of greed that had spawned John Rigas? Like the Adelphia CEO, Berman stole because he wanted to live well. The loot had financed lavish vacations in Colorado ski resorts and places like Antigua and Puerto Vallarta. In the end his motive didn't matter very much. He went through the ritual of admitting guilt, just as Eddie had done, and was sentenced to five years in a federal penitentiary.

■ ■ ■

Before his sentencing on May 31, 1994, Sammy told Judge Politan that "Mr. Mautone's advice basically saved my life." He was deeply grateful that he had been counseled to tell everything he knew to Paul Hayes, and his gratitude was reciprocated. Stacked before Politan were letters from the US Attorney in New Jersey, the SEC, lawyers for aggrieved investors, and even attorneys for Crazy Eddie's new, humbled overlords. They were simply glowing. They read more like job recommendations written by old fraternity buddies, or perhaps award citations, than letters to a judge concerning the punishment of a person who had pleaded guilty to felonies. Lawyers for the Oppenheimer-Palmieri partnership and burned shareholders lauded Sammy for his wholehearted cooperation. Chertoff wrote that Sammy's assistance was "extraordinary in its scope, its significance and its steadfast dedication." His testimony in court was "forthright and effective, and demonstrated his commitment to cooperating with the government."

The SEC's enforcement director, William McLucas, contrasted Sammy's full-fledged cooperation with the deception and evasiveness of other witnesses in the Crazy Eddie case "who either have provided no assistance at all or, in the case of two individuals, lied under oath to conceal aspects of the fraud and thereby protect their co-conspirators." The two individuals were not named, but Sammy had a pretty good idea who they were.

The letters had their intended effect. In one of his last actions in a Crazy Eddie case before he was removed, Politan sentenced Sammy to three years' probation, including six months of house arrest with an electronic monitor, twelve hundred hours of community service, and imposed fines totaling $10,000. "If you come forward, you will be rewarded," the judge commented.

Antar defense lawyers weren't happy with the light sentence. Arsenault called Sammy "the architect of the fraud." He had made the same argument at the trial, to no avail. There was a crucial difference between Sammy and Eddie that had not worked well for the defense. He had not gotten rich as Eddie had done by dumping Crazy Eddie stock. He had not reaped the insider-trading whirlwind. He had committed crimes, for sure. But he had done them for the family. For Eddie.

Like other reformed fraudsters such as Frank Abagnale of *Catch Me If You Can* fame, Sammy is one of the good guys now. He is friends with Paul Hayes, his former SEC adversaries, and the prosecutors and private attorneys who had pursued Crazy Eddie. He gives lectures to universities, accounting firms, regulators, and law enforcement on how to detect and prevent corporate fraud. He works as a consultant to law firms seeking to root out accounting fraud on behalf of their clients. He is quoted frequently by the press as an expert on white-collar fraud.

Sammy is still as flinty and unfiltered as he was on the witness stand. The post-Eddie years had taught him to stand his ground, and when a trader acquaintance whitewashed the behavior of Patrick Byrne, the subject of that comment on my blog, Sammy fought him on social media. Byrne scoffed at Sammy's criticism of Overstock's accounting, but his analysis was borne out in 2010, when the company restated its earnings, saying its previous filings could not be relied upon. In 2019 Byrne resigned from the company, sold his stock, and departed for Indonesia. He reemerged in subsequent years as a proponent of "stolen election" conspiracy theories, fictions on a grand scale that shredded his reputation, turning him into a "pariah" and earning him another libel suit. When Byrne imploded, and the underling who had stalked Sammy copped a plea to eight felony counts of forgery, the taste of vindication was as sweet as it was when Eddie was convicted.

■ ■ ■

Eddie died on September 10, 2016. He was buried by the Syrian Jewish community's *chevra kadisha* burial society, Congregation Rodfeh Zedek, at the destination on Staten Island he had feared but could not indefinitely postpone. He was interred at United Hebrew Cemetery on Staten Island near his deceased daughter, his parents, uncles, cousins, and grandparents. Various possible causes of death were whispered within the family—cirrhosis of the liver by one account, liver cancer by another. His drinking had caught up with him, or perhaps not.

There was an immediate outpouring of nostalgia. A *New Yorker* writer confessed that he was "wistful for Crazy Eddie." As a *Wall Street Journal* columnist observed, Crazy Eddie "evoked a less slick and knowing era." Eddie's brainchild was a screaming ghost of the past, emblematic of a vanished working-class New York, when newspapers thick with advertising weighed the line of succession to Carlo Gambino, when Times Square was a red-light district and entire neighborhoods resembled Berlin in 1945. It was a filthy, litter-strewn city of muggers and Fox Police Locks and graffiti on subway cars, a lethal, exciting city that was deeply, exuberantly crooked, from the political clubhouses to the police precincts to the bureaucracy that processed parking tickets. Eddie was not an outlier. He was a product of his times. And he had a quality lacking in the scoundrels who followed him.

Bernie Madoff stole a lot more. Enron's Jeffrey Skilling and WorldCom's Bernard Ebbers committed a higher dollar volume of fraud. The faceless bankers who precipitated the 2008 financial crisis overshadowed all who came before them, even the Enron crooks and certainly Eddie. But they and their ilk were colorless and odorless, carbon monoxide in human form.

Madoff was the nightmare you try to forget. Eddie Antar was the fever dream you try to remember even though it was strange and scary and made no sense. His story arose in the mists of the past like a mirage in the deserts of northern Syria—rich, complex, and nuanced, punctuated by larceny so outrageous that it seemed ripped from the script of *The Producers*. But Eddie Antar was no Max Bialystock. He wasn't hated, but he hurt people.

Eddie epitomized the duality of the American Dream. With only a junior high school education, blessed with imagination and guts, he built a company that was remembered by people who were kids when he was running Crazy Eddie. That alone was a remarkable achievement. Yet his criminal acts were so prolific that some of the most serious were never prosecuted. He turned decent people into criminals, people who were weak, people who were loyal. The closer you were to him, the more likely it was that you would become either an accomplice or a victim, sometimes both.

Eddie considered writing a memoir, but he dropped the idea. He wanted to forget what he had done. "The past to me is a black hole," he said on CNBC when he confronted Sammy in 2007. "People live in the past. A black hole—you know what it does to you. It sucks you in and destroys you; it crushes you." Eddie had put Crazy Eddie behind him, and he wanted the same from the people he had harmed. Especially one person.

On February 29, 2000, a New York court finally gave Debbie Rosen Antar her long-sought "equitable." Ruling on a suit the Felders had filed against Eddie and Solomon in 1987, New York Supreme Court justice Ira Gammerman awarded her $486,700. Eddie had meant what he said that night in January 1985: "You will get nothing." He was right. She got nothing. The lawyers from hell were thwarted in straightforward fashion. Eddie and Solomon did not want to pay, so they didn't.

"They simply welched on their indebtedness," Debbie said in an affidavit in 2019. Yes, 2019. Early that year, Debbie, now self-employed as a therapist, sued the eighty-one-year-old Solomon to enforce her 2000 judgment against him and Eddie. For obvious reasons, there was no point in naming Eddie's estate in the suit.

On May 21, 2019, thirty-five years after signing the separation agreement that Judge Hurowitz had called an act of "civil theft," yet another New York

State Supreme Court justice gave Debbie yet another empty courtroom victory. The judgment, with accrued interest, now stood at $1,315,002.19. Her chances of collecting the money she was owed were not good. But she was not giving up.

Some might call that futile, perhaps even obsessive. They would be wrong. Deborah Rosen Antar was merely seeking her share of the American Dream, the one that had been denied her since 1984. It was so basic, so elemental that it was taught in the civics classes Eddie cut when he worked in clip joints to create his first victims.

She demanded justice.

ACKNOWLEDGMENTS

Sam E. Antar helped immeasurably in binding together all the strands of the Crazy Eddie story. I became well acquainted with Sam after he showed up at my blog in December 2006, and I am grateful for his generosity in sharing his recollections in many hours of interviews.

My agent, Richard Morris of Janklow and Nesbit Associates, was a fierce advocate and sound editorial voice. *Retail Gangster* could not have been published without his dedication and hard work. And I mean that literally, because the title was his idea! That was but one facet of his fine editorial judgment and sound commercial instincts.

At Hachette Books, I owe a special debt of gratitude to Ben Schafer, executive editor, for his expert guidance of this book through the editorial process. I know that writing a book during a pandemic was a challenge, and I don't envy what it must have been like to run a publishing company while the world was going mad. He and Carrie Napolitano whipped this book into shape with amazing dexterity and staggering attention to detail, and they have my deepest appreciation and heartfelt thanks. My thanks also go to Amber Morris, senior production editor, and to Annette Wenda for copyediting the manuscript. Elisa Rivlin provided a painstaking legal review.

In addition to personal recollections, this book draws on thousands of pages of public records—the trial transcript, depositions, affidavits, naturalization and Census records—as well as news accounts and Sammy's contemporaneous handwritten notes while he was pleading his case to prosecutors. I also relied on the decisions handed down by three now deceased jurists who tried pivotal cases—Barry Hurowitz of the New York State Supreme

Court and US District Court judges Nicholas H. Politan and Harold M. Ackerman. Their detailed accounts are invaluable to any researcher. Judge Politan was roundly and, in my opinion, unfairly criticized for his handling of the Crazy Eddie case. Some of the attacks on him by Eddie Antar and others were irresponsible, and as far as I know he never responded. I hope that this book may help to correct the record.

During the time I lived with this story, I found it to be a kind of *Rashomon* tale. To some of the people who knew him, Eddie Antar was and always will be a hero. To others who experienced the same person, Eddie was the embodiment of evil. Some view him as a little of each. My aim was to portray all facets of his persona. But since I necessarily relied heavily on court transcripts and the public record, which are scathingly negative, this book does tilt in that direction. There's little doubt that Eddie was a brilliant man, probably a genius. But he left many victims in his wake.

In exploring the criminal case, I am deeply grateful for the help provided to me by one of the unsung heroes of the Crazy Eddie saga—Paul Weissman, former Assistant US Attorney in Newark. He shared freely his insights and recollections and provided me with the 1993 trial transcript that aided immeasurably in telling this story. The court reporter had died and his old firm had none of his work, which made it difficult to obtain this necessary document.

I'm grateful as well for the assistance provided by Paul Hayes, the FBI agent in charge of the Crazy Eddie investigation, who was generous with his time and recollections in the midst of the pandemic and shared with me his extensive files. His remarkable career probably deserves a book all its own, and I was privileged to tell the Crazy Eddie elements of his long and productive work in law enforcement.

I would also like to extend my warmest thanks to Larry Weiss, whose pivotal role in the marketing of Crazy Eddie has been unfairly neglected over the years. His successor, Harry Spero, who was there through the bitter end, was tremendously helpful in sketching out the remainder of the story.

Dozens of other people were of great assistance to me in the years I worked on this book, but a number stand out: Nick Zippilli, Richard Wallace, Ira Weiss, Andrea Carroll, Jack Arsenault, Michael Chertoff, Gerald

Krovatin, Rori Sassoon, Dan Gibbons, Michael Cohen, Irit Cohen, Robert Crumb, Alexander Wood, Lora Fountain, Mary Conte, Richard Zuckerman, Stu Friedman, and Amir Toossi.

And, of course, this book would have been impossible without the love and support of Anjali.

NOTES

Prologue

Gold Coast, Regency Whist Club: Norval White, Elliot Willensky, and Fran Leadon, *AIA Guide to New York City*, 5th ed. (New York: Oxford University Press, 2010), 419, 431; Tom Miller, "The Cortlandt Field Bishop House—15 East 67th Street," *Daytonian in Manhattan* (blog), December 28, 2019, http://daytoninmanhattan .blogspot.com/2019/12/the-cortlandt-field-bishop-house-15.html.

meeting with Milton Petrie: Sam E. Antar trial testimony, *USA v. Eddie Antar et al.*, US District Court for the District of New Jersey, no. 92-347, June 28, 1993; Sam E. Antar, interviews with the author, November 23 and December 20, 2021.

1985 survey: Kirk Johnson, "Our Towns: Best and Worst of Times in Tale of 2 Crazy Eddies," *New York Times*, June 22, 1993.

99 percent name recognition: "How Crazy Eddie Begs for Business," *Mart*, September 1986, 13.

Crazy Eddie heroin brand: Paul J. Goldstein et al., "The Marketing of Street Heroin in New York City," *Journal of Drug Issues* (Summer 1984): 553.

Petrie background, philanthropy: "Utah Collateral Bank, J. Petrovitzky, Proprietor," *Salt Lake City Directory* (Salt Lake City: R. L. Polk, 1899); "Notice of Trustee Sale in Bankruptcy," *Salt Lake Herald*, November 28, 1902; Charlotte Curtis, "The Tireless Milton Petrie," *New York Times*, May 15, 1984; David Moin and Mark Tosh, "Milton Petrie Dead at 92," *Women's Wear Daily*, November 9, 1994; Douglas Martin, "A Tale of Giving, with a Surprise for One Reader," *New York Times*, July 19, 1989; Sidney Rutberg, "Milton Petrie Still Runs on the Fast Track," *Women's Wear Daily*, May 28, 1986; Geraldine Fabrikant, "He Sure Didn't Take It with Him," *New York Times*, November 20, 1994.

Robert Crumb rip-off: Emails to author from Robert Crumb and Alexander Wood, January 2022.

Chapter One

family background, Sam M. and nehkdi: Sam E. Antar, interview with the author, September 28, 2012.

"obtained a rather clear sense": Opinion by Judge Harold M. Ackerman, *Securities and Exchange Commission v. Sam M. Antar et al.*, 15 F. Supp. 2d 477, 1998 US Dist. LEXIS 21474, July 16, 1998.

Murad anecdote: Antar interview, September 28, 2012.

conditions in Aleppo: Joseph A. D. Sutton, *Magic Carpet: Aleppo-in-Flatbush; The Story of a Unique Ethnic Jewish Community* (New York: Thayer Jacoby, 1979), 7, 155–199.

"were sent to 'squeeze'": Sephardic Heritage Museum, *The History of the Jewish Community of Aleppo Through the Mid-Nineteenth Century* (New York: Sephardic Heritage Museum, 2019), 82.

"quite unfit for human habitation": "Allen Street, Again!," *New York Times*, February 14, 1929, 26.

"there beneath the roar": Leon Kobrin quoted in Irving Howe and Kenneth Libo, *How We Lived: A Documentary History of Immigrant Jews in America, 1880–1930* (New York: R. Marek, 1979), 28–29.

Murad and Tera Antar arrival: Passenger manifest, SS *France*, June 20, 1920.

second-class travel by immigrants: Ronald H. Bayor, *Encountering Ellis Island* (Baltimore: Johns Hopkins University Press, 2014), 27–28.

Syrian Jews on the Lower East Side: "In New York Is a City Set Apart Where Live Jews Who Know No Yiddish," *New York Tribune*, September 22, 1912; Rev. D. DeSola Pool, "The Levantine Jews in the United States," *American Jewish Yearbook, 1913–1914* (Chicago: American Jewish Congress), 207.

"Eastern European Jews showed": Nathan Glazer and Daniel P. Moynihan, *Beyond the Melting Pot: The Negroes, Puerto Ricans, Jews, Italians, and Irish of New York City*, 2nd ed. (Cambridge, MA: MIT Press, 1970), 155.

Syrian Jews versus Ashkenazis on education, "Americanization," tendency to pursue mercantile careers: Sutton, *Magic Carpet*, 149–151.

Sam M. marriage to Rose Tawil: New York, New York, Marriage License Indexes, 1907–2018, Ancestry.com.

Syrian Jewish naming conventions: Antar interview, August 5, 2007.

Murad's "dream": Antar interview, September 29, 2007.

Matile Auebe immigration, age, and occupation: Passenger manifest, SS *Byron*, February 24, 1930; Matile Davis in the 1940 Census, Youngstown, OH, 7:605; Petition for Naturalization, Matile Antar, October 10, 1944.

marriage to Sam M. Antar: Bernalillo County, New Mexico, Marriage Index, 1888–2017, Ancestry.com.

"absolutely invalid and worthless": S. Zevulun Lieberman, "A Sephardic Ban on Converts," *Tradition: A Journal of Orthodox Jewish Thought* 23, no. 2 (1988): 22–25.

birth of Mark Daniel Antar: California birth records, Ancestry.com.

Sam M. divorce from Matia Antar: "Decrees Granted," *Nevada State Journal*, November 8, 1945.

Matia Kooy remarriage: Amendment to Certificate of Naturalization, Matia Kooy, February 20, 1963.

Danny Mark Kooy death: Listing in US Veterans' Gravesites, ca. 1775–2019, Ancestry.com; listing in Findagrave, https://www.findagrave.com/memorial/232959052/danny-mark-kooy.

"An Aleppine can sell even a dried camel skin": Joseph T. Wells, *Frankensteins of Fraud* (Dexter, MI: Obsidian, 2000), 218, 217.

Eddie Antar dropping out in ninth grade, early background: Antar interviews, August 5 and September 29, 2007, and September 28, 2012; Wells, *Frankensteins of Fraud*,

218–219; statement by Eddie Antar, sentencing hearing, *USA v. Eddie Antar et al.*, US District Court for the District of New Jersey, no. 92-347, May 8, 1996.

age fifteen when he "officially" quit school, "battles": John T. Ward, "Eddie Speaks," *Asbury Park (NJ) Press*, December 11, 1994.

mandatory attendance laws: Gertrude Samuels, "The Schools, the Children, the Dilemma," *New York Times Magazine*, February 16, 1958.

Zookie background, marriage: Antar interview, August 31, 2012; Irving Antar in marriage license indexes, 1907–2018, Ancestry.com.

1946 reaffirmation of conversion ban: Lieberman, "Sephardic Ban on Converts."

$1,000 a week: Ward, "Eddie Speaks."

saffo customers: Antar interview, September 21, 2013.

details of leasing deals: Antar interview, December 20, 2012.

Chapter Two

"don't have to go to a favorite hangout": General Electric youth program; Marilyn Hoffman, "Young Buyers 'Dig' Electronics," *Christian Science Monitor*, August 5, 1968.

manufacturers confronting discounters: "Growth and Variety of Discount Houses Challenge Shopper and Store Alike," *New York Times*, January 30, 1962.

General Electric tracking down off-price retailers: Associated Press, "Backers Deny That Fair Trade Dying," *Montgomery Advertiser*, January 27, 1957.

Ronnie selling stake in Sights and Sounds: Sam E. Antar monograph, "The Crazy Eddie Fraud: Confessions of a White Collar Criminal," September 21, 2014.

deliveries to Corner: Sam E. Antar, interviews with the author, December 5, 2012, and March 1, 2013.

"serving Bronx and Manhattan players for 40 years": Alice McQuillan and Jorge Fitz-Gibbon, "Cops Go by Numbers, Nab 25," *New York Daily News*, January 17, 1997.

"Hundreds of hours": William H. Rashbaum, "Collecting's His Racket," *New York Daily News*, January 18, 1997.

"pivotal to the success": Patrice O'Shaughnessy, "Treasures from 2-Bit Bets?," *New York Daily News*, January 25, 1997.

the Vegliantes' East Harlem operations: Anthony Marino and Kermit Jaediker, "2 Roof-Hopping Cops Land KO on $3,000,000 Numbers Bank," *New York Daily News*, September 6, 1951; Anthony Marino, "Boss Cop Knocks Off 6 Million Policy HQ," *New York Daily News*, January 15, 1954.

"exceptional and exceptionally decent gentleman": Rashbaum, "Collecting's His Racket."

Eddie buying from other retailers: Gary Belsky and Phyllis Furman, "Calculated Madness: The Rise and Fall of Crazy Eddie Antar," *Crain's New York Business*, January 5, 1989.

Nick Zippilli background, work at Crazy Eddie: Nick Zippilli, interview with the author, October 19, 2012.

bait and switch, lunching: Antar interviews, August 5, 2007; March 1, 2013; May 1, 2013.

Sam E. Antar's pay at Crawford's: Antar interview, August 5, 2007.

"The customers gave me the [Crazy Eddie] name": David Lee Preston, "For 'Crazy Eddie' a New World," *Philadelphia Inquirer*, November 7, 1994.

"plastered the US with billboards": *Madman Muntz: American Maverick* (Offbeat Trilogy Productions, 2005).

"Car 54" episode: "Harry's Men's Shop" is at the fourteen-minute mark of "Toody and Muldoon Crack Down," air date January 21, 1962.

"even if he sells at cost or below cost," sticking it to Sony: Antar interviews, September 28, 2012, and December 20, 2021.

large-scale gasoline tax thievery: Robert I. Friedman, "The Organizatsiya," *New York*, November 7, 1994, 52.

"I sold the turntable for C-line": Zippilli interview.

Chapter Three

"helped shape a political agenda," "flipside of television": Charles Kaiser, *1968 in America: Music, Politics, Chaos, Counterculture, and the Shaping of a Generation* (New York: Weidenfeld and Nicolson, 1988), 190–191.

Larry Weiss background: Larry Weiss, interview with the author, March 6, 2020.

"Lonnie": L. Weiss interview, April 15, 2020.

Eddy brought in to keep the books: Sam E. Antar, interview with the author, August 5, 2007.

"Eddie was very crude": L. Weiss interview, April 15, 2020.

"showed his appreciation by not firing you": L. Weiss interview, April 15, 2020.

increasing reliance on Jerry Carroll: L. Weiss interview, April 15, 2020.

"He'd be hanging there upside down": L. Weiss interview, April 17, 2020.

Jerry Rosenberg: Isadore Barmash, "Hard-Hat Huckster," *New York Times*, March 17, 1974.

doo-wop commercial: L. Weiss interview, April 13, 2020.

"Eddie freaked out": L. Weiss interview, April 15, 2020.

Chapter Four

Sammy ejected from store: Sam E. Antar, interview with the author, April 13, 2020.

sale of cassette tapes with Mitchell: Antar interview, August 5, 2007.

"We need a brain in the business": Antar interview, September 28, 2012.

Salim Chera as El Maz: Antar interview, August 31, 2012.

Salim Chera arrival in New York, early years in United States: Passenger manifest, SS *Chicago*, February 16, 1921; US Census, 1930, 1940; Antar interview, August 31, 2012.

"making them sit in garbage cans": Antar interview, August 5, 2007.

Abraham Briloff background: Gary Weiss, "Abraham J. Briloff: Champion of Accounting and Accountability," *Barron's*, May 19, 2012, 38; Antar interview, March 3, 2012.

"pooling of interest accounting": Floyd Norris, "Abe Briloff, an Accountant Who Saw Through the Games," *Economix* (blog), December 13, 2013, https://economix.blogs.nytimes.com/2013/12/13/abe-briloff-an-accountant-who-saw-through-the-games/.

Sammy appreciation of Briloff: Antar interview, March 2, 2012.

Chapter Five

"'Be-in,' 'love-in'": Paul Vitello, "Howard Smith, Trend-Spotting Columnist, Dies at 77," *New York Times*, May 2, 2014.

"Beyond repetition": Howard Smith and Brian Van der Horst, "Scenes: Crazy Eddie Revealed," *Village Voice*, March 21, 1977.

"flashlight waved in front of the eyes": Vance Packard, *The Hidden Persuaders* (New York: D. McKay, 1957), 93.

Mary Hartman, Mary Hartman: Larry Weiss, interview with the author, April 15, 2020.

"people will do what we tell them to do": L. Weiss interview, April 30, 2020.

"a mob mentality to generate hate": L. Weiss interview, April 30, 2020.

"'buying the week's business'": L. Weiss interview, April 17, 2020.

"Remember our name": L. Weiss interview, April 17, 2020.

Eddie stabbing: Sam E. Antar, interview with the author, December 5, 2012; Joseph T. Wells, *Frankensteins of Fraud* (Dexter, MI: Obsidian, 2000), 224; Gary Belsky and Phyllis Furman, "Calculated Madness: The Rise and Fall of Crazy Eddie Antar," *Crain's New York Business*, January 5, 1989.

"Mylar dome tweeter": Acousti-Phase advertisement, *Hi Fi Review*, November 1977, 104.

partner's complaint: Susan Smallheer, "Judge Dismisses False Arrest Count in Acousti-Phase Business Lawsuit," *Rutland (VT) Herald*, January 18, 1980.

Eddie changes after stabbing: Nick Zippilli, interview with the author, October 19, 2012.

fair trade laws ending: Eileen Shanahan, "'Fair Trade' Laws Coming to an End," *New York Times*, December 13, 1975.

"We were flying by the seat of our pants": L. Weiss interview, April 15, 2020.

James Brown contacts: L. Weiss interview, April 17, 2020.

East Brunswick store opening: Mark Schoifet, "Bedlam Reigns at 'Audio Supermarket,'" *Home News* (New Brunswick, NJ), November 12, 1978.

"These store openings": Harry Spero, interview with the author, July 6, 2020.

Chapter Six

July 13, 1977: Miss Rosen, "How the Blackout of 1977 Helped Hip Hop Blow Up," Mandatory.com, July 13, 2017, www.mandatory.com/culture/1294849 -blackout-1977-helped-hip-hop-blow-up.

Eddie and insurance, spiking claims: Sam E. Antar, interview with the author, January 31, 2013.

"budgeted for a calculated amount of fraud": Tom Hall, "The Billion-Dollar Bent Fender," *Chicago Tribune*, June 25, 1972.

Vinnie Badalamenti and Crazy Eddie: Antar interview, July 20, 2020.

Badalamenti Advertising Agency, Ltd.: New York State Department of State, Corporate Records, DOS ID #531534, incorporated January 8, 1979.

Robad Distributors: New York State Department of State, Corporate Records, DOS ID #722644, incorporated September 16, 1981.

products stocked by Robad: *New York Daily News* display advertising, November 28, 1982, April 22, May 13, 1988.

clients in New Jersey and Connecticut, eleven employees: Transcript of statement of Ronald Fischetti, arraignment hearing, *USA v. Vincent Badalamenti*, 02 CR 1399, December 10, 2002.

rise in Bonanno family: Transcript of statement of Assistant US Attorney Thomas Siegel, arraignment hearing, *USA v. Vincent Badalamenti*, 02 CR 1399, December 10, 2002.

Badalamenti criminal history: USA v. Vincent Badalamenti, 12 CR 50, letters to court by Ronald Fischetti, August 15, 2012, to Assistant US Attorney Jack Dennehy, July 18, 2012; statement by Vincent Badalamenti, sentencing hearing, April 9, 2012.

administrative body of Bonanno family: Superseding indictment, *USA v. Vincent Badalamenti*, 12 CR 50, March 22, 2012.

"street boss": Statement of Assistant US Attorney Nicholas Argentieri, detention hearing, *USA v. Vincent Badalamenti*, 12 CR 50, February 13, 2012; Frank Donnelly, "5 Staten Islanders Accused After Raids on Bonanno Mob Family," *Staten Island Advance*, January 27, 2012; Frank Donnelly, "Mob Boss from Staten Island Sentenced to 18 Months Behind Bars," *Staten Island Advance*, September 25, 2012.

Gotti beat up a guy over horn-honking: Andrew Kershner, "John Gotti and Associate Beat Road Rage Rap in 1986 When Victim Kept Quiet at Trial," *New York Daily News*, March 14, 2017, www.nydailynews.com/new-york /gotti-associate-beat-road-rage-rap-victim-quiet-article-1.2997096.

Michael "the Nose" Mancuso: John Marzulli, "A Get Out of Jail Pass? Mafia Killer Wants to See His Kid," *New York Daily News*, May 18, 2006, 4.

Badalamenti plea deal: Transcript of statement by Ronald Fischetti, detention hearing, *USA v. Vincent Badalamenti*, 12 CR 50, February 13, 2012.

December 2009 social club raid: Transcript of statement by Fischetti.

Chapter Seven

"wagon of gold": Sam E. Antar, interview with the author, August 5, 2007.

nehkdi tapering: Testimony of Sam E. Antar, *USA v. Eddie Antar et al.*, US District Court for the District of New Jersey, no. 92-347, June 25, 1993; Antar interviews, September 28, 2012, May 1, 2013, and December 20, 2021; Sam E. Antar monograph, "The Crazy Eddie Fraud: Confessions of a White Collar Criminal," September 21, 2014, 30.

"my time to shine": Antar interview, May 1, 2013.

"You have to understand": Antar interview, May 1, 2013.

officials "would devise a temporary solution": Ken Auletta, *The Streets Were Paved with Gold* (New York: Vintage Books, 1980), 29.

tax-collection date moved back: Vincent Cannato, *The Ungovernable City: John Lindsay's New York and the Crisis of Liberalism* (Cambridge, MA: Basic Books, 2001), 101.

$700 million placed in capital budget: Congressional Budget Office, "The Causes of New York City's Fiscal Crisis," *Political Science Quarterly* 90, no. 4 (1975–1976): 662.

"tolerated or even suggested": Congressional Budget Office, "Causes of New York City's Fiscal Crisis," 659–674.

"An investor looking solely": Edward M. Gramlich, "The New York City Fiscal Crisis: What Happened and What Is to Be Done?," *American Economic Review* 66, no. 2 (1976): 415–429.

"budgetary, accounting and financial practices": Auletta, *Streets Were Paved with Gold,* 93.

"handling its money like a heroin addict": Joshua Brustein, "The Fiscal Crisis After 30 Years," *Gotham Gazette,* October 10, 2005, www.gothamgazette.com/index.php /economy/3016-the-fiscal-crisis-after-30-years.

"If there is one name that incites fear": N. R. Kleinfeld, "The All-Electronics Department Store," *New York Times,* March 7, 1982.

WRVR argument: Larry Weiss, interview with the author, April 17, 2020.

"hope that if it's not stuck behind a bowling alley": Peter Lynch with John Rothchild, *One Up on Wall Street* (New York: Simon and Schuster, 1989), 190.

"Crazy Eddie's Greatest Whatever-It-Is Sale Ever!": L. Weiss interview, April 15, 2020.

"never was a sale": L. Weiss interview, April 17, 2020.

"Whenever winter weather": Larry Weiss, "Crazy Eddie Advertising Memories," LinkedIn, September 15, 2016, www.linkedin.com/pulse/crazy-eddie -advertising-memories-from-guy-who-created-larry/.

Ira Weiss background: Ira Weiss, interview with the author, May 8, 2020.

Milky Way Lounge: Advertisement, *Yonkers (NY) Herald Statesman,* June 11, 1976, 43.

salesmen earnings: Nick Zippilli, interview with the author, October 19, 2012.

"High-end audio equipment is what I did": I. Weiss interview, May 8, 2020.

"The whole store persona was on making the sale": I. Weiss interview, May 8, 2020.

"Eddie was a character": I. Weiss interview, May 8, 2020.

"He wanted to call it Westbury": L. Weiss interview, April 21, 2020.

"Eventually, I found out": L. Weiss interview, April 21, 2020.

Gerald Newman claims: Decision of Appellate Division, New York State Supreme Court, Second Department, *Newman v. Crazy Eddie Inc.,* 119 A.D.2d 738 (1986); Antar interview, February 18, 2021; Crazy Eddie 10-K annual report for 1987, 17.

Robert Crumb rip-off: Emails to author from Robert Crumb and Alexander Wood, January 2022.

trademark registration: Service Mark Serial No. 73189630, Filing Date October 17, 1978, US Patent and Trademark Office, accessed through the Trademark Electronic Search System, www.uspto.gov/trademarks/search.

Chapter Eight

"brightly lit, 200-pound Big Apple ball": Larry Sutton, "'84 Here We Come," *New York Daily News,* January 1, 1984.

TV viewing: John J. O'Connor, "TV Weekend," *New York Times,* December 30, 1983.

Eddie called Debbie I to cancel: Joseph T. Wells, *Frankensteins of Fraud* (Dexter, MI: Obsidian, 2000), 228.

Eddie not at hospital for birth of child: Deposition of Deborah Rosen Antar, *Deborah Antar v. Eddie Antar,* New York State Supreme Court, Kings County, January 5, 1989, Index No. 6755/88, 1151.

"constantly changing existence": Deposition of Deborah Rosen Antar, *Deborah Antar v. Eddie Antar,* 1168.

"Eddie did what he wanted to do": Deposition of Deborah Rosen Antar, *Deborah Antar v. Eddie Antar,* 1153.

Sam M.'s jealousy: Sam E. Antar, interview with the author, September 29, 2007.

"He told me that they should not be living together": Deposition of Solomon E. Antar, *Deborah Antar v. Eddie Antar,* January 6, 1989, 75.

"a very, very big uproar": Deposition of Solomon E. Antar, *Deborah Antar v. Eddie Antar,* 95.

"upon arriving at Sam M.'s house that evening": Opinion by Judge Harold M. Ackerman, *Securities and Exchange Commission v. Sam M. Antar et al.,* 15 F. Supp. 2d 477, 1998 US Dist. LEXIS 21474, July 16, 1998.

"raging in obscenities": Wells, *Frankensteins of Fraud,* 229.

"in a position to receive 50 percent": Deposition of Solomon E. Antar, *Deborah Antar v. Eddie Antar,* March 9, 1989, 220.

"arguments, phone calls at all hours": Supreme Court justice Barry Hurowitz, Memorandum Decision, *Deborah Antar v. Eddie Antar,* January 24, 1990.

"He told her 'it was one year'": Hurowitz, Memorandum Decision.

"designed to take care of the children": Hurowitz, Memorandum Decision.

"was frightened and confused": Hurowitz, Memorandum Decision.

"judge will do the Equitable Distribution": Hurowitz, Memorandum Decision.

"the agreement was never mentioned again": Deposition of Deborah Rosen Antar, *Deborah Antar v. Eddie Antar,* 1161.

"Don't worry, you will get your money": Deposition of Deborah Rosen Antar, *Deborah Antar v. Eddie Antar,* 1188.

provisions of separation agreement: Hurowitz, Memorandum Decision.

Chapter Nine

Journal of Accountancy article: Ronald S. Barden et al., "Going Public—What It Involves: A Framework for Providing Advice to Management," *Journal of Accountancy* (March 1984): 63.

impact of nehkdi reduction: Opinion by Judge Harold M. Ackerman, *Securities and Exchange Commission v. Sam M. Antar et al.,* 15 F. Supp. 2d 477, 1998 US Dist. LEXIS 21474, July 16, 1998.

"dealing in blocked German currencies after World War II": "Max Oppenheimer, Investment Broker" (obituary), *New York Times,* June 4, 1964.

Zofnass background: Bob Rozycki, "Profits & Passions: Paul Zofnass," *Westchester County Business Journal* 44, no. 5 (2005): 40.

Berman background: David Robinson, "President of New York's Chartwell Investments Quits," *Knight-Ridder Tribune Business News,* September 30, 2003.

Zofnass friendship with Al Gore: Ellen Nakashima and David Maraniss, "Gore Adapted to Army, Dad's Defeat," *Washington Post,* December 30, 1999.

"The due-diligence guys, Berman and Zofnass, come over": Sam E. Antar, interview with the author, August 5, 2007.

"They said, 'Let's let Sam come along'": Antar interview, August 5, 2007.

road show: Sam E. Antar trial testimony, *USA v. Eddie Antar et al.*, US District Court for the District of New Jersey, no. 92-347, June 25, 1993.

working off cue cards: Antar trial testimony.

questions came up about bait-and-switch sales practices: Deposition of Sam E. Antar, *Oppenheimer Palmieri L.P. v. Peat Marwick Main*, 87 Civ. 0033, 88 Civ. 3481, January 14, 1992, 1859.

"educate the customer": Deposition of Sam E. Antar, *Oppenheimer Palmieri L.P. v. Peat Marwick Main*, 1860.

Zofnass and Berman aware of bait and switch: Deposition of Sam E. Antar, *Oppenheimer Palmieri L.P. v. Peat Marwick Main*, 1851–1853.

"did not want us to use the words 'bait and switch' to describe our sales practices": Deposition of Sam E. Antar, *Oppenheimer Palmieri L.P. v. Peat Marwick Main*, 1855, 1856.

Chapter Ten

Barron's article: Gigi Mahon, "Not-So-Crazy Eddie: Hard-Sell Retailer Going Public," *Barron's*, June 4, 1984, 14.

Eddie's reaction: Sam E. Antar, interview with the author, August 5, 2007.

price move after offering: Floyd Norris, *Barron's*, September 17, 1984, 93.

Eddie meets with Colloton: Testimony of John Edmund Colloton, *USA v. Eddie Antar et al.*, US District Court for the District of New Jersey, no. 92-347, July 6, 1993.

"There is no benchmark for corporate excellence": Testimony of Colloton, *USA v. Eddie Antar et al.*

Colloton background: Testimony of Colloton, *USA v. Eddie Antar et al.*; "John E. Colloton" (death notice), *Journal News*, White Plains, NY, August 1, 2002. His trial testimony conflicts with claims made in the death notice. The author has relied on the former over the latter.

Colloton's alcoholism: Sam E. Antar, interview with the author, July 26, 2013.

drunk-driving incident: "Mamaroneck: DWI Charged After Wreck," *Port Chester (NY) Daily Item*, May 22, 1987.

"He was the best: smooth, enthusiastic, helpful": Kathryn F. Staley, *The Art of Short-Selling* (New York: Wiley, 1997), 216.

medical school admission standards: Jack Dolan, "Schools Lower the Bar," *Hartford (CT) Courant*, June 30, 2004.

Water Club reception: Kristen Kelch and Joe Calderone, "Crazy Eddie's Medical School Flops," *New York Newsday*, March 21, 1984.

"They really sold the place": Kelch and Calderone, "Crazy Eddie's Medical School Flops."

Sammy's trip to St. Lucia: Antar interview, September 28, 2012.

Chapter Eleven

"if he could have children with someone else": Deposition of Deborah Rosen Antar, *Deborah Antar v. Eddie Antar*, New York State Supreme Court, Kings County, January 5, 1989, Index No. 6755/88, 1142, 1171.

remained in bed three days: Deposition of Deborah Rosen Antar, *Deborah Antar v. Eddie Antar*, 1142, 1171.

"You will get nothing, and I will break your arms and legs!": Deposition of Deborah Rosen Antar, *Deborah Antar v. Eddie Antar*, 1237.

hits her on face: Deposition of Deborah Rosen Antar, *Deborah Antar v. Eddie Antar*, 1215.

Solomon drafted the divorce papers; "You wanted a divorce, here it is": Deposition of Deborah Rosen Antar, *Deborah Antar v. Eddie Antar*, 1253.

"The judge takes care of the equitable division": Deposition of Deborah Rosen Antar, *Deborah Antar v. Eddie Antar*, 1258.

divorce decree signed: Second Amended Complaint, *Deborah Antar v. Eddie Antar and Solomon Antar*, Supreme Court of the State of New York, County of New York, Index No. 15910/87, May 16, 1991.

"Trust me": Deposition of Deborah Rosen Antar, *Deborah Antar v. Eddie Antar*, 1265.

"I will come down with Richie to check": Deposition of Deborah Rosen Antar, *Deborah Antar v. Eddie Antar*, 1319.

Al Dayon background: "City Ends Racket in Old Watches," *New York Times*, November 22, 1957; "4 Indicted Here on Stock Conspiracy," *New York Times*, January 21, 1971.

"Let's go": Deposition of Deborah Rosen Antar, *Deborah Antar v. Eddie Antar*, 1334.

"when the case goes to court": Deposition of Deborah Rosen Antar, *Deborah Antar v. Eddie Antar*, 1368.

claim Debbie learned about divorce in filing with SEC (footnote): Opinion of Judge Nicholas H. Politan, *Securities and Exchange Commission v. Deborah Rosen Antar et al.*, Civ. 89-3773, August 23, 1993.

"Don't worry, you will have plenty": Deposition of Deborah Rosen Antar, *Deborah Antar v. Eddie Antar*, 1402.

"The stock sold, and he made a lot of money, and he came home": Deposition of Deborah Rosen Antar, *Deborah Antar v. Eddie Antar*, 1580.

"I believed him": Deposition of Deborah Rosen Antar, *Deborah Antar v. Eddie Antar*, 1581.

Lillian signed Debbie's name: Opinion of Judge Politan, *Securities and Exchange Commission v. Deborah Rosen Antar et al.*

"preparatory effort": Opinion of Judge Politan, *Securities and Exchange Commission v. Deborah Rosen Antar et al.*, quoting Debbie's lawyer.

Chapter Twelve

"Do you know what co-op advertising is?": Harry Spero, interview with the author, July 6, 2020.

Harry Spero background: Spero interview.

argument with Eddie over not broadcasting one day: Spero interview.

Forbes *piece:* "His Margins Are Insaaaaaaane," *Forbes*, October 8, 1984, 39.

article quoting Richard Lilly: John Henry, "Sell Like Crazy," *New York Daily News*, December 11, 1984.

"underlying assumption": Testimony of John Edmund Colloton, *USA v. Eddie Antar et al.*, US District Court for the District of New Jersey, no. 92-347, July 6, 1993.

Chapter Thirteen

"Analysts liked the feel of pulling the wool over the consumers' eyes": Kathryn F. Staley, *The Art of Short-Selling* (New York: Wiley, 1997), 212–213.

warranty fraud, details, constituted 40 to 50 percent of claims, yielded $150,000 to $200,000 a year: Testimony of David Panoff, *USA v. Eddie Antar et al.*, US District Court for the District of New Jersey, no. 92-347, July 8, 1993.

Dave Panoff background, Audio Clinic, Eddie assenting to his continuing it at Crazy Eddie: Testimony of Panoff, *USA v. Eddie Antar et al.*

auto-warranty trial in Boston: Robert J. Anglin, "Edgerly Planned Car Warranty Fraud, Jury Told," *Boston Globe,* March 9, 1976.

"Rip their eyes out": Testimony of Panoff, *USA v. Eddie Antar et al.*

"I need you to do me a favor": Testimony of Panoff, *USA v. Eddie Antar et al.*

"I didn't know exactly what he meant at first": Testimony of Panoff, *USA v. Eddie Antar et al.*

approach to Neiderbach, "Will you be able to do it?": Testimony of David Neiderbach, *USA v. Eddie Antar et al.*, US District Court for the District of New Jersey, no. 92-347, June 22, 1993.

"I don't know exactly how": Testimony of Neiderbach, *USA v. Eddie Antar et al.*

pretax profits would be boosted 20 percent: Sam E. Antar monograph, "The Crazy Eddie Fraud: Confessions of a White Collar Criminal," September 21, 2014.

polygraph tests: Nick Zippilli, interview with the author, October 19, 2012.

"give the auditors a hand": Testimony of Neiderbach, *USA v. Eddie Antar et al.*

"we would change them back, but we couldn't do it yet": Testimony of Neiderbach, *USA v. Eddie Antar et al.*

reports of Eddie transshipping goods: Testimony of John Edmund Colloton, *USA v. Eddie Antar et al.*, US District Court for the District of New Jersey, no. 92-347, July 6, 1993.

"The sale of stock by the chief executive": Testimony of Colloton, *USA v. Eddie Antar et al.*

"Eddie was very persuasive": Testimony of Colloton, *USA v. Eddie Antar et al.* The identity of the money manager is garbled in the trial transcript.

"I normally taped CEO addresses": Testimony of Colloton, *USA v. Eddie Antar et al.*

"Don't ever do that again": Testimony of Colloton, *USA v. Eddie Antar et al.*

"A doubt is a process": Testimony of Colloton, *USA v. Eddie Antar et al.*

"above-average growth prospects": Barry Bryant, "Consumer Electronics Retailing," equity research, Drexel Burnham Lambert, December 1985, 43.

"relishes beating earnings estimates": Staley, *Art of Short-Selling,* 213.

"We judge the results": Staley, *Art of Short-Selling,* 213.

Chapter Fourteen

childhood recollections: Rori Sassoon, interview with the author, April 12, 2021.

corporate filings reviewed climbed 71 percent: "U.S. Securities and Exchange Commission Fifty-Second Annual Report," March 2, 1987, 2.

1985 SEC statistics: 51st Annual Report of the US Securities and Exchange Commission, December 31, 1985, ii, 9.

"more likeable to our auditors and corroded their professional skepticism": Sam E. Antar monograph, "The Crazy Eddie Fraud: Confessions of a White Collar Criminal," September 21, 2014.

"comparable store sales growth in the low double digits": Joseph T. Wells, *Frankensteins of Fraud* (Dexter, MI: Obsidian, 2000), 236.

"anything with a battery or a plug": Testimony of Leonard Rubin, *USA v. Eddie Antar et al.*, US District Court for the District of New Jersey, no. 92-347, June 24, 1993.

mechanics of Wren fraud: Testimony of Leonard Rubin, *USA v. Eddie Antar et al.*

"could do basically the same thing I had did the year before": Testimony of David Neiderbach, *USA v. Eddie Antar et al.*, US District Court for the District of New Jersey, no. 92-347, June 22, 1993.

involvement of Arnie Spindler: Testimony of Arnold Spindler, *In the Matter of Crazy Eddie Inc.*, Securities and Exchange Commission, November 20, 1987, 58–100; Testimony of Neiderbach, *USA v. Eddie Antar et al.*; Testimony of Sam E. Antar, *USA v. Eddie Antar et al.*, US District Court for the District of New Jersey, no. 92-347, June 25, 1993.

"not in great shape at that point": Testimony of Neiderbach, *USA v. Eddie Antar et al.*

"You'll have to do it again this year": Testimony of David Panoff, *USA v. Eddie Antar et al.*, US District Court for the District of New Jersey, no. 92-347, July 8, 1993.

"It was explained to me": Testimony of Panoff, *USA v. Eddie Antar et al.*

$200,000 sold to Gateway Marketing: Opinion by Judge Harold M. Ackerman, *Securities and Exchange Commission v. Sam M. Antar et al.*, 15 F. Supp. 2d 477, 1998 US Dist. LEXIS 21474, July 16, 1998.

Sammy came up with the idea: Sam E. Antar, interview with the author, May 1, 2013.

money shunted through Panama: Testimony of Sam E. Antar, *USA v. Eddie Antar et al.*, June 25, 1993; Opinion of Judge Nicholas H. Politan, *Securities and Exchange Commission v. Deborah Rosen Antar et al.*, Civ. 89-3773, August 23, 1993.

overshot their targets: Testimony of Sam E. Antar, *USA v. Eddie Antar et al.*, June 25, 1993.

outside auditors' recommendation: Testimony of Sam E. Antar, *USA v. Eddie Antar et al.*, June 25, 1993; Affidavit of Sam E. Antar, *In re Crazy Eddie Securities Litigation*, 87 Civ. 0033, May 29, 1992.

"rainy day fund": Antar, "Crazy Eddie Fraud," 23; Affidavit of Sam E. Antar, *In re Crazy Eddie Securities Litigation*.

"money in the bank": Testimony of Sam E. Antar, *USA v. Eddie Antar et al.*, June 25, 1993.

"No public company got sued for underreporting earnings": Antar, "Crazy Eddie Fraud," 23.

stock-sale proceeds: *USA v. Eddie Antar et al.*, superseding indictment, June 11, 1993; Antar, "Crazy Eddie Fraud," 22.

"Not bad for a $2 million 'reinvestment'": Antar, "Crazy Eddie Fraud."

Allen Antar on outs with the family: Antar interview, September 29, 2007.

Allen depositing funds: Testimony of Sam E. Antar, *USA v. Eddie Antar et al.*, June 25, 1993; Opinion of Judge Ackerman, *Securities and Exchange Commission v. Sam M. Antar et al.*

Sam M. came up short: Testimony of Sam E. Antar, *USA v. Eddie Antar et al.*, June 25, 1993.

Chapter Fifteen

Cohen background: Testimony of Sasson Cohen, *USA v. Eddie Antar et al.*, US District Court for the District of New Jersey, no. 92-347, June 30, 1993.

agreed that they would work together: Testimony of Cohen, *USA v. Eddie Antar et al.*

"the first to receive all new merchandise that comes on the market": Testimony of Cohen, *USA v. Eddie Antar et al.*

"He explained to me": Testimony of Cohen, *USA v. Eddie Antar et al.*

80 percent of its merchandise from Crazy Eddie: Testimony of Sam E. Antar, *USA v. Eddie Antar et al.*, US District Court for the District of New Jersey, no. 92-347, June 25, 1993.

checks were undated: Testimony of Sam E. Antar, *USA v. Eddie Antar et al.*

$650,000 in small, undated checks: Opinion by Judge Harold M. Ackerman, *Securities and Exchange Commission v. Sam M. Antar et al.*, 15 F. Supp. 2d 477, 1998 US Dist. LEXIS 21474, July 16, 1998.

anonymous call, Purcell reaction: Affidavit of Sam E. Antar, *In re Crazy Eddie Securities Litigation*, June 4, 1992.

"merchandise was being skimmed," "call in": Memorandum to file, James Purcell, March 8, 1987 (Exhibit B to Affidavit of Sam E. Antar, *In re Crazy Eddie Securities Litigation*).

phony excuse to KMG and Ferrara denial: Affidavit of Sam E. Antar, *In re Crazy Eddie Securities Litigation*.

Eddie depriving his stores of prime merchandise: Testimony of Sam E. Antar, *USA v. Eddie Antar et al.*

"The comparison to Wal-Mart": Mary Kay Ribi, "Wall Street's Just Wild About Crazy Eddie," *Home News* (New Brunswick, NJ), July 27, 1986.

"even a high school dropout could rise to upper management": William Westhoven, "Crazy Eddie Turned Me into a Journalist," *Morris County (NJ) Daily Record,* September 16, 2016, www.dailyrecord.com/story/news/2016/09/16/crazy-eddie-turned-me-into-journalist/90346610/.

"didn't have the benefit of a proper education": Harry Spero, interview with the author, July 20, 2020.

"manager meetings": Ribi, "Wall Street's Just Wild About Crazy Eddie."

Chapter Sixteen

price-cutting: Richard Sherwin, "Prices Are Insane!," *New York Daily News*, July 22, 1986.

comp-store sales padded from 6.8 percent to 15 percent: Opinion by Judge Harold M. Ackerman, *Securities and Exchange Commission v. Sam M. Antar et al.*, 15 F. Supp. 2d 477, 1998 US Dist. LEXIS 21474, July 16, 1998.

Sam M. stock dump: Opinion by Judge Ackerman, *Securities and Exchange Commission v. Sam M. Antar et al.*

5 to 10 percent decline expected: Testimony of Sam E. Antar, *USA v. Eddie Antar et al.*, US District Court for the District of New Jersey, no. 92-347, June 28, 1993.

"Now, you issue financial statements": Testimony of Sam E. Antar, *USA v. Eddie Antar et al.*, June 25, 1993.

memo concerning stock sales: Testimony of Sam E. Antar, *USA v. Eddie Antar et al.*, June 25, 1993.

"Maybe I'm being a little bit too pessimistic": Testimony of Sam E. Antar, *USA v. Eddie Antar et al.*, June 28, 1993.

Morgan Stanley Retail Forum: Testimony of Sam E. Antar, *USA v. Eddie Antar et al.*, June 28, 1993.

"I didn't even know if I could do that": Testimony of Sam E. Antar, *USA v. Eddie Antar et al.*, June 28, 1993.

"Better that you didn't know": Testimony of Sam E. Antar, *USA v. Eddie Antar et al.*, June 28, 1993.

New York Times *feature on Crazy Eddie home shopping network:* Richard W. Stevenson, "Crazy Eddie Sets Network," *New York Times*, July 29, 1986.

"straight from a tax-planner's manual": John R. Dorfman, "Firm Insiders Are Not Selling Despite '87 Rise in Tax on Gains," *Wall Street Journal*, December 1, 1986.

Eddie leaves Laguna Beach: Testimony of John Edmund Colloton, *USA v. Eddie Antar et al.*, US District Court for the District of New Jersey, no. 92-347, July 6, 1993.

Chapter Seventeen

"a philandering sort of 'Crazy Eddie' television huckster": Vincent Canby, "'Peggy Sue Got Married,' Time Travel by Francis Coppola," *New York Times*, October 5, 1986.

Springsteenmania: Alan Mirabella, "Born to Run Out!," *New York Daily News*, November 11, 1986.

timing of Eddie's remarriage: Supreme Court justice Barry Hurowitz, Memorandum Decision, *Deborah Antar v. Eddie Antar*, January 24, 1990.

"I will give you everything": Deposition of Deborah Rosen Antar, *Deborah Antar v. Eddie Antar*, New York State Supreme Court, Kings County, January 13, 1989, Index No. 6755/88, 1586.

Eddie coming to Debbie's house during the summer: Deposition of Deborah Rosen Antar, *Deborah Antar v. Eddie Antar*, 1608.

"He got into a fight with me": Deposition of Deborah Rosen Antar, *Deborah Antar v. Eddie Antar*, 1620.

"Put the piece of shit on the phone": Deposition of Deborah Rosen Antar, *Deborah Antar v. Eddie Antar*, 1621.

"So I thought to myself": Testimony of Sam E. Antar, *USA v. Eddie Antar et al.*, US District Court for the District of New Jersey, no. 92-347, June 28, 1993.

actual versus real comp-store sales: Testimony of Sam E. Antar, *USA v. Eddie Antar et al.*, June 28, 1993.

"We gave up hope": Testimony of Sam E. Antar, *USA v. Eddie Antar et al.*, June 28, 1993.

"informed me that Eddie had decided": Testimony of David Panoff, *USA v. Eddie Antar et al.*, US District Court for the District of New Jersey, no. 92-347, July 8, 1993.

"all of his wishes should still be followed": Testimony of Panoff, *USA v. Eddie Antar et al.*

Scott "asked stupid questions": Sam E. Antar, interview with the author, May 18, 2021.

"fall goy": Antar interview, May 17, 2021.

"he didn't want to pick up the pieces": Testimony of Sam E. Antar, *USA v. Eddie Antar et al.*

"He said, 'Fuck Jim Purcell'": Antar interview, May 18, 2021.

"powers and responsibilities": Crazy Eddie press release, January 9, 1987.

Sammy as source for illness rumor: Antar interview, May 19, 2021.

"Eddie was the real entrepreneurial spirit of the company": Todd Beamon, "Chief Steps Down at Crazy Eddie," *New York Times*, January 10, 1987.

debit memo fraud, involvement of Spindler, Grinberg, and Mitchell Antar: Testimony of Sam E. Antar, *USA v. Eddie Antar et al.*, June 28, 1993.

$5 million–$6 million from Wren: Testimony of Sam E. Antar, *USA v. Eddie Antar et al.*, June 28, 1993.

"People were losing faith": Testimony of Sam E. Antar, *USA v. Eddie Antar et al.*, June 28, 1993.

"No one has seen or heard from Eddie": Robin Schatz, "Crazy Eddie's Stock Slides After Disquieting Christmas," *New York Newsday*, January 7, 1987.

analyst conflicts of interests: Jill E. Fisch, "Fiduciary Duties and Analyst Scandals," *Alabama Law Review* 1083 (2007).

"shockingly poor": Barbara Demick, "Puzzle of Crazy Eddie Driving Analysts 'Insa-a-ane," *Philadelphia Inquirer*, January 26, 1987.

"fundamentally sound company with tremendous opportunities": James B. Stewart, "Crazy Eddie's Founder Resigns as Chief amid Rumors That He Is Seriously Ill," *Wall Street Journal*, January 12, 1987.

"felt entitled to a larger share of the business": Testimony of Sam E. Antar, *USA v. Eddie Antar et al.*, June 28, 1993.

"he made them all rich": Antar interview, September 29, 2007.

"I became like a Henry Kissinger": Testimony of Sam E. Antar, *USA v. Eddie Antar et al.*, June 28, 1993.

Chapter Eighteen

"courtier of rich, unhappily wed New Yorkers": Susan Brenna, "You're Rich? Not Boring? He'll Take Your Case," *New York Newsday*, January 14, 1987.

the Capassos and the "Bess Mess": Jack Newfield and Wayne Barrett, *City for Sale: Ed Koch and the Betrayal of New York* (New York: Harper and Row, 1988), 388–486.

"might be called the Felder gambit": Michael Gross, "Trouble in Splitsville," *New York*, December 13, 1999.

"or they will all go down": Deposition of Deborah Rosen Antar, *Deborah Antar v. Eddie Antar*, New York State Supreme Court, Kings County, January 16, 1989, Index No. 6755/88, 1782.

warranty fraud subpoena: Testimony of David Panoff, *USA v. Eddie Antar et al.*, US District Court for the District of New Jersey, no. 92-347, July 8, 1993; Sam E. Antar, interview with the author, July 13, 2007.

"They came into our repair center": Testimony of Panoff, *USA v. Eddie Antar et al.*

warranty claims had gotten sloppy: Paul Hayes, interview with the author, April 28, 2020.

"There was something about that whole meeting": Testimony of Panoff, *USA v. Eddie Antar et al.*

"we had the other records": Testimony of Panoff, *USA v. Eddie Antar et al.*

"The profitability of Crazy Eddie was going down the tubes": Testimony of Sam E. Antar, *USA v. Eddie Antar et al.*, US District Court for the District of New Jersey, no. 92-347, June 28, 1993.

"in case anything happens": Sam E. Antar, notes, May 14, 1989.

comp-store sale decline in fiscal 1987: Testimony of Sam E. Antar, *USA v. Eddie Antar et al.*, June 28, 1993.

store-inventory inflation: Testimony of Sam E. Antar, *USA v. Eddie Antar et al.*, June 28, 1993.

key dropped in paper clips: Testimony of Sam E. Antar, *USA v. Eddie Antar et al.*, June 29, 1993; Antar interview, December 5, 2012.

"Eddie's going to be crossing the goal line": Testimony of Panoff, *USA v. Eddie Antar et al.*

"We decided to overship": Testimony of Sam E. Antar, *USA v. Eddie Antar et al.*, June 29, 1993.

falsification of earnings announced in March 1987: Testimony of Sam E. Antar, *USA v. Eddie Antar et al.*, June 29, 1993.

troubles with the home shopping network: Harry Spero, interview with the author, July 6, 2020.

Bo Dietl background: Nicholas Pileggi, "The Cop Who Came in from the Heat," *New York*, August 26, 1985, reprinted in the Stacks Reader, www.thestacksreader .com/the-cop-who-came-in-from-the-heat/.

Dietl hired: Deposition of Deborah Rosen Antar, *Deborah Antar v. Eddie Antar*, January 16, 1989, 1717.

"What is your mother's number?": Deposition of Deborah Rosen Antar, *Deborah Antar v. Eddie Antar*, January 16, 1989, 1731.

"We were both very upset": Deposition of Deborah Rosen Antar, *Deborah Antar v. Eddie Antar*, January 16, 1989, 1736.

confrontation with Dietl's men and police: Deposition of Deborah Rosen Antar, *Deborah Antar v. Eddie Antar*, January 16, 1989, 1740–1766.

order of protection: Deposition of Deborah Rosen Antar, *Deborah Antar v. Eddie Antar*, January 16, 1989, 1786–1787.

firing of Lillian Rosen: Testimony of Sam E. Antar, *USA v. Eddie Antar et al.*, July 1, 1993; Deposition of Sam E. Antar, *SEC v. Sam M. Antar, Allen Antar and Benjamin Kuszer*, US District Court, District of New Jersey, Civ. 93-3988, February 7, 1995, 371–372.

Sam M. fired: Crazy Eddie 10-K annual report for 1987, 7.

Mitchell meets Scott: Testimony of James Scott, *USA v. Eddie Antar et al.*, US District Court for the District of New Jersey, no. 92-347, July 13, 1993.

Mitchell quits: Crazy Eddie 10-K annual report for 1987.

Mitchell Antar letter: Testimony of Sam E. Antar, *USA v. Eddie Antar et al.*, January 30, 1993.

"concerned that my former wife": Opinion of Judge Nicholas H. Politan, *Securities and Exchange Commission v. Deborah Rosen Antar et al.*, Civ. 89-3773, August 23, 1993.

Chapter Nineteen

"no one would suspect": Deposition of Sam E. Antar, *SEC v. Eddie Antar, Sam E. Antar, Mitchell Antar, Isaac Kairey, David Panoff, Eddie Gindi and Kathleen Morin*, US District Court, District of New Jersey, Civ. 89-3773, December 3, 1991, 846–847.

"repackage the company": Testimony of Sam E. Antar, *USA v. Eddie Antar et al.*, US District Court for the District of New Jersey, no. 92-347, June 28, 1993.

"You don't like me because I'm Jewish": James R. Hagerty, "Bache CEO Repelled Raider but Lost Job," *Wall Street Journal*, May 30–31, 2020.

"Meet with the Belzbergs": Testimony of Sam E. Antar, *USA v. Eddie Antar et al.*, June 28, 1993.

"I said we were being 'conservative'": Sam E. Antar, interview with the author, June 5, 2021.

10 to 20 percent share: Testimony of Sam E. Antar, *USA v. Eddie Antar et al.*, June 30, 1993.

"raised many questions": Isadore Barmash, "Founder Joins Bid for Crazy Eddie," *New York Times*, May 21, 1987.

"question Eddie's integrity": Jeffrey A. Tannenbaum, "Crazy Eddie Gets $7-a-Share Buyout Bid from Group Led by Founder, Belzbergs," *Wall Street Journal*, May 21, 1987.

"opportunism at the expense of shareholders": Jeffrey A. Tannenbaum, "Crazy Eddie's Founder Antar Is Back, with a Price That Has People Talking," *Wall Street Journal*, May 22, 1987.

"earned accolades," "scroungy, makeshift": Paulette Thomas, "Crazy Eddie Suitor: 'Money Heals All,'" *Wall Street Journal*, June 4, 1987.

air-conditioning "is set too low": Bill Crawford, "E. Z. Goes Crazy," *Texas Monthly*, November 1987, 150–154.

"cultural affinity": Thomas, "Crazy Eddie Suitor."

Chapter Twenty

"to take over the company": Testimony of Sam E. Antar, *USA v. Eddie Antar et al.*, US District Court for the District of New Jersey, no. 92-347, June 28, 1993.

"We didn't consider it anything": Testimony of Sam E. Antar, *USA v. Eddie Antar et al.*, June 28, 1993.

Chemical Bank line of credit cut off: "SEC Probes Crazy Eddie; Credit Halted," *New York Newsday*, June 18, 1987.

Newsday *article:* Robin Schatz, "Eddie's Crazy World: Family Airs Dirty Laundry in New Jersey Court," *New York Newsday*, August 1, 1987.

"Crazy Eddie's Family Feud Blowout Blitz": Display advertisement, *New York Daily News*, August 6, 1987.

Manufacturers Hanover Trust withdraws: Deposition of Sam E. Antar, *SEC v. Sam M. Antar, Mitchell Antar and Benjamin Kuszer; Rori Antar, Sam A. Antar, Michelle*

Antar, Adam Kuszer, et al., Relief Defendants, US District Court, District of New Jersey, Civ. 93-3988, February 8, 1995, 721–722.

electronic stalking of Debbie: Sam E. Antar, interview with the author, June 5, 2021.

Mitchell meeting with Zinn: Testimony of Marvin Gersten, *USA v. Eddie Antar et al.,* US District Court for the District of New Jersey, no. 92-347, July 13, 1993.

"The Antar family was positioning itself": Antar interview, July 13, 2007.

"Arnie came to me perceiving": Deposition of Sam E. Antar, *SEC v. Sam M. Antar, Mitchell Antar and Benjamin Kuszer; Rori Antar, Sam A. Antar, Michelle Antar, Adam Kuszer,* et al., Relief Defendants, February 7, 1995, 373–374.

"He threatened to spill the beans": Antar interview, July 13, 2007; Joseph T. Wells, *Frankensteins of Fraud* (Dexter, MI: Obsidian, 2000), 244–245.

"I felt that since Arnie was not a family member": Antar interview, September 3, 2007.

"I told both of them": Testimony of Arnold Spindler, *In the Matter of Crazy Eddie Inc.,* Securities and Exchange Commission, November 27, 1987, 216–217.

Spindler testimony re debit memos: Testimony of Spindler, *In the Matter of Crazy Eddie Inc.,* November 20, 1987, 183–207.

"Destroy everything and anything": Testimony of Sam E. Antar, *USA v. Eddie Antar et al.,* June 28, 1993.

six tractor trailers: Testimony of David Neiderbach, *USA v. Eddie Antar et al.,* US District Court for the District of New Jersey, no. 92-347, June 22, 1993.

not all documents shredded: Testimony of Sam E. Antar, *USA v. Eddie Antar et al.,* June 28, 1993.

"They came and I lied under oath": Antar interview, July 13, 2007.

"we had the shredding machines": Antar interview, July 13, 2007.

disclosure of SEC investigation and warranty probe: Gregory A. Robb, "Crazy Eddie Is Facing 2 Federal Investigations," *New York Times,* October 29, 1987.

"bad feeling in your stomach": "Crazy Eddie Antar Plans to Sell Half of 9.1% Stake," *Wall Street Journal,* September 15, 1987.

"a big bicycle": Daniel F. Cuff and Peter H. Frank, "Bidder for Crazy Eddie Confident of Success," *New York Times,* June 3, 1987.

Palmieri background: Alison Leigh Cowan, "A Corporate Doctor Is Getting Fewer Calls," *New York Times,* July 6, 1990; "Carter Names L.A. Man to Refugee Affairs Post," *Los Angeles Times,* December 1, 1979; John D. Williams, "Victor Palmieri Finds a Nugget of Gold in the Ashes of the Penn Central Railroad," *Wall Street Journal,* January 27, 1978.

"black hole": Antar interview, June 21, 2021.

Palmieri exchange with Eddie: Antar interview, June 21, 2021; Sam E. Antar, "My Crazy Eddie Story," unpublished essay dated May 5, 2006; Wells, *Frankensteins of Fraud,* 242.

Chapter Twenty-One

Robert Marmon education, professional background: Testimony of Robert Marmon, *USA v. Eddie Antar et al.,* US District Court for the District of New Jersey, no. 92-347, June 15, 1993.

considered putting Crazy Eddie into bankruptcy: Sam E. Antar, notes, November 16, 1987.

"to observe and validate the count": Testimony of Marmon, *USA v. Eddie Antar et al.*, June 15, 1993.

"took me into an office": Testimony of Marmon, *USA v. Eddie Antar et al.*, June 15, 1993.

"There were no files": Testimony of Marmon, *USA v. Eddie Antar et al.*, June 15, 1993.

$45 million shortfall: Testimony of Marmon, *USA v. Eddie Antar et al.*, June 15, 1993.

"we have no indication now what caused this": "Crazy Eddie Deficit in Inventory Disclosed," *New York Times*, November 20, 1987.

"poor management, inaccurate bookkeeping": "Crazy Eddie Deficit in Inventory Disclosed."

Sammy doubts $45 million figure: Sam E. Antar, interview with the author, December 5, 2012; Sam E. Antar monograph, "The Crazy Eddie Fraud: Confessions of a White Collar Criminal," September 21, 2014.

"My father said, 'I want to make peace'": Antar interview, July 13, 2007.

confrontation at Tera's house: Antar interview, July 13, 2007.

"He was making wild accusations": Antar interview, July 13, 2007.

"At the time, even though they may have had their doubts": Antar interview, July 13, 2007.

no knowledge of brothers' involvement: Testimony of Arnold Spindler, *In the Matter of Crazy Eddie Inc.*, Securities and Exchange Commission, November 20, 1987, 101.

"directly invited": Testimony of Spindler, *In the Matter of Crazy Eddie Inc.*, November 20, 1987, 109.

"I basically said, 'I'll tell you the truth, it didn't happen'": Antar interview, July 13, 2007.

Barron's article: Joe Queenan, "Positively Insane: The Absolutely Incredible Saga of Crazy Eddie," *Barron's*, June 15, 1988, 15.

Eddie takes precautions to avoid being followed: Antar interview, July 12, 2007; Testimony of Sam E. Antar, *USA v. Eddie Antar et al.*, US District Court for the District of New Jersey, no. 92-347, June 28, 1993.

"So I would go to his lawyers and act like nothing happened": Testimony of Sam E. Antar, *USA v. Eddie Antar et al.*, June 25, 1993.

Chapter Twenty-Two

feeling pressure from lawsuits and investigations: Sam E. Antar, interview with the author, May 21, 2013.

Sammy's indebtedness: Antar interview, July 12, 2007.

"No, you did it for yourself": Antar interview, July 12, 2007.

"You're on your own": Antar interview, July 12, 2007.

conversation with father: Antar interview, July 13, 2007.

meeting with Nolan: Antar interview, July 13, 2007.

Pentek case: Linda Moss, "Garfield Man Innocent," *The Herald-News* (Passaic, NJ), July 22, 1982; Kathleen Sullivan, "Terror Victim Freed in Killing," *The Record* (Hackensack, NJ), July 22, 1982.

first meeting with Gibbons: Antar interview, July 13, 2007.

"nerdy cousin they needed to help": Paul Hayes, interview with the author, April 29, 2020.

second meeting with Gibbons: Antar interview, July 13, 2007.

Chapter Twenty-Three

Paul Hayes background: Paul Hayes, interview with the author, April 27, 2020.

"This case is going to be a real mess": Hayes interview, April 28, 2020.

cover almost blown: William M. Carley, "How the FBI Snared Two Scientists Selling Drug Company Secrets," *Wall Street Journal*, September 5, 1991.

"so that they see you more as a friend": Hayes interview, April 27, 2020.

Gilbert Schulman: Hayes interview, April 27, 2020.

Sammy thrown at the mercy of the FBI: Sam E. Antar, interview with the author, July 13, 2007.

not in anyone's loop: Antar interview, July 12, 2007.

"My impression": Hayes interview, April 29, 2020.

"kept running in": Hayes interview, April 28, 2020.

"harsh, unbending prosecutor": Joseph T. Wells, *Frankensteins of Fraud* (Dexter, MI: Obsidian, 2000), 247.

Gibbons description of relationship with Gersten (footnote): Dan Gibbons, interview with the author, July 19, 2021.

"extremely hyper and nervous": Hayes interview, April 29, 2020.

the SEC civil suit: Complaint in *SEC v. Eddie Antar, Sam E. Antar, Mitchell Antar, Isaac Kairey, David Panoff, Eddie Gindi and Kathleen Morin*, US District Court, District of New Jersey, Civ. 89-3773, September 6, 1989.

New York Times *article:* Stephen Labaton, "S.E.C. Files Fraud Case on Retailer," *New York Times*, September 7, 1987.

Daily News *article:* Andrew M. Gluck, "Crazy Charge: SEC Hits Eddie on Fraud," *New York Daily News*, September 7, 1987.

no grand jury convened: Hayes interview, April 28, 2020.

"They seemed more interested": Robert Fachet, "For Touring Soviets, Times Are Changing," *Washington Post*, January 1, 1989.

"a sound survival strategy": Ricki Fulman, "Eddie's a Bit of a Shut Case," *New York Daily News*, March 30, 1989.

1989 loss: Christine Dugas, "$50M Loss Hits Chain," *New York Newsday*, June 1, 1989.

Chapter 11: Associated Press, "Crazy Eddie in Chapter 11," *New York Times*, June 21, 1989.

"he had a major bogie to overcome": Harry Spero, interview with the author, July 6, 2020.

"He was a Texan": Spero interview, July 6, 2020.

"I believe we made tremendous progress": "Revamped Crazy Eddie Gets Change at the Top," *New York Times,* February 2, 1989.

Spero notified of Crazy Eddie closing: Spero interview, July 6, 2020.

demise disclosed by a supplier: Nina Andrews, "Crazy Eddie to Liquidate, Ending Move to Reorganize," *New York Times*, October 4, 1989.

auction: John Richardson, "400 Bidders Take Home Remnants of Crazy Eddie," *Home News* (New Brunswick, NJ), November 29, 1989.

final Jerry Carroll commercial: Richardson, "600 Bidders Take Home Remnants of Crazy Eddie."

Chapter Twenty-Four

Debbie testimony on Israeli bank account: Deposition of Deborah Rosen Antar, *Deborah Antar v. Eddie Antar*, New York State Supreme Court, Kings County, December 1988–January 1989, Index No. 6755/88, 445–448, 1406.

Crain's *article:* Gary Belsky, "U.S. May File RICO Charges Against Antar," *Crain's New York Business*, September 11, 1989, 1.

"that they may soon seek an indictment": Laurie P. Cohen, "U.S. Threats to Seize Fees Scare Lawyers from Cases," *Wall Street Journal*, October 27, 1989.

"someone in government": Sam E. Antar, notes, October 27, 1989.

SEC put on the money trail by Sammy's lawyer: William R. McLucas to Judge Nicholas H. Politan *USA v. Sam E. Antar*, US District Court, District of New Jersey, Crim. 92-614, March 14, 1994.

decision in divorce case: Supreme Court justice Barry Hurowitz, Memorandum Decision, *Deborah Antar v. Eddie Antar*, January 24, 1990.

Solomon Antar testimony on signing of divorce papers: Deposition of Solomon E. Antar, *Deborah Antar v. Eddie Antar*, May 22, 1989, 329–330.

Eddie claimed he gave Debbie cash: Antar notes, September 4, 1989.

"he will have to give 1/2": Antar notes, January 30, 1990.

Gibbons comment (footnote): Dan Gibbons, interview with the author, July 19, 2021.

Eddie not fazed, invites friends to Florida: Antar notes, February 26, 1990.

transfiles in disarray: Paul Hayes, interview with the author, April 30, 2020.

meeting with Alito: Sam E. Antar, interview with the author, April 2, 2020.

Gibbons on transfer to civil division: Gibbons interview, July 19, 2021.

"The reality was that Spindler": Paul Weissman, email to the author, August 21, 2021.

plea agreement: Michael Chertoff to Anthony Mautone, "re: Plea Agreement with Sam E. Antar," *USA v. Sam E. Antar*, August 22, 1991.

began meeting with SEC lawyers in March 1991: Testimony of Sam E. Antar, *USA v. Eddie Antar et al.*, US District Court for the District of New Jersey, no. 92-347, June 29, 1993.

SEC settlement: McLucas to Judge Politan, *USA v. Sam E. Antar*, March 14, 1994.

"He'd make a comment based upon what was happening in the news": Jack Arsenault, interview with the author, April 9, 2021.

Hayes visits Arsenault: Hayes interview, April 29, 2020.

Chapter Twenty-Five

"David Jacob Levi Cohen" and "Solemn Declaration": Testimony of Joseph Moshkovsky, *USA v. Eddie Antar et al.*, US District Court for the District of New Jersey, no. 92-347, July 9, 1993.

"the error and negligence": Quoted in summation by Michael Chertoff, *USA v. Eddie Antar et al.*, July 15, 1993.

SEC Enforcement Division receives package: Richard Wallace, interview with the author, May 11, 2020.

identification of Eddie Antar: Wallace interview; Paul Hayes, interview with the author, April 30, 2020.

bank transfers: Testimony of Moshkovsky, *USA v. Eddie Antar et al.*, July 9, 1993.

"nearly all of them either numbered": Summation by Paul Weissman, *USA v. Eddie Antar et al.*, July 14, 1993.

Lansky immigrating to Israel: Robert Lacey, *Little Man: Meyer Lansky and the Gangster Life* (Boston: Little, Brown, 1991), 323–356.

Israeli citizenship applications: Testimony of Yossef Zamory, *USA v. Eddie Antar et al.*, US District Court for the District of New Jersey, no. 92-347, July 9, 1993.

"probably paid off someone to get it": Hayes interview, April 29, 2020.

"Providing false documentation": Hayes interview, April 30, 2020.

"big bolts like a battleship": Hayes interview, April 28, 2020.

Eddie's arrest: Testimony of Zamory, *USA v. Eddie Antar et al.*, July 9, 1993; Michael Rotem, "'Crazy Eddie' Nabbed in Yavne by Police," *Jerusalem Post*, June 25, 1992.

"lists of holding companies": George Anastasia, "A Chaotic Empire Crumbles," *Philadelphia Inquirer*, November 2, 1992.

Eddie's bags were packed: Testimony of Zamory, *USA v. Eddie Antar et al.*, July 9, 1993.

"He was on the move again": Jack Arsenault, interview with the author, April 9, 2021.

niece's impressions of prison: Rori Sassoon, interview with author, April 12, 2021.

"fight tooth and nail": Associated Press, "'Crazy Eddie' Will Fight Extradition," *Home News* (New Brunswick, NJ), July 9, 1992.

Ministry of Justice approves extradition: Associated Press, "Israel Moves Closer to Ousting Antar," *Asbury Park (NJ) Press*, August 25, 1992.

Chapter Twenty-Six

"looking weak and sickly": Andrew Meisels, "Israel Not So Hot for Eddie," *New York Daily News*, August 25, 1992.

"had a dirt floor": Jack Arsenault, interview with the author, April 9, 2021.

"kind of basically looked at me": Arsenault interview, April 9, 2021.

New York Times *article mentioning illness:* Isadore Barmash, "Founder Joins Bid for Crazy Eddie," *New York Times*, May 21, 1987.

Eddie gives interview to the New York Post: Daphna Barak, "'I'm Going to Die!': 'Crazy Eddie' Wasting Away in Israeli Prison," *New York Post*, September 25, 1992.

"liver and kidney disorders": George Anastasia, "A Chaotic Empire Crumbles," *Philadelphia Inquirer*, November 2, 1992.

"private medical report": Raine Marcus, "Crazy Eddie's Wife, Lawyer, Worried He'll Die If Forced to Await Extradition Hearing in Jail," *Jerusalem Post*, November 10, 1992.

"lost the will to live": Marcus, "Crazy Eddie's Wife, Lawyer, Worried He'll Die."

reported suicide attempts: "'Crazy Eddie' Tried Suicide Before," Jewish Telegraphic Agency, November 11, 1992.

Israeli police believe Eddie faked suicide attempt: Uri Dan, "Cops: Not-So-Crazy Eddie Faked Suicide Try," *New York Post*, November 9, 1992.

"So I flew over": Arsenault interview, April 9, 2021.

"the judge who conducted the [Israeli] hearing": Paul Weissman, email to the author, August 21, 2021.

speculation about Likud attitude: Barak, "'I'm Going to Die!'"; Ron Scherer, "'Crazy Eddie' Fights Extradition from Israel," *Christian Science Monitor*, December 9, 1992.

Reso kidnapping: Catherine S. Manegold, "Twisted Tale of a Kidnapping and of Dreams Gone Wrong," *New York Times*, July 1, 1992; Charles Strum, "Man Sentenced to Life in Killing of Exxon Executive," *New York Times*, December 1, 1992; Frances Ann Burns, "Irene Seale Gets 20 Years in Exxon Kidnapping," United Press International, January 25, 1993.

"As far as I was concerned": Paul Hayes, interview with the author, May 4, 2020.

phone call from Vinnie Badalamenti: Sam E. Antar, interview with the author, July 22, 2020.

Chapter Twenty-Seven

Paul Weissman background: Paul Weissman, interview with the author, March 30 and April 1, 2020, and email to the author, August 22, 2021.

"I tried to describe to Paul": Paul Hayes, interview with the author, April 28, 2020.

"during breaks in the depositions": William R. McLucas to Judge Nicholas H. Politan, *USA v. Sam E. Antar*, US District Court, District of New Jersey, Crim. 92-614, March 14, 1994.

Grinberg indictment: "Grand Jury Indicts Ex-Crazy Eddie Aide on Perjury Charges," *Wall Street Journal*, May 29, 1992.

Grinberg guilty plea: Associated Press, "Plea by Official of Crazy Eddie," *New York Times*, May 12, 1993.

"the perjury to which Grinberg pled guilty": McLucas to Judge Politan, *USA v. Sam E. Antar*, March 14, 1994.

"encompassing a more recent time frame": Anthony Mautone to Judge Nicholas H. Politan, *USA v. Sam E. Antar*, US District Court, District of New Jersey, Crim. 92-614, March 22, 1994.

meeting with Gindi in Florida: Hayes interview, May 4, 2020.

"made defense witnesses cower": John T. Ward, "Antar Trial Lawyers Compete Intensively," *Asbury Park (NJ) Press*, July 11, 1993.

Paul Berkman sentence: David A. Vise, "Fraud Case Defendants Sentenced," *Washington Post*, November 7, 1989.

"pale, bony and balding": Ward, "Antar Trial Lawyers Compete Intensively."

"known for his one-liners": Victoria St. Martin, "Known for His One-Liners, Former N.J. Judge Nicholas H. Politan Dead at 76," *Newark (NJ) Star-Ledger*, February 22, 2012.

"Every jury I've ever had": Judge Nicholas H. Politan remarks, *USA v. Eddie Antar et al.*, US District Court for the District of New Jersey, no. 92-347, June 15, 1993.

"strong prima facie showings": Richard Sherwin, "Calling on Eddie," *New York Daily News*, January 24, 1990.

"Please stop playing to the Third Circuit": Politan remarks, *USA v. Eddie Antar et al.*, June 22, 1993.

"trial-long impersonation of Judge Roy Bean": Joseph T. Wells, *Frankensteins of Fraud* (Dexter, MI: Obsidian, 2000), 253.

cross-examination of Sam E. Antar: USA v. Eddie Antar et al., June 29, 1993.

"He's Orthodox": *USA v. Eddie Antar et al.*, June 17, 1993.

"a feigned issue": *USA v. Eddie Antar et al.*, October 18, 1993.

Arsenault summation: USA v. Eddie Antar et al., July 14, 1993.

"skirt-wearing friend of J. Edgar Hoover": Hayes interview, April 30, 2020.

"the Mad Faxer": Wells, *Frankensteins of Fraud*, 239.

"though he had violated the rules of the Bar": Wells, *Frankensteins of Fraud*, 257.

analysts would not testify: Weissman, interview with author, December 14, 2020.

SEC case against Allen, Sam M., and Ben Kuszer: Complaint in *SEC v. Sam M. Antar, Allen Antar and Benjamin Kuszer*, US District Court, District of New Jersey, Civ. 93-3988, September 8, 1993; Opinion by Judge Harold M. Ackerman, *Securities and Exchange Commission v. Sam M. Antar et al.*, 15 F. Supp. 2d 477, 1998 US Dist. LEXIS 21474, July 16, 1998.

$53 million repatriated: US Attorney for District of New Jersey, "Petition for Panel Rehearing and Suggestion for Rehearing in Banc," *USA v. Eddie Antar and Mitchell Antar*, US Court of Appeals, Third Circuit, Docket Nos. 94-5228 and 94-5230, June 1, 1995.

"Darth Vader of capitalism" and Eddie's response: John T. Ward, "'Crazy Eddie' Jail Term 12 Years," *Asbury Park (NJ) Press*, April 30, 1994.

Chapter Twenty-Eight

Cindy Adams interview: Cindy Adams, "Behind Bars, Eddie Claims: 'I'm Not Crazy'—or Guilty," *New York Post*, May 18, 1994.

"Sure, I'm not perfect": Seamus McGraw, "Antar Claims Judge Treated Him Unfairly," *The Record* (Hackensack, NJ), May 26, 1994.

"I was not what you would call, I guess, a model citizen": David Lee Preston, "For 'Crazy Eddie,' a New World," *Philadelphia Inquirer*, November 7, 1994.

"a blatant anti-Semite": John T. Ward, "Eddie Speaks," *Asbury Park (NJ) Press*, December 11, 1994.

appellate court reversal: Opinion of the court, *USA v. Antar*, 53 F.3d 568 (3d Cir. 1995), decided April 12, 1995.

"Haven't we had a good life together?": Paul Weissman, interview with the author, April 7, 2020.

Weissman legal arguments: US Attorney for District of New Jersey, "Petition for Panel Rehearing and Suggestion for Rehearing in Banc," *USA v. Eddie Antar and Mitchell Antar*, US Court of Appeals, Third Circuit, Docket Nos. 94-5228 and 94-5230, June 1, 1995.

"You reached for that honey pot": Douglas Martin, "Harold A. Ackerman, Federal Judge in New Jersey, Dies at 81," *New York Times*, December 10, 2009.

Eddie Antar admissions of guilt: Transcript of Proceedings before Judge Harold A. Ackerman, *USA v. Eddie Antar et al.*, plea, US District Court for the District of New Jersey, no. 92-347, May 8, 1996.

Epilogue

comment on blog: "I would have loved to work for you," author's blog, December 22, 2006, http://garyweiss.blogspot.com/2006/12/sam-antars-letter-to-patrick-byrne .html.

mentioned in previous book: Gary Weiss, *Wall Street Versus America* (New York: Portfolio, 2006), 205–206.

Byrne background: Joe Nocera, "Overstock's Campaign of Menace," *New York Times*, February 25, 2006.

Byrne employee: Joe Nocera, "The Patrick Byrne Show Distracted from Overstock's Woes," Bloomberg, August 23, 2019, www.bloomberg.com/opinion /articles/2019-08-23/overstock-com-s-patrick-byrne-distracted-from-company-s -troubles; Gary Weiss, "Closing the File on a Criminal and Junkie Named Judd Bagley," author's blog, March 30, 2015, http://garyweiss.blogspot.com/2015/03 /closing-file-on-criminal-and-junkie.html.

al-Qaeda financier: Nazerali v. Mitchell, 2016 BCSC 810, Supreme Court of British Columbia, Reasons for Judgment, May 6, 2016, www.bccourts.ca/jdb-txt/sc /16/08/2016BCSC0810cor1.htm; "Vancouver Businessman Wins $1.2 Million for Internet Libel," *Vancouver Sun*, May 7, 2016; M. L. Nestel, "Gold-Hoarding Boss Wants to Become Governor," *Daily Beast*, November 28, 2015, www.thedaily beast.com/gold-hoarding-boss-wants-to-be-governor.

"giving Goldman [Sachs] traders blowjobs": Bethany McLean, "Phantom Menace," *Fortune*, November 14, 2005, https://money.cnn.com/magazines/fortune/fortune _archive/2005/11/14/8360711/index.htm; Damaris Colhoun, "The Shadowy War on the Press: How the Rich Silence Journalists," *Columbia Journalism Review* online, June 16, 2016, www.cjr.org/analysis/shadowy_war.php.

"If the purpose of this was to silence us": Nocera, "Patrick Byrne Show."

"using the courts": Nocera, "Overstock's Campaign of Menace."

CNBC confrontation: "Crazy Eddie Antar and His CFO/CPA Cousin Sam Antar Meet for First Time in 30 Years," www.youtube.com/watch?v=Y_7ntzgTvhs.

Herschkopf report: Text of letter from Dr. Isaac Herschkopf to Sam M. Antar, August 2001, courtesy of Joe Nocera.

"There is perhaps no more insidious drain," Sam M. testimony on lying: Opinion by Judge Harold M. Ackerman, *Securities and Exchange Commission v. Sam M. Antar et al.*, 15 F. Supp. 2d 477, 1998 US Dist. LEXIS 21474, July 16, 1998.

SEC litigation: Litigation Release No. 15251, Securities and Exchange Commission, February 10, 1997.

Politan rules against Debbie I: Opinion of Judge Nicholas H. Politan, *Securities and Exchange Commission v. Deborah Rosen Antar et al.*, Civ. 89-3773, August 23, 1993.

$3.9 million settlement: Litigation Release No. 14028, Securities and Exchange Commission, March 25, 1994.

cash found in ceiling panels: Richard Wallace, interview with the author, May 11, 2020.

SEC cash hunt, restitution: Litigation Release No. 15251; Report Pursuant to Section 308(c) of the Sarbanes Oxley Act of 2002, Securities & Exchange Commission, 2003; Ted Sherman, "The Long and Wild Crazy Eddie Investor Fraud Case Nears the End," NJ.com, March 4, 2012, www.nj.com/news/2012/03/the_long_and _wild_crazy_eddie.html.

cash found in 2009: Agreed Order to Liquidate Account, *USA v. Eddie Antar*, Criminal Action 92-347, US District Court, District of New Jersey, June 11, 2010.

Deborah Antar gives birth: David Lee Preston, "The Scene in South Jersey," *Philadelphia Inquirer*, May 13, 1996.

Crazy Eddie revival, 1998: Steve Klein, "Are These Guys Crazy?," *Asbury Park (NJ) Press*, January 29, 1998; Lisa W. Foderaro, "Crazy Eddie's Returning, Minus Two Jailed Founders," *New York Times*, January 20, 1998.

Crazy Eddie revival, 2001: James Covert, "Crazy Eddie Chain Originator Returns to Retail with Website," Dow Jones News Service in *Philadelphia Inquirer*, June 19, 2001; Lisa Marsh, "Insaaane Comeback—Convicted Crazy Eddie Returning to Retailing," *New York Post*, June 6, 2001, https://nypost.com/2001/06/06 /insaaaane-comeback-convicted-crazy-eddie-returning-to-retailing/.

"It was moving": Larry Weiss, interview with the author, April 23, 2020.

investor aversion to Eddie: L. Weiss interview, April 23, 2020.

Crazy Eddie website taken down: Joseph P. Fried, "Following Up: Crazy Prices Gone, One More Time," *New York Times*, September 19, 2004.

"three or four TV pilots": David Behrens, "The Crazy World of Jerry Carroll," *Newsday*, July 31, 1986.

EuroDance website: "EuroDance Masterfully Mixed by Jerry," www.jerrycar rolldj.com (defunct), archived August 18, 2000, https://web.archive.org /web/20000818222036/http://www.jerrycarrolldj.com:80/; and March 2, 2001, https://web.archive.org/web/20010302005338/http://www.jerrycarrolldj.com:80/.

Jerry Carroll's death: Andrea Carroll, interview with the author, January 21, 2022.

"decidedly sweeter disposition": Joseph T. Wells, *Frankensteins of Fraud* (Dexter, MI: Obsidian, 2000), 259.

Sam A. Antar SEC complaint: Complaint in *Securities and Exchange Commission v. Sam A. Antar*, US District Court, Southern District of New York, Civ. 19-11527, December 17, 2019; Ted Sherman, "Nephew of Crazy Eddie Founder Gets Prison in His Own Investment Scam," *Newark (NJ) Star-Ledger*, August 8, 2013, www .nj.com/news/2013/08/nephew_of_crazy_eddie_founder_gets_prison_in_his _own_investment_scam.html.

2019 criminal charges: "New York City Man Charged with Stealing Approximately $794,000 from Investors in New Jersey and New York," Office of Attorney General, State of New Jersey, https://web.archive.org/web/20210112192635/https://www .nj.gov/oag/newsreleases19/pr20191217b.html (archived January 12, 2021); William H. Trizano, attorney for Sam A. Antar, to Judge Alison J. Nathan, indictment attached, *Securities and Exchange Commission v. Sam A. Antar*, November 30, 2021.

ABC News segment: Enjoli Francis et al., "At Snack Business, Young People with Autism Find Work and Skills for the Future," ABC News, November 14, 2017, https:// abcnews.go.com/Business/snack-business-young-people-autism-find-work-skills /story?id=51152031.

Debbie II divorce: Online docket entries for *Deborah Antar v. Eddie Antar*, New York State Supreme Court, Docket No. 0303372/2009.

Debbie II remarriage: Deborah Susan Ehrlich Antar in the New York, New York, Marriage License Indexes, 1907–2018, Spouse: Jerald Ehrlich, Date of Marriage License: June 11, 2010.

Sam Cohen sentence: Docket entry, *USA v. Cohen*, US District Court, Eastern District of New York, 94 cr 00143, March 6, 1997.

Dick Lewis indictment, sentencing: Richard Perez-Pena, "100 Are Linked to Huge Insurance Scheme," *New York Times*, September 23, 1993; Estelle Lander Smith, "Insurance Fraud: Ex-Envoy and Former Electronic Retailer Plead Guilty," *Newsday*, September 4, 1993; Docket entry, *USA v. Lewis*, US District Court, Eastern District of New York, 93 cr 00970, April 30, 1997.

Berman and Sabres: Brad Meikle, "Chartwell Skates in as White Knight for Sabres," *Buyouts*, December 16, 2002, www.buyoutsinsider.com/chartwell-skates -in-as-white-knight-for-sabres/.

John Rigas siphoning funds from company: Barry Meier, "Ex-Accountant Testifies on Dealings with Rigas: Personal Expenses Charged to Adelphia," *New York Times*, March 30, 2004.

Todd Berman's downfall: David Robinson, "Buffalo's Business," *Buffalo News*, March 28, 2005; David Robinson, "President of New York's Chartwell Investments Quits," *Knight-Ridder Tribune Business News*, September 30, 2003; Todd Berman profile, Chartwell Investments, archived April 10, 2003, https://web.archive.org /web/20030410215727/http://www.chartwellinvestments.com/berman.html.

Berman sentence: David Robinson, "Berman Gets Five Years in Penalty Box," *Buffalo News*, July 10, 2005, https://buffalonews.com/news/berman-gets-5-years-in -penalty-box/article_c9234792-f93d-54e8-acb2-e63581009939.html.

"Mr. Mautone's advice basically saved my life": Tim O'Brien, "Footnote to Crazy Eddie Case: You Talk, You Walk," *New Jersey Law Journal*, June 13, 1994, 7.

letters from Oppenheimer-Palmieri partnership and investors: C. Stephen Howard, Milbank, Tweed, Hadley & McCloy to Judge Nicholas H. Politan, *USA v. Sam E. Antar*, US District Court, District of New Jersey, Crim. 92-614, March 11, 1994; Howard E. Sirota, Sirota & Sirota, to Judge Politan, *USA v. Sam E. Antar*, March 8, 1994.

"extraordinary in its scope, its significance and its steadfast dedication": Michael Chertoff, Paul Weissman, and Jayne Blumberg to Judge Politan, *USA v. Sam E. Antar*, March 14, 1994.

"If you come forward, you will be rewarded": O'Brien, "Footnote to Crazy Eddie Case."

"the architect of the fraud": O'Brien, "Footnote to Crazy Eddie Case."

restated Overstock.com earnings: Sam E. Antar, "My Reporting of a Financial Statement Manipulation Scheme at Overstock.com Is Vindicated by Latest Company Announcement," *White Collar Crime Blog*, February 4, 2010, https://white collarfraud.blogspot.com/2010/02/my-reporting-of-financial-statement.html.

Byrne and "stolen election" conspiracy theories: Will Sommer, "Overstock Founder Will Sell You Election Fraud for $5 Per Month," *Daily Beast*, May 24, 2021, www.thedailybeast.com/overstock-founder-will-sell-you-election -fraud-for-dollar5-per-month; Brian Schwartz, "Trump Allies Are Helping Overstock Founder Patrick Byrne Run a Group That Pushes False Election Claims," CNBC.com, December 20, 2021, www.cnbc.com/2021/12/20

/trump-allies-help-overstock-founder-patrick-byrne-push-false-election-claims
.html.

election libel suit: Kristine Phillips, "Dominion Sues OAN, Newsmax, Ex-Overstock
CEO Patrick Byrne for $1.6 Billion over Voter Fraud Claims," *USA Today*, August 10, 2021, www.usatoday.com/story/news/politics/2021/08/10/dominion
-sues-newsmax-oan-trump-ally-patrick-byrne-over-fraud-claims/5551561001/;
A. J. Vicens, "Mojo Wire: Former Overstock CEO Patrick Byrne Gets Sued for
Pushing Election Lies," *Mother Jones*, August 10, 2021, www.motherjones.com
/mojo-wire/2021/08/patrick-byrne-dominion-defamation/.

"pariah": Ja'han Jones, "After Faking Jan. 6 Outrage, Big Companies Still Donate
to GOP Election Deniers," MSNBC.com, January 6, 2022, www.msnbc.com
/the-reidout/reidout-blog/corporations-funding-jan-6-republicans-rcna11115.

Overstock aide's plea deal: Weiss, "Closing the File on a Criminal and Junkie Named
Judd Bagley; *State of Utah v. Judson Montgomery Bagley*, Case No. 131400924,
www.scribd.com/doc/260361037/Judd-Bagley-Confessed-Drug-Addict-and
-Criminal; Lehi City Police, "Officer Report for Incident LE01597, Forgery,"
www.scribd.com/document/261999238/Judd-Bagley-Arrest-Record.

"wistful for Crazy Eddie": Michael Schulman, "Remembering Crazy Eddie: His Prices
Were Insane," *New Yorker*, September 17, 2016.

"evoked a less slick": Ralph Gardner Jr., "Wistful for Era of 'Crazy Eddie,'" *Wall Street
Journal*, September 14, 2016.

Gammerman decision: Affidavit of Deborah Antar in Support of Motion for Summary
Judgment in Lieu of Complaint, *Deborah Antar v. Solomon E. Antar*, Supreme
Court of the State of New York, County of New York, Index No. 650482/2019,
January 23, 2019, Exhibit 1.

Deborah Antar 2019 lawsuit: Affidavit of Deborah Antar in Support of Motion for
Summary Judgment in Lieu of Complaint, *Deborah Antar v. Solomon E. Antar*,
Second Amended Complaint, *Deborah Antar v. Eddie Antar and Solomon
Antar*, Supreme Court of the State of New York, County of New York, 15980/87,
May 16, 1991.

INDEX